Adventures in Spirituality

Adventures in Spirituality

A Journey from Belief to Faith

ROBERT P. VANDE KAPPELLE

WIPF & STOCK · Eugene, Oregon

ADVENTURES IN SPIRITUALITY
A Journey from Belief to Faith

Copyright © 2020 Robert P. Vande Kappelle. All rights reserved. Except for brief quotations in critical publications or reviews, no part of this book may be reproduced in any manner without prior written permission from the publisher. Write: Permissions, Wipf and Stock Publishers, 199 W. 8th Ave., Suite 3, Eugene, OR 97401.

Unless otherwise noted, Bible quotations are from the *New Revised Standard Version of the Bible*, copyright © 1989 by the Division of Christian Education of the National Council of the Churches of Christ in the United States of America. Used by permission.

Wipf & Stock
An Imprint of Wipf and Stock Publishers
199 W. 8th Ave., Suite 3
Eugene, OR 97401

www.wipfandstock.com

PAPERBACK ISBN: 978-1-7252-6388-8
HARDCOVER ISBN: 978-1-7252-6389-5
EBOOK ISBN: 978-1-7252-6390-1

Manufactured in the U.S.A.   02/07/20

The visible world is an active doorway
to the invisible world, and the invisible world
is much larger than the visible.
—Richard Rohr, OFM

Seek grace, not instruction; desire, not understanding.
Seek the groaning of prayer over diligent reading.
Seek the Spouse more than the teacher.
Seek God, not man; darkness, not clarity:
not light, but the fire itself.
—Bonaventure of Bagnoregio

Yearning for a new way will not produce it.
Only ending the old way can do that.
You cannot hold onto the old,
all the while declaring that you want something new.
There is only one way to bring in the new.
You must make room for it.
—Neale Donald Walsch

We live forward, but we understand it backward.
—Søren Kierkegaard

Contents

Preface ix

Part I: Hope Revealed

Chapter 1: Love Never Fails 3
Chapter 2: Dark Splendor 21
Chapter 3: The Invisible Mountain 36

Part II: Truth Revealed

Chapter 4: Into Thin Places 57
Chapter 5: Beyond Belief 66
Chapter 6: Refined by Fire 85

Part III: Wisdom Revealed

Chapter 7: Securing Life 105
Chapter 8: The Scandal of Divine Love 119

Part IV: Grace Revealed

Chapter 9: Living Graciously 139
Chapter 10: The New Creation 151

Part V: Power Revealed

Chapter 11: In the Potter's Workshop 165
Chapter 12: Walking on Water 183
Epilogue 202
Appendix A: The Road of Life 209
Appendix B: Chronological List of Publications by Dr. Vande Kappelle 211
Bibliography 213
Index 217

Preface

LIFE IS GRAND—A GIFT of nature, society, and family, but above all, of our Creator. As we age, we look backward, nostalgically, idealistically: the highs seem higher, and the lows smaller and shallower. And that's the way it should be. For we are blessed, and our backward glance should be filled with gratitude and not with regret.

The title of this book is taken from the life enabling advice imparted to graduating seniors by Howard J. Burnett, former president of Washington & Jefferson College, words that serve as my mantra: "Life is an adventure to be lived, not a problem to be solved."

Two necessary paths move us forward in life: a journey outward and a journey inward. To live adventurously means to take risks, to try new things, to embrace uncertainty, to remain forever open to newness—outwardly and inwardly, physically and spiritually. At birth, a lifetime of adventure beckons. Initially, most of us focus on the tasks at hand: establishing an identity, a home, career, relationships, friends, community, and security, all foundational for getting started in life. If we have good health and financial means, we add travel to the mix. Later in life, many focus increasingly on the inward journey. This book tells my story of spiritual adventure, following the pastoral advice in 1 Timothy 6:12, "Fight the good fight of the faith."

Our society is deeply divided, not only by politics, race, gender, lifestyle, culture, region, country of origin, social standing, and economic status, but also by religion. When Americans of different faiths disagree, they tend to distrust one another, and even conservatives and liberals of the same denomination are known to regard one another as ignorant, misguided, or diseased. I use that last word intentionally, for people across the denominational spectrum often view those theologically different from themselves—even fellow Christians—as possessing a dangerous and potentially contagious virus destined to bring America to ruin.

Religion, the one factor capable of restoring harmony, unity, and vitality, seems the most divisive and flawed. Designed as a vehicle of hope and grace, religion is being used today to vilify those with alternative lifestyles and views: Protestants versus Catholics, conservatives versus liberals, fundamentalists versus progressives, religionists versus secularists, devout versus nones, literalists versus metaphorists, believers versus atheists, saved versus lost. The solution, I believe, is in storytelling. Each person is a story waiting to be told and heard. As we take time to identify and own our story, that story needs to be shared and appreciated. As we listen to one another's stories, we will find in these narratives our common humanity.

Recently I received an email from a long lost college friend. In college, we had a casual friendship. Possessing gregarious personalities, we both had close friends and common acquaintances. We also shared an evangelical upbringing. We had lost touch for over fifty years, until she came across a reference to my writings and decided to contact me. When I heard she had earned a PhD in psychology and had taught on the collegiate level, I felt we could resume our friendship on an intellectual level.

"You would never have thought of me as deeply spiritual," my friend noted in a recent email, "yet I was." When I told her of my intent to "woo people away from biblical literalism," I was surprised to hear her say, "I can't think why you would want to 'woo me away' from what the Bible says. Honestly, the Bob Vande Kappelle I knew wouldn't have wanted to do so. I am very surprised, Bob, at how your belief system has changed. I have spent much of my life seeking God's face, and I have found God in my Bible and in my heart. And I am quite content to remain securely rooted right there. Further, it seems to me that Jesus was strong on biblical literalism. Although I read various books and Bible studies, the Bible wins out every time."

When she concluded, "At this point in my life, I'm pretty firmly set in my faith, which includes biblical literalism, or at the very least, biblical inerrancy," I sensed an insuperable divide in our faith and approach to scripture. Thinking about her disappointment over my progressive biblical approach, I thought it might be obvious why I had changed, and why I was no longer naively evangelical. Wouldn't someone change after eight years of graduate study and forty years of research, teaching, and writing volumes on faith, theology, and spirituality? Not necessarily so, and certainly not if one is conservatively orthodox.

Although I have written at length about my theological views, notably in *Beyond Belief* (2012) and more recently in *Refined by Fire* (2018), my friend's comments triggered a desire to tell anew the story of my journey from belief to faith. Hence, *Adventures in Spirituality* provides a singular account of my spiritual journey, indicating where I stand theologically, how and why my theological sensibility has changed, and how such changes have transformed my living and thinking. The result, I trust, will revitalize your thinking and living as well.

PICTURES AT AN EXHIBITION

Perhaps you are familiar with Modest Mussorgsky (1839–1881), a soldier by trade and a Russian musician associated with the nationalist movement known as "The Five." Famous for his opera *Boris Godunov*, Mussorgsky also composed a set of piano miniatures called "Pictures at an Exhibition." Originally written for solo piano but later orchestrated by the French composer Maurice Ravel, the work refers to a memorial exhibit of pictures by a friend of Mussorgsky who had recently died, the Russian painter Victor Hartman. Like Mussorgsky, Hartman cared deeply about incorporating Russian "themes" into his work, themes such as the Russian nutcracker or gnome, a ballet, the witch Baba-Yaga, and the great gate at Kiev. To provide thread or unity to the set of ten different musical pieces, Mussorgsky hit upon an ingenious plan, creating a theme called "Promenade," thereby depicting the composer strolling around the picture gallery. The theme returns several times in free variations to show the viewers' change of mood as they contemplate Hartman's varied work.

Like "Pictures at an Exhibition," *Adventures in Spirituality* displays concepts from my books, recalling titles and topics that elucidate my spiritual journey. My goal is to inspire readers to tell their own story and to facilitate their transformation from an independent, egoic creature to nourishing, adventurous waves on the ocean of reality. My "promenade" theme, called "nonduality," appears frequently in variation form throughout this work.

Why "nonduality"? Because duality thinking, also called polarity thinking or all-or-nothing thinking, is the bane of spirituality. More than with any other personality trait in our lives, all-or-nothing thinking causes huge mistakes and bad judgments. It results in withholding love, misinterpreting situations, and hurting both others and ourselves. This pattern of dualistic or polarity thinking is deeply entrenched in most of us, despite its severe limitations. Dualistic thinking is not wrong or bad in itself—in fact, it is necessary in most situations. However, it is completely inadequate for the major questions and dilemmas of life.

Dualistic people use knowledge, even religious knowledge, for the purposes of ego enhancement, shaming, and the control of others and themselves, for it works very well in that way. Nondual people are both courageous and creative. Seeing reality with a new eye and heart, they use knowledge for the transformation of persons and structures, but especially to experience transformation. They are "yes/and" thinkers who avoid getting trapped in the small world of "either/or," except in the ways of love and courage, where they are "all in."

GUIDING PRINCIPLES

As stars guided navigators in the past, the following principles have proven reliable in my faith journey. These principles, stated in the first person plural, are defined in future chapters.

1. *All truth is God's truth.*
   This principle encourages us to remain open to truth wherever it may be found and wherever it leads, and to recognize that human truth is progressive and never final.

2. *Faith, like truth, is a journey, not a destination.*
   This principle encourages us to transcend conventional spirituality to a wholesome faith that is trust-based rather than belief-based.

3. *The faith journey is a two-stage process, from first- to second-half-of-life experience.*
   This principle encourages us to view human personhood as an organic participation in the Selfhood of God.

4. *Transformative spirituality values postcritical understanding, as embodied in the Postcritical Paradigm.*
   This principle encourages us to be nondualist in perspective, nonliteral in our interpretation of scripture, and non-legalistic in practice.

5. *Transformative spirituality is holistic, embracing body, mind, soul, and spirit equally.*
   This principle emphasizes the importance of connecting body and spirit for living fully, and connecting mind (head) and soul (heart) for thinking wisely.

6. *Creation spirituality fully explains the origin, nature, and destiny of human beings.*
   Opposing the fall/redemption paradigm, also known as "the heaven-and-hell framework," this principle emphasizes original goodness and creativity over original sin and conformity.

7. *Panentheism explains God's nature and relationship to humanity and the cosmos.*
   Opposing the traditional doctrine of hell, this principle encourages

us to view God as neither personal nor impersonal but rather as transpersonal, who communicates primarily by persuasion rather than verbally or directly.

8. *The concept of God's Two Books clarifies the relationship between science and religion.*
Acknowledging that the Book of Nature and the Book of Scripture proceed alike from the creative Word of God, this principle embraces biological evolution and scientific discoveries equally with religious insights.

9. While instructed by many scriptures and teachings, *the Bible is our primary scripture.*
Acknowledging the Bible as human creation, this principle encourages us to consider the Bible as "holy" not because of its origin but rather because of its power to transform.

10. *Jesus of Nazareth, a Jewish faith teacher of the first century, is our model, guide, and mentor,* though other religious figures are also primal to our spirituality.
Considering Jesus as the human bridge to God, this principle emphasizes that to understand the meaning of Jesus, we must start with the humanity of Jesus ("christology from below").

DISTINCTIVE FEATURES

Adventures in Spirituality is organized around five concepts, captions borrowed from titles of my biblical commentaries: Hope Revealed, Truth Revealed, Wisdom Revealed, Grace Revealed, and Power Revealed. These headings are not to be followed slavishly or taken literally. Signs or beacons, their intention is to move us onward, shedding light on our path. Likewise, the twelve chapter headings are taken from titles of my other books, generally following their order of publication, though not exclusively. Literary tropes, these titles are suggestive rather than determinative of content.

PART I
Hope Revealed

Chapter 1

Love Never Fails

Promenade. Faith demands living with uncertainty, ambiguity, and a fair degree of tension. We have to be trained how to do this. Only two things are strong enough to accomplish this training: great love and great suffering. They are the primary spiritual teachers, more than the Bible, church, clergy, sacraments, or theology. Only love and suffering are strong enough to decentralize the ego and superego, break down our dual thinking, and open us to Mystery. Ironically, to find one's True Center, one must first go to the edge. As sages, mystics, and prophets invariably know, only by living at the edges of our lives—not grasping at the superficial or protecting the surface of things—do we encounter our essence.

IN 1935, AT THE height of the Depression, my parents, Jacob (Jake) and Bertha (Bert) Vande Kappelle, became married and three weeks later they left every security—family, friends, most of their meager belongings, even their country—for the adventure of a lifetime as missionaries in Costa Rica, then a world far away. They went by faith to a foreign land, staking their lives on the promises of scripture. There they began a new vocation, immersing themselves in a new culture, eating different food, observing different traditions, learning a different language, and even worshipping in a different manner.

My parents' story, spanning the twentieth century and told in my biographical tribute, *Love Never Fails*, contains a myriad of shorter stories, happy ones and sad, triumphant and tragic, entertaining and inspiring. My father, a man of few words, articulated with his hands. He was utterly patient and self-controlled; those who knew him cannot remember unkind or belittling remarks. When he spoke he probed, thinking carefully, cautiously, and insightfully. My mother was a storyteller. She spoke from the heart, viscerally, bluntly, but always with conviction. Her energy was boundless. Blessed with the "gift of gab," she was at home entertaining audiences with anecdotes or illustrations, usually from her own experience. I wrote *Love Never Fails* out of love but also with appreciation and deep respect. Christ before others, others before self, character before career, success through service, making things last, doing more with less, enjoying the moment—these were their priorities, this their legacy.

As their son, I came to rely daily upon the strength and guidance coming through their prayers. They taught me a poem long ago; its words sum up their lives: "Only one life, 'twill soon be past; only what's done for Christ will last."

Most of us, I trust, had exciting childhoods. I certainly did. I grew up the only child of missionary parents in Costa Rica, a rugged and peaceful country in Central America. I spent my first eight years in a mountainous area of that country, on an orphanage/farm we called La Finca (The Farm) or El Hogar Bíblico (The Bible Home), where on a clear day one could see both the Atlantic and the Pacific oceans. Working for the Latin America Mission (LAM), my parents served as houseparents, teachers, and worship leaders, and my father oversaw the local workers who tended the 180-acre farm, including the vegetable gardens and the dairy cows and livestock, enough to provide for the needs of sixty to eighty orphans. The farm also served as a coffee plantation, the coffee bushes used to produce income for the orphanage.

I never regretted growing up in that land of haunting beauty, often called "The Switzerland of the Americas." Bilingualism and biculturalism, inherited gifts, exposed me to diverse perspectives and lifestyles. A byproduct of that upbringing was a healthy curiosity about the world, its people, cultures, and terrain.

Missionaries going overseas need to be resourceful as well as adaptable. At one time mission boards expected their recruits to possess rudimentary mechanical skills, some knowledge of carpentry and agronomy, and the ability to handle medical emergencies, together with communication skills. Noticeable deficiencies were generally overcome on location.

Before my parents could proceed to their awaited duties at the orphanage, they needed to learn the Spanish language. During that period they lived at the LAM complex in the capital city of San José, which included a hospital and dormitories and other facilities for the staff and students training at the Seminario Bíblico (the Biblical Seminary), the mission's theological seminary.

One day the Vande Kappelles were put to an extraordinary test. They were taken to the Seminary kitchen preparation room, where they were handed aprons and given their orders for the day. Their job was to butcher a cow. They couldn't believe their eyes as the carcass of a recently slaughtered cow, brought from the LAM farm, was placed before them. This was no task for the squeamish. Jake, who had once run a poultry business with his father, got right down to business. But Bert found the job repulsive; the experience nearly transformed her into a vegetarian.

Susan Strachan, co-founder and co-director of the Latin America Mission, had devised the gruesome ordeal. This petite, highly motivated pioneer had begun her career as a single missionary in Argentina. Even after her marriage to Harry and their relocation to Costa Rica, she often administered the Mission's affairs on the home front for weeks and even months at a time while her husband pursued his urgent calling to evangelize the rest of Latin America.

Mrs. Strachan had a flair for life, and there wasn't an LAM missionary left unsinged by the fire burning within her Irish heart. Putting neophyte missionaries through the paces was one of her specialties. According to her perspective, missionaries had to learn quickly that they could not enter a foreign land expecting natives to convert and to step out by faith unless they themselves were willing to adjust culturally and lead by example.

When the LAM purchased the farm in the late 1920s, that it was a working coffee plantation added to its value. The laborers whom Jake supervised were responsible not only for the farm's general maintenance but also for the cultivation of its coffee plants, spread over seventy acres. Their other duties included hand cutting special grasses used for cattle feed, cultivating sugar cane, tending the farm's large vegetable garden, milking the cows, and churning the butter. The farm provided remarkably for the needs of the orphanage, underscoring a unique symbiotic relationship.

Though the scenery was spectacular, living conditions at the Home were rather primitive. The newcomers faced the prospect of unheated buildings, cold-water showers, dim lighting, the lack of electrical appliances, and the unavailability of telephone service. The region surrounding the farm was even less developed. Most of the homes dotting the hillsides were simple, thatch-roofed, adobe huts, built by squatters. The dirt floors, pounded to a hard finish and regularly scrubbed, were generally kept quite clean. Even the *pueblo*, the nearby village, lacked electricity. The orphanage, with its cozy setting, looked attractive and inviting by comparison.

As Bert and Jake approached the farm on the unpaved roadway leading from the *pueblo*, they saw the orphanage below them, its four red-roofed buildings quaintly nestled together. To the left stood a small schoolhouse, its tiny bell tower glistening in the sunlight. The central building, La Esperanza (The Hope), was a large double-gabled building that served as home to the school-age girls but also contained the kitchen, dining room, and laundry. Behind La Esperanza stood El Nido (The Nest), home to preschool children, and across the street from La Esperanza stood El Porvenir (The Future), a dormitory for boys of school age, generally from six to fourteen years of age.

The schoolhouse also doubled as a chapel. Though the children made a ready congregation, the missionaries were eager for growth and pursued their goal by evangelizing the surrounding area. Their task was formidable, for the rural population, consisting mostly of peasants and dirt farmers, had little interest in spiritual matters. Though reared as Catholics, few attended Mass regularly, in part because the nearest resident priest was in Barva, an hour's walk away. Despite their laxness in attending church, their religious views, generally a combination of Catholic dogma and superstitious beliefs, were rigidly held. The majority maintained an antipathy towards evangelicals (Protestants), especially the missionaries, whom they considered heretics.

Though the missionaries gave evangelism high priority, progress came slowly. Initially every step was met with opposition. As farm superintendent, Jake began with his workers, cultivating their friendship, gaining their trust, and achieving a reputation for fairness. Bert's approach was more direct. Having overcome her fear of horses, she traveled widely on horseback, accompanied by Victoria, a teacher at the orphanage. Together they canvassed the area, going from door to door, making friends, meeting needs, but always looking for opportunities to share the gospel. The friendliness and hospitality innate to Latin Americans opened many doors for them.

My earliest memory is about the time I got lost. As a toddler, I was often under the watchful eye of older children whose maternal and paternal instincts were already in bloom. My parents, with their busy schedules, appreciated those helping eyes and hands. However, youngsters are easily distracted, and it was during a careless moment that I wandered off. By the time my absence was discovered, I had vanished.

"*¿Donde está Roberto?*" The cry of alarm quickly spread among the children, "Where did Robert go?"

They looked everywhere, inside the house, in the school, and on the playground. Concern mounted as a search through the familiar haunts proved futile. They finally found me, lying next to a cow, fast asleep.

The pace of life at the orphanage quickened for my parents in the late 1940s, for in addition to the dozen or more children under their direct care, they had a youngster of their own to rear. They appreciated the helping hands of the older children, which not only eased their load but also enabled the blossoming MK (missionary kid) to become one with his orphan companions.

Spanish became my first language, the only one I spoke as a youngster. When I reached school age, I began attending the Home's tiny schoolhouse, where I learned to speak, write, read, and think as a native. When I was six, a year before my parent's furlough in the United States, they decided it was time that I learn English. However, they found me most uncooperative; for whenever they tried to teach me English my response was "*Tan feo, no!* (Something that ugly, no)." I heard in that language a dissonance not present in the melodious strains of my beloved Spanish.

While my parents were undergoing adjustments of their own, due to additional challenges and increased responsibilities, I, too, was changing, not just physically and emotionally, but spiritually. At an early age, my parents had impressed upon me the importance of recognizing my own sinfulness and of accepting God's grace. Throughout their evangelistic work my parents had witnessed the transformation of many lives. They understood conversion as both a foundation for personal life and as a relationship that brought humans closer to one another and to God. Conversion—professing one's faith in Jesus as Savior and yielding to Christ's Lordship—was an elixir, God's remedy for all of humanity's needs. It seemed most natural, given my upbringing, that I should make a profession of faith at an early age, and I did so, genuinely, at the age of four.

My first dramatic encounter with God, however, occurred two years later, when we were living in *La Esperanza*. It was siesta time, and my parents were inside, resting. Though I was free to play outdoors, I was warned not to climb trees, and especially not to eat the fruit of the *níspero* trees. However, like that young alchemist in the fables who was warned not to think of pink elephants whenever he attempted to make gold from base metals, lest the magical transformation be foiled, I couldn't resist the thought of juicy *nísperos* melting in my mouth.

Behind *El Nido*, isolated from view, were several *níspero* trees, and on that day no one was around. I climbed one of the trees and began eating the forbidden fruit. However, in that moment, I was overcome by an eerie feeling. Everything was quiet, too quiet. The birds had stopped their singing, the insects their chirping, and I was existentially alone. Then I heard a rumbling sound. The trees began to shake and the earth convulsed. My heart pounded while I grasped the limb as tightly as possible. *El Nido*, its flooring resting on three-foot-high columns, was shaking from the tremors. By then my entire body trembled with fear. My arms and legs shook like JELL-O, and I was unable to hang on to the limb any longer.

As soon as I hit the ground, the tremors subsided. The earthquake, quite common in that seismic region, was not particularly severe, but that day I understood the wrath of God, and I was sure that the earth had moved as punishment for my disobedience. God had been watching, and my guilt was exposed. Two years earlier I had experienced the embracing love of God, but this time it was God's wrath. I am thankful that my first experience with God, one of faith and not of fear, became the lasting one, for my relationship with God has remained one of affirmation and love.

When I was eight years old, my parents moved to the capital city of San José. Following World War II, the LAM embarked on a bold campaign to extend its evangelistic outreach. In February of that year the Mission radio station TIFC went on the air, becoming the first evangelical station in Central America and the second missionary station in the world. To support the interests of the listening audience, a literature department was established, and *Editorial Caribe* (Caribbean Publishers) soon became one of the leading evangelical publishing houses in Latin America.

In 1952 Jake began to oversee an ambitious construction program that included building a headquarters for the *Editorial Caribe*, followed by a three-story Annex for the hospital and the renovation of the Biblical Seminary complex. The Latin America Biblical Seminary, founded in 1923, shortly after the Mission was established, was arguably the LAM's most vital institution. From the beginning, the Mission's primary emphasis had been to evangelize the Latin American continent, and the Seminary's role, training young converts and preparing Latin America's future church leaders, was pivotal. By 1952 the Seminary's graduates were located in most Latin American countries, including a large number in the Caribbean island of Puerto Rico and others among Hispanics in the United States. The forty-five male students enrolled in 1950 came from twelve countries, including three who were full-blooded Indians.

Bert's activities during her five-year term in San José were both challenging and diverse. Her primary job was at the *Clínica Bíblica*, the Mission hospital, where she functioned as receptionist and personal secretary to her friend, Doctor Marie Cameron. While on break or during off-hours she visited the patients, supporting them with prayer and encouraging them to grow in their faith. For two of those years, while she continued with reduced responsibilities at the hospital, Bert also served as Dean of Women at the Seminary, where she supervised some fifteen students annually. As Dean, Bert was expected to provide her charges with personal and academic advice, but primarily with spiritual guidance. The Mission, managed by a small staff, encouraged its members to take risks, to live boldly and thus exercise their abilities fully.

Bert found those years to be immensely fulfilling. Despite holding two jobs simultaneously, she taught a women's class each Sunday at the Templo Bíblico, the Mission's downtown church, and participated in weekly Women's Association meetings. She also continued to make time for her trademark home-to-home visitations, a priority since her teenage years in Paterson, New Jersey.

A highlight of my youth was when my parents purchased a three-speed bicycle on sale at a nearby fire station, its lightweight frame and narrow tires promising adventure. Regular commutes to school several miles away, coupled with occasional excursions on weekends, gave me the confidence to go on longer rides. In this mountainous country, I acquired the curiosity to see what was on the other side of the hill.

During those formative years, I engaged regularly in home devotions, reading scripture and praying daily before meals at home Bible studies. These practices didn't ensure perfection, however, for as an active and willful child, I occasionally resorted to lying, stealing, and even cheating. If caught, I was corrected, disciplined, and forced to make amends. As an eleven-year-old, I worked at an ice-cream factory, but that money went into savings. I had no allowance, and consequently no money to spend, so I constantly desired things I couldn't have. As missionaries, my parents lived frugally, sustained solely by the sacrificial support of friends in the States. Consequently, my parents never acquiesced to spend money frivolously on my childhood whims.

On one occasion, after admitting to stealing from a store, I was required to return the items and make restitution. On another occasion, after stealing stamps from a friend's stamp collection, I was required to turn over my entire collection to the boy, including stamps my father had brought me from a recent trip to Colombia. One time, when I was disrespectful to a Sunday School teacher, I spent that Sunday afternoon walking to his house to apologize. Both as Christians and as missionaries, my parents were committed to respect and absolute honesty. That trip cost my mother more than it cost me, and I remember that incident with admiration for her consistently high theological and ethical standards.

During those formative years in Costa Rica I was introduced to the Gospel of John, with its dual emphasis on a loving God who desires the salvation of the world and its unique presentation of Jesus as fully God and fully man. The Latin America Mission, with whom my parents served for thirty-three years in the mid-twentieth century, emphasized biblical literacy, using their publishing house to distribute literature that promoted its evangelistic endeavors. When free correspondence courses were created to disseminate biblical perspectives, the Fourth Gospel had a prominent role. I was encouraged to take those courses, and I did so willingly, for my love affair with scripture began at an early age. That encounter with the Gospel of John enhanced my understanding of God, the cosmos, and the Christian life, as well as my identity as a child of God.

Those years in San José brought sweeping changes into our family life. Earlier, my parents had not wanted to leave the orphanage but now, five years later, as they prepared for furlough, Bert and Jake felt fulfilled in their ministries, confident that they would return to San José, where they believed they would complete their missionary careers. That, however, would not be the case. The late 1950s became a time of transition for our family. While each of us expected to return to Costa Rica after the furlough, God—and the Latin America Mission—had another plan. A huge adjustment awaited us in the United States.

Several months later, as I returned from school in Paterson, New Jersey, I picked up the mail as usual, bringing it upstairs to our apartment. My mother was home alone at the time, for Dad was away on Mission business. When Mom saw that one of the letters was from the Field Office in Costa Rica, she opened it immediately. The dramatic change in her facial expression as she began reading the letter prompted me to ask what was wrong.

"Oh Bob!" she exclaimed. "The Mission is asking us to go to Colombia."

"But I don't want to go to Colombia," was all I could say. Adapting to another country and another home, to new friends and another school, was more than I felt I could handle, particularly after the adjustments of the past five years. And going to the torrid Colombian coast, with its unbearable heat and high humidity, was something neither of us wanted.

My mother's thoughts raced far ahead of mine as an idea entered her mind, an idea so drastic that she decided to wait for Dad's return before even mentioning it. But when I pressed her to tell me she finally blurted it out. "Bob, if we go to Colombia, you won't be able to go with us. There are no suitable schools nearby where you can continue your education."

When Dad came home that night and read the letter he said very little, but it was obvious what he was thinking. The LAM had decided to rebuild a private secondary school for girls in Cartagena, Colombia, and Dad was needed to supervise its construction.

"Do we have to go?" I asked. "Is the Mission making you go?"

"No," Mom responded, "but they think we are the right ones for the job, and they've asked us to pray about it."

My parents' decision was compounded by the news that the Field Board had voted unanimously in favor of this assignment. Had there been any dissenting votes, even one, there might have been room to question whether this decision represented God's will, but that option was not available.

My parents knew what Colombia represented, for Dad had just visited that country, and he had no desire to return. And Mom, who knew about the climate, had no desire to visit the place, let alone go there to live. In addition, Colombia was considered unsafe, for that country had just emerged from the "ten years of violence," a period of social and political upheaval during which time the Protestant community had undergone violent persecution. That night none of us slept very well.

The pieces began to fall into place. As my parents prayed about leaving me behind, the matter of my schooling became paramount. I enrolled at The Stony Brook School , a private Christian preparatory school in Long Island, not far from New York City, and that school, with its supportive environment, became my home for the next three and a half years. The transition from dependence to independence is generally easier for a child than for a parent, and I made my adjustment faster than my mother.

During those years of separation, my parents prayed for me on a daily basis. And I could feel, across the miles, the efficacy of their prayers. Though I was alone, I never felt betrayed or abandoned, nor did I feel sorry for myself. From the moment of her dramatic conversion as a young adult, my mother believed that God had a plan for her life, a plan to be realized by faith. "If you want to sit in a corner and feel sorry for yourself," she stated, "if you want to say 'I can't do this' or 'I can't do that,' you will never get anywhere as a Christian." For her, life's meaning unfolds as one claims God's promises.

As she turned to the scriptures for comfort, she thought about the biblical passage that speaks of the blessedness of leaving houses and lands for Christ's sake, knowing she had already done that. The passage also spoke about leaving loved ones, brothers, sisters, father, and mother, and she knew she had done that as well. But did the passage mention leaving children? She thought so, but she wasn't sure. So she turned to Matthew 19:29 and refreshed her memory: "And every one who has left houses or brothers or sisters or father or mother *or children* or fields, for my name's sake, will receive a hundredfold, and will inherit eternal life."

Yes, the word "children" was there. God had not asked her to do something impossible when he asked her to leave her only child. Every sign seemed to confirm that parting. Finally, she experienced the peace she sought.

At Stony Brook, I receive a first-rate education. It took me a few years to develop my intellectual sea legs, but when I did, I was ready to take on the world. At that boarding school, known for its adherence to Christian values, I grew physically, intellectually, and spiritually, all under the watchful care of a distinctive Christian staff. Learning to read, write, and investigate critically, I acquired a love of history and a deep appreciation for classical literature.

My faith deepened during that period, due in part to compulsory daily chapel and to additional opportunities for spiritual growth such as leading a Christian youth group in the community, representing the school at religious conferences, and embarking on a summer cross-country tour with a teacher and several international students. In school I excelled in religious and theological studies; my religious zeal was such that I was one of two seniors to complete the headmaster's challenge to memorize Paul's letter to the Philippians in the New Testament in order to receive a Bible of my own choice. When the headmaster asked me what version of the Bible I desired, I had no answer, for I had not given it any thought; my only goal being to complete the task. The headmaster indicated he would surprise me, and at graduation I received a genuine morocco red-leather copy of the Bible, with my name inscribed on the front—correctly spelled. I treasure that Bible, having read it cover to cover many times.

In 1961, when I graduated from The Stony Brook School, my parents were present to celebrate the occasion. Though distance prevented me from celebrating my birthdays or Christmas holidays with my parents during their ten-year stay in Colombia, they never missed my graduations. Essentially self-educated, my parents made numerous sacrifices to ensure that I should have every opportunity to progress as far as my academic ability might take me. Their gift to me—an open door to learning and the confidence to walk through it—was my inheritance. This gift was surely better than monetary or material presents for it never tarnishes, breaks down, or falls out of fashion.

From 1961 to 1965, The King's College (TKC) was my home. Located in a former resort on the outskirts of exclusive Briarcliff Manor, New York, I thrived in this Christian setting, excelling academically and spiritually. My years at TKC were some of the best of my life. I made great friends, had wonderful experiences, and befriended many, from the resident custodian in the men's dorm to the maintenance crew to members of the faculty and administration. In addition to serving in student government, I also played varsity soccer. My faith was nurtured at daily chapel services, Sunday evening services, and accompanying the college president, Dr. Bob Cook, on his speaking and preaching engagements. I also spent two summers traveling the country representing the college as pianist for musical gospel teams. One summer, in addition to musical accompaniment, I preached over sixty times at church services and other church related events.

One night, following a program at a church in Minnesota, a member of the Billy Graham Evangelistic Association invited me to attend the next day's staff meeting and lead in devotions. Due to an engagement in Iowa later that day, I was forced to decline, wondering if by rejecting the invitation I was forgoing a life-altering career opportunity.

After their furlough to attend my graduation from high school, my parents relocated to the city of Sincelejo, the site of LAM's pioneer work in Colombia. Dad had finished the construction of the girls' school in Cartagena, and now his skills were needed at the Caribbean Bible Center (CBC) in Sincelejo, an institute that had long served as a base for the training of evangelists and church workers in northern Colombia.

In 1963, after my sophomore year in college, I returned to Colombia to spend the summer vacation with my parents. The summer went by quickly, for I was kept busy. During my stay in Sincelejo, I found the doors to ministry opening more widely than ever before for me. My piano-playing abilities enabled me to travel extensively, participating in special services and evangelistic campaigns. When I was not involved in ministry, traveling, assisting in church, or playing soccer with friends, I was learning to play the guitar. One of the national teachers at the CBC had published a guitar manual, and with the help of friends and the encouragement of my mother, who also played the guitar, I quickly mastered the basics. I purchased a light, hand-painted instrument and soon I was accompanying the youth at church, participating in their services and activities.

One Sunday, after I had preached in Spanish for the Sincelejo congregation, my parents discussed with me a problem in the Protestant church at El Carmen, a city some fifty miles from Sincelejo. The church, founded a decade earlier, was currently without a pastor, and the congregation was divided by doctrinal disputes. A cultic group, an extreme form of Pentecostalism, had made inroads among the believers, particularly among the recent converts.

When the small evangelical congregation was established, only a few of the town's twenty-eight thousand Catholics were churchgoers. About one hundred people attended the Roman Catholic Church, a handful was Seventh Day Adventists, and the rest displayed no faith whatsoever. The recent Protestant converts lacked religious roots. Like the converts in the city of Corinth, they remained in a state of spiritual infancy (cf. 1 Corinthians 3:1–3). Their emotional Latin temperament, coupled with spiritual immaturity, made them susceptible to dissension.

Early one morning, during an electrical storm, lightning killed one of the leaders of the congregation. The church members were divided in their interpretation of the event. Some saw the tragedy as an act of divine justice, as God's way of punishing the traditionalists for opposing the new teaching. Others saw it only as a natural occurrence. The strife threatened to split the congregation.

"Bob," my parents said, explaining the situation, "Some of the elders in the Sincelejo church are wondering whether you would be willing to lead the congregation of El Carmen in worship for the remainder of the summer. Most of the members wish to maintain ties with the mission and the church's evangelical roots, but some are threatening to leave. If we send a missionary, there most certainly will be a schism, but if an indigenous worker sympathetic to the charismatic minority leads them, they will not achieve unity. As an outsider, and because of your youth, you may be able to minister effectively to these people while remaining neutral. A few months of solid biblical preaching in that church could provide the basis for unity."

Wanting to follow God's leading and recognizing the logic in their argument, I accepted the challenge, and for several weeks, twice a week, I traveled to El Carmen by bus. As I rode, I contemplated the divided congregation, the slain elder, and the remarkable challenge awaiting me. I prayed for guidance and decided to keep a journal of my experiences and insights. One day, following an inspiring service, I wrote these words in my pocket diary: "Right now, as I perform this task, I believe I am in the center of God's will. There is nothing I would rather be doing than what I am doing. I could not be any happier than I am at this moment." Pondering the meaning of life, I concluded that each day, and every moment of each day, is a unique point of contact with the divine.

Each year my mother selected a biblical passage to serve as her motto for that year; one New Year's Day she chose the verse, "But godliness with contentment is great gain" (1 Timothy 6:6 KJV). This is the truth I learned during the summer of '63.

Graduating with a major in Modern Foreign Languages, I remained at The King's College for a year, assisting the language department and serving as resident director of an off-campus dormitory. I also audited a class in church history taught by world-renowned Yale professor Kenneth Scott Latourette at General Theological Seminary in New York City. A disappointment occurred at the start of the term when my Baptist church in Paterson, New Jersey denied my request for funds to study at the seminary on account of the church's policy to support only students attending conservative denominational seminaries. I concluded that my denominational affiliation lay elsewhere.

The following year I enrolled in a graduate program in Latin American Studies at Indiana University. Though I found the topic fascinating, I remained undecided about a career and applied to Princeton Theological Seminary, one of America's leading theological institutions, intending to study ethics and ecumenism. During my first year in the divinity program my attention gravitated to biblical studies, partly because of my strong background in the subject but also through the influence of one of the leading scholars at the institution, Dr. Bruce Metzger, a gracious scholar with a stellar international reputation and a conservative approach to the Bible.

Upon completing a divinity degree, I transferred my church membership to the Presbyterian Church and remained at Princeton Seminary, enrolling in the PhD program in biblical studies. Discerning a call to ministry, I sought ordination in my adoptive denomination and accepted the pastorate of a small congregation while I completed the dissertation phase of my program. Though my work at the church was meaningful, I found the administrative side tedious. Aware that my gift definitely lay in academics, I accepted a teaching position at Grove City College, a Presbyterian-related liberal arts college.

For the next forty years, I taught a college course in either Old or New Testament every semester. That vision started during family devotions, and it was fostered by my correspondence course on the Gospel of John, by my commitment to memorize Philippians, and through religion classes and preaching opportunities in high school and college. My fervor was nurtured through daily reading and study of that red Bible that I kept at my desk at all times.

An area of theological study that had fascinated me for a long time was the topic of eschatology, which dealt with the end of history and the return of Christ. This topic had also intrigued the earliest Christians and many others throughout church history. My evangelical upbringing emphasized the imminent return of Christ, which led to a literalistic interpretation of eschatological passages in the Bible, particularly apocalyptic passages in the Gospels (see Mark 13, Matthew 24, and Luke 21), in the epistles (2 Thessalonians 2), and in the books of Daniel and Revelation.

Princeton Seminary, known for its commitment to a Reformed and amillennial approach to eschatology,[1] encouraged less literal approaches to the topic. Seminarians at Princeton, after all, were training for careers in ministry and society, and not for the impending end of history.

---

1. Amillennialism utilizes a symbolic interpretation to the early Christian focus on the concept of a millennium, a reference to the restored earthly kingdom that was understood to last for a period of one thousand years between the first coming of Christ and the establishment of a totally new cosmic order at his second coming.

Nevertheless, the centrality of eschatology in the Bible and for early Christianity was undisputed by scholars at the seminary. While some students believed in an imminent "rapture" (the expectation that believers would soon be "caught up in the clouds" to meet Christ at the time of his return, a view based upon a literal interpretation of 1 Thessalonians 4:15–17), I no longer agreed. My changing views on eschatology resulted in fervent debates with my evangelical parents, who clung tenaciously to literal premillennialism.[2] They disagreed with my interpretation of scripture and feared that my understanding of eschatology indicated an alarming compromise with biblical principles. Prolonged disputes on the topic, with neither side relenting, led to the conclusion that it was best to avoid the topic altogether.

A corollary to eschatology is the doctrine of heaven and hell, a topic with important implications for soteriology (salvation). Though I still maintained a traditional understanding of salvation (that individuals are saved through Christ's work on the cross), the doctrine of hell kept resurfacing, and the more I thought about it, the more inclined I felt to abandon it. C. S. Lewis's witty and subtle approach to heaven and hell described in his allegory, *The Great Divorce*, became increasingly attractive at that time. Questioning eschatology led to my questioning other religious topics as well, particularly biblical prophecy.

Despite these concerns, the bedrock of my belief was intact and continued to be based on scripture. While the Bible seemed largely the product of human authorship, I saw no need to question the doctrine of divine inspiration. I no longer believed in verbal inspiration—the notion that the actual words of scripture were inspired—but I still maintained that the Bible was a product of special revelation, and that it was sufficient for faith and practice.

Upon completion of my doctorate at Princeton, I became ordained as a Presbyterian minister and worked as a pastor for two years in New Jersey before relocating to Pennsylvania to teach religion and philosophy at Grove City College (1975–1980). In 1980 I accepted my dream job, serving as Chair and Professor of Religious Studies and College Chaplain at Washington & Jefferson College in Washington, Pennsylvania. I met Susan while preparing for ministry, and found a partner with whom I could grow through life. Together we reared two amazing children and currently enjoy our six grandchildren.

If this account of my life sounds ideal, it does not tell the whole story, for many details have been overlooked. My life to that point—and that of my parents—was far from ideal. When my parents left for a foreign land in

---

2. Premillenialism refers to the view that the imminent "rapture" of believers will be followed by a seven-year period of tribulation for those "left behind" during the rule of the antichrist.

1935, they went by faith. They staked their lives on the promises of scripture and on the faithfulness of God. As career missionaries, first in the idyllic country of Costa Rica, then in turbulent Colombia, they trusted God implicitly. They did not know what lay ahead—the glorious highs and the gut-wrenching lows—but they trusted God implicitly. And they were not disappointed.

Yet I remember the traumatic, life-changing calamities that struck my parents, how my father lost an eye in a sledding accident when he was ten years of age, or how my mother contracted cancer at the age of forty-eight, while in the prime of her life, at a time when she was fully engaged in a caregiving ministry for the God she loved and served. And it was breast cancer, quite possibly a woman's worst fear. A mastectomy was performed, and after several months of improving health, my mother discovered another lump forming in her other breast. Was this spreading of cancer an indication that her ministry, perhaps even her life, was at an end? Or was this experience a "wound of love," like the limp that the Old Testament patriarch Jacob received when he wrestled with God, when he received a new name (Israel) and a renewed promise for himself and his posterity?

This event came at a time when my parents were about to experience a deepening of their faith and an enlarging of their ministry. My mother would go on to live forty additional years as a cancer survivor. My father became ordained to the gospel ministry in 1966, two years before his retirement, and he spent the next twenty-five years teaching himself Greek and Hebrew, eventually reading the entire Bible in the original languages, something few seminary graduates or Bible scholars have ever accomplished. And he did this with the use of only one eye.

UNSUNG HEROES

Our culture's stock of heroes, particularly, moral heroes, is dwindling. According to Allan Bloom, author of the 1987 bestselling book, *The Closing of the American Mind*, when asked to name their heroes, college students go mute. It seems that today's young people have inserted celebrities into the roles and places once occupied by real heroes.

What occurs when the imagination loses Odysseus and Joan of Arc, or forgets more recent heroes such as Albert Schweitzer, Dietrich Bonhoeffer, Dorothy Day, or Mother Teresa? What happens when the imagination loses contact with the time-tested heroic tales that vividly display courage, honesty, service, and faithfulness? Inevitably, the mind and spirit find fuel elsewhere. Many young people escape into a world of fantasy; others imitate celebrities. If there is an instinct to copy what we admire, then today our culture looks to celebrities as heroes. We model their hairstyles, clothing, makeup, and even, their lifestyles.

While heroes are known for their accomplishments, celebrities need be neither good nor bad, but only famous. And what is truly startling is that most celebrities are extraordinarily average. Look at their sins—extramarital affairs, multiple divorces, drinking binges; they are so like us.

I wrote *Love Never Fails* as a biographical tribute to my parents, Jacob and Bertha Vande Kappelle, career missionaries in Latin America at a dangerous time in history when democracy and Marxism battled for the soul of that land. My parents were flesh-and-blood saints, and I believe, twentieth-century heroes. To ensure their legacy in my heart, as well as the hearts and minds of those they loved and served, I have listed seven reasons why they were unsung heroes.

1. *They had a love affair with people in need.* Whether on the mission field, or during retirement, they never stopped serving and loving people in need. Utterly selfless, they believed that Christ lived through their lives and that his life—including his priorities, vision, compassion, and transforming love—continues through all who claim to be his followers.

2. *They lived life courageously*—by faith, not by fear. David Howard, who worked with my parents in Colombia, described my mother as "fearless and direct." She did not hesitate to expose herself to situations or places of danger, for she felt she had been commissioned to do God's work and that with God as her companion, "all things are possible."

3. *They lived with a remarkable blend of depth and simplicity*, exemplifying the slogan: "character before career." My parents valued relationships far more than possessions. They took little with them to Latin America and they returned with even less. They could say, like the apostle Paul: "I have learned to be content with whatever I have" (Phil. 4:11).

4. *They were guided by faith, hope, and love.* They embodied a "purpose-driven life" long before the phrase became the title of a best-selling book. They proved that those three simple, but powerful principles can transform anyone's life, enabling ordinary people to live extraordinary lives. In tough times their fueling faith came through their hopeful reminder that "the best is yet to come."

5. *They encouraged me to live life with a sense of adventure.* In 1935, at the height of the Depression, they left every security they knew—their family, friends, jobs, most of their meager belongings, and even their

country—to head for a lifetime of adventure in a world far away. There they began new vocations, immersed themselves in a new culture, learned to communicate in a new language, observed different traditions, and even worshipped in a different manner. For them, life was "an adventure to be lived, not a problem to be solved."

6. *They established a clear pattern of life that I could imitate* while still maintaining my own identity. Putting Christ before others and others before self, doing more with less, making things last, enjoying the moment—these were their priorities, this their template for life. They answered God's call upon their lives, detecting in their lives a spiritual story that they learned to communicate in an inspiring and compelling way. They acquired a burning passion to share their story—which they understood to be an extension of the biblical story—through love and service to others. This pattern enabled me to discern God's call upon my life and discover my place in the ongoing story of faith.

7. *They gave themselves to God without reservation and were willing to be remade by God.* They did not gain their reputation in heroic feats, by thinking new thoughts, or by formulating breakthroughs in the fields of science, medicine, or some other important modern endeavor. Their names will likely never appear on the marquees of Christianity, but their story is "an outstanding account of two people who loved and served the Lord without public recognition, without fame or fortune, but with all their heart, soul and body."[3]

In our modern culture, self-centered celebrities flourish. Such a culture lacks the courage and imagination to be concerned with others, while traditional heroes demand it of themselves. With celebrities there are few surprises, and only rarely vision. With them, we can continue to be as we are. Saints and heroes, on the other hand, find their lives by losing them.

Jesus said, "Turn the other cheek." Without his example, and the saints and heroes who followed him, that command has no meaning. As Paul once wrote, the letter without the Spirit kills. The Spirit, however, the animator of heroes, gives life. My parents are my heroes because they introduced me to that Spirit through their priorities and by the quality of life they lived.

---

3. This assessment of my parents, by missionary colleague David Howard, appears in the Foreword to Love Never Fails, 10–11.

QUESTIONS FOR REFLECTION

1. After reading this chapter, what did you learn about compassion and service to others?
2. My parents' motto was, "Only what's done for Christ will last." What is your motto? If you don't have one, find one to which you can commit.

Chapter 2

Dark Splendor

Promenade. In nondual spirituality, acting precedes understanding: first, we must act, and then we will understand, meaning we will understand intuitively. However, we will never truly know *why* we know, nor will we be able to prove it to others. The mysterious wisdom of faith is not learned in abstraction, or by reflection, but only when one is on the way. It is not a lesson anyone else can teach us; we must go down this road ourselves. This is the place of the soul, the place of wisdom, toward which we must move. Once we let go of control, we will come to the inner place of compassion. In this place, we will notice how much the suffering of the world is our suffering, and how committed we are to this pain. At this inner place of compassion, we will find the peace that the world cannot give. We won't need to win anymore; we just do what we need to do as simply and joyfully as possible. That is why Augustine could make such an outrageous statement as "love God and do what you want." People who are living from a God-centered place instead of a self-centered place are dangerously free precisely because they are tethered at the center. When one lives in this manner, from this center, all is possible, because all is permitted. However, if it is true that "with God all things are permitted," how do we decide right from wrong? The answer is simple: by focusing on the biblical command to love God, self, and neighbor equally. That is our sole priority. The aim of this study is to present alternative responses to rigid, either/or approaches that narrow the possibilities for seekers at all stages of their journey.

During the twentieth century, physical science became increasingly dissatisfied with prevailing views of reality, thereby challenging and transforming many cherished scientific beliefs. In his 1962 book, *The Structure of Scientific Revolutions*, T. S. Kuhn, a trained physicist and one of the most influential historians of science, introduced the concept of "paradigm shift," demonstrating that modern science does not provide nearly the certainty that scientists had formerly thought. Likewise, Werner Heisenberg, one of the greatest revolutionaries of modern science, has written that science has discarded many concepts that it thought were final and certain.

Using his uncertainty principle, Heisenberg affirmed the ultimate mysteriousness of reality, challenging science's hegemony on certainty. For example, time and space were no longer viewed as constants, and light was said to be both a particle and a wave. Even though most humans cannot comprehend such a paradox, they accept it as somehow real. As Heisenberg notes, these descriptions of light, while paradoxical, are complementary. The brilliant mathematician Kurt Gödel, known for Gödel's Proof, has demonstrated that even mathematics does not provide absolute certainty. In 1933, as a young man of only twenty-seven, he confirmed that two quite different answers could be obtained from the same group of mathematical data. If mathematics could not lay claim to absolute certainty, as Gödel claimed, surely people must remain open to truth, whatever its source.

OLD AND NEW

Each person is unique, with a distinct personality. Despite their uniqueness, individuals share personality traits, qualities, and preferences that can be defined and typed into distinct categories. Like cyclists on a tandem, personality and spirituality travel together through the journey of life. Riding in tandem, they are deeply influenced by conditions both internal (goals, moods, desires) and external to the self. When one leans, the other leans; where one starts, the other starts; if one stops, the other stops. Though not identical, they strive to be in sync, balancing one another in profound and intimate ways. Personality takes the lead, and where personality goes, spirituality follows, though not blindly or passively. Spirituality has its own voice, and when its desires are addressed and heeded, personality thrives. When the two disagree, they must communicate, or the consequences can be disastrous. Cooperation always enhances the ride.

In 2015 I published my tenth book, *Dark Splendor*, a volume on "depth spirituality." Examining the relationship between personality and spirituality, I presented various psychological developmental models, focusing on the contributions of Swiss psychiatrist Carl G. Jung and Jungian personality type theory. That book also explores the notion of the two halves of life, noting how the perspectives and experiences of the first half of life either inhibit or enhance the vibrant maturity called "the second half of life."

This talk of the first and second half of life is not new. It has been embodied for centuries in the scriptures, tales, and experiences of men and women who found themselves on the further journey. In Matthew 13:52, at the close of a chapter dealing with parables of the kingdom, Jesus presents his followers with one of his most significant interpretive principles: "Every scribe who has been trained for the kingdom of heaven is like the master of a household who brings out of his treasure what is new and what is old." The principle, in modern terms, might read something like this: "If something is true once, it is always true. Honor the old, but in a way that makes spiritual sense now, in a modern psychological and sociological context."

While some beliefs are helpful, others may be harmful. We need to know what to build upon, and what to discard or reinterpret. Rather than seeing "old and new" dualistically—that is, as opposites—the term "evolving" acknowledges their relationship. What happens when we see our lives in this way, as works of art expressing creativity and newness? As Mirabai Starr writes, "A miraculous event unfolds when we throw the lead of our personal story into the transformational flames of creativity. [When we do so], our hardship is transmuted into something golden. With that gold we heal ourselves and redeem the world . . . When we allow ourselves to be conduits for creative energy, we experience direct apprehension of that energy. We become a channel for grace. To make art is to make love with the sacred."[1]

During my studies at Princeton Theological Seminary, I read about John Goddard, an adventurer who spent his life pursuing 127 goals that he had devised at the age of fifteen. These goals, amazingly varied, included exploring the Nile River; writing a book; composing music; learning to play "Clair de Lune" on the piano; teaching a college course; studying primitive cultures in New Guinea; learning French, Spanish, and Arabic; running a five-minute mile; climbing the Matterhorn; circumnavigating the globe; and flying an airplane. I found such an approach to life quite compelling, although I knew I would never be that adventurous.

During midlife, settled into a career and a parent with children of my own, I took to heart Dr. Howard J. Burnett's advice about living live adventurously, engaging in challenging and creative activities such as road

---

1. Starr, Wild Mercy, 159–60.

cycling, white-water kayaking, cross-country skiing, and playing the saxophone with the college wind ensemble.

Though I had biked most of my life, cycling became a routine during my midlife. Around the age of forty, when I began experiencing discomfort in my lower back, I discovered that cycling offered therapeutic benefits, when accompanied by stretching and massage. A love of sports and an obsession with exercise rekindled my dreams and sparked the passion for adventure and independence I had experienced as a child. During the summer of 1989, I translated my dream of a cross-country cycling trip into a solo trek on behalf of Habitat for Humanity, utilizing adventure as a means to help disadvantaged citizens. As I cycled across the "northern tier" of the North American continent, I matured as an individual and grew spiritually by going "Homeless for Habitat." The trek resulted in a book contract, resulting in my second book, *The Invisible Mountain*.

Cycling became integral to the postcritical phase of my life, as daily rides created experiences that provided powerful personal and emotional lessons for life, including heightened self-motivation, better self-control, improved decision-making, strategic planning, respect for others, care for the environment, and judicious cooperation with motorists. Simply put, road cycling enhanced my physical conditioning, self-confidence, self-awareness, and my spirituality. Finding the rhythmic pedaling meditative, lengthy rides provided moments of reflection that were both therapeutic and creative, helping me solve problems while allowing me to ponder my sense of purpose and the meaning of life.[2] In 2005, after twenty years of cycling, I reached 75,000 miles, averaging nearly 4,000 miles a year. I set a lifetime goal of 100,000 miles. These activities included serving as a board member of the local Habitat for Humanity and resulted in receipt of the "Citizen of the Year" award from Community Action of Southwest Pennsylvania for Washington County.

While teaching at W&J, I also learned to play the saxophone and clarinet. I requested permission to enroll as a student in music classes, with the intention of completing the requirements for a major course of study in music. The music department sent my request to the president of the college, who granted permission to enroll as an auditor as time allowed, subject to permission from each instructor and to all course requirements. However, he denied my petition to enroll in the degree program. I was already performing double duty as professor and chair of Religious Studies, in addition to serving as college chaplain. Those duties were deemed sufficient to the

---

2. For more on this topic, see appendix A, "The Road of Life."

terms of my contract. I agreed, enrolling eventually in four classes while playing with the wind ensemble for six years.

Classes in jazz music and in jazz improvisation provided another creative outlet, the writing of *Blue Notes*, a volume on jazz styles and jazz history featuring 365 biographical entries of jazz artists by date of birth, one for each day of the year.

ALTERNATIVE ORTHODOXY

The spiritual transformation I have undergone since early adulthood has resulted in an amalgam I characterize as progressive orthodoxy, a form of Christian orthodoxy based on the new order that Jesus announced. Can orthodoxy be progressive or alternative? Does it strike you as impossible or as oxymoronic? For dualists, one is either orthodox (true and right) or heterodox (wrong and false). But heterodoxy is precisely a third possibility, a middle ground between orthodoxy and heresy, rejecting the extremes of institutional Christianity, corporate and individual, Catholic and Protestant.

Heterodoxy represents a "third way," the creative and courageous role that is both active *and* contemplative, prophetic *and* mystic. At the heart of orthodoxy is paying attention to correct teaching and behavior, where the opposite is wrong and false, focusing on principles, precepts, and standards. Alternative orthodoxy deemphasizes hierarchicalism, power, institutionalism, ceremonialism, ostentation of any kind. It pays attention to different things, such as nature, simplicity, the outsider, humility, compassion, affirmation, and nonduality, where the opposite is accepted, at times even embraced. Going back to the basics, rightly understood; that's what I have in mind by "alternative orthodoxy."

In my estimation, this alternative orthodoxy is closer to the order that Jesus' first followers believed had already arrived than to the religio-political forms that emerged in the Western world during the Middle Ages, developed from imperial forms of Christianity and shaped by emperors such as Constantine in the West and Justinian in the East. When Jesus called his disciples, he was not asking others to join a new security system, a religious club, denomination, or order. He did not invite them to a belief system, but rather to a lifestyle: "Follow me." Where faith was elicited, it was in the form of trust, not belief. When he called his first disciples, Jesus was talking about further journeys to people who were already settled, socially and religiously.

The Gospels are essentially resurrection accounts, written after the fact. Their purpose is to unify Christian believers by evoking faith in Christ. The Gospels can be misleading, particularly for those who view faith systematically, as a set of doctrines and beliefs, for they were not intended to be read doctrinally or dogmatically. It took Christians several centuries to create a systematic understanding of Jesus and his mission, one that, in my estimation, they got wrong. When I think of Jesus, it is not how he is dissimilar from other human beings that I seek to understand, but rather how he serves as the model and metaphor for all humanity. In my estimation, the historical Jesus embodies the universal Christ, the Reality that gives all humans final meaning and definition.

According to the New Testament, Christians are kind of hybrid creatures who live in two dimensions. They are citizens of the present age while at the same time living under the dominion of Christ's kingdom. As Paul put it somewhat paradoxically, Christians live "in the flesh" (human nature) as well as "in the Spirit" (the new dimension introduced by Christ). Awareness of this dual citizenship led early Christians to say that they were "strangers" in the historical era on earth (Heb. 11:13). Ever since the New Testament period, Christianity has had to steer between two dangers: the temptation (1) to withdraw from society, on the assumption that Christ's kingdom is not of this world (John 18:36), and (2) to make a too easy identification of the kingdom with something in this world, such as the institutional church or the ideal human society. However, the essential message of the New Testament is this: The kingdom is not of this world, yet it has been manifest in this world through the life, death, and resurrection of Christ.

Every verse of the New Testament presupposes the new people of God, a new community called the church. From the beginning, Christians were characterized as "the body of Christ," followers of Jesus who showed by their lifestyle that they were a part of the new order that Jesus had announced and that they believed had now arrived. Theologically, the church was a microcosm of the transformation that God's new order would bring for the whole world. To be in the church was to have a foretaste of life as God's new people. Socially, the church in the Roman Empire was an alternative society, based not on selfishness, greed, and exploitation, but on the new freedom and fellowship that Jesus had announced: freedom to love God and to love and serve others (Mark 12:29–31). As the church expanded across the Mediterranean world, it was indeed a new society—a context in which people of diverse social, racial, and religious backgrounds were united in a new and radical friendship. Because they had been reconciled to God, they found themselves reconciled to each other.

The church is aware of living in an interim, "between the ages." It cannot bring in the kingdom; it can only testify to its reality, living by the spiritual and ethical principles established by Jesus. Because the citizens of the kingdom belong to a community of believers and are not isolated individuals, they are responsible to maintain the four "notes" or marks of the church, that is, its four defining characteristics as noted in the creeds of Christendom:

- *One*: the unity of the church.
- *Holy*: the purity of the church (to be "holy" is to be set apart for and dedicated to service).
- *Catholic*: the universality of the church (every Christian is part of an inclusive and welcoming whole).
- *Apostolic*: the faithfulness of the church to its founding principles.

Through discipleship, the church models God's "new creation," exhibiting the presence of the kingdom of God to the world, thereby fulfilling individually and communally the cultural mandates associated with the covenant of creation (see Gen. 1:26—2:3). These ordinances, instituted for human wellbeing, include family, labor, and worship. The covenant of creation binds all humans to God and to one another. It entails that, as image-bearers, humans are to reflect God's concern for all of life.

HETERODOXY

More serious than religious opposition from Judaism and persecution from Rome, the early church's internal struggles were caused primarily by minorities who wanted to remain free and charismatic in their interpretation of Christianity. The majority opposed heterodox beliefs and practices, favoring factors that would define orthodoxy, such as apostolic succession, institutional authority, and a binding notion of "the faith." However, when dogma is equated with truth, the container is mistaken for the content, the husk for the kernel.

Throughout religious history, people who disagree or dissent from the norm have been called heretics. The term "heresy," meaning "choice" in the Greek language, usually refers to a person or movement that "stands apart" or deviates from orthodoxy. Historically viewed, a heterodox belief is what we now call a minority opinion. It is not deemed wrong or rebellious as such, but is simply not the mainstream perspective. If Jesus is the primary teacher and reference point for Christianity, then "heresy" would surely be lack of love and not simply disbelief or disobedience.

When a dominant group or religion labels a movement "cultic" or an individual "heretical," this usually indicates amnesia or a short memory, for at its source, almost every distinct movement goes back to someone branded "heretic" on account of novel thoughts or innovative ideas. In the Judeo-Christian tradition alone, Abraham would have been a heretic to the religions of ancient Mesopotamia; Moses to the Egyptians; Jesus and Paul to Judaism; Martin Luther to Catholicism; John Wesley to Anglicanism; William Wilberforce to slavery; Elizabeth Cady Stanton and Susan B. Anthony to patriarchy; Martin Luther King, Jr. to racism; and so forth. Heresy, not apathy, drives history. In the grand scheme of things, nonconformists spark newness and change.

It is that group of alternative Christians—progressive by some standards, conservative by others, but all heterodox in their day—that I wish to join and represent in my living and thinking.

KIERKEGAARD'S EXISTENTIAL MODEL

Søren Kierkegaard, the noted Danish Christian existentialist, made an important contribution to the religious journey in his formulation of three levels of existence or stages through which humans go in their ascent toward God. On the first level, which he labeled the *aesthetic stage*, individuals are ruled by their senses, in which case they can be called "sensual aesthetes." Such persons live solely for the present, and particularly for self-gratification. Aesthetes, characterized by the absence of either moral standards or religious faith, remain detached and uncommitted. Kierkegaard extends this attitude to include the "intellectual aesthete," the contemplative person who tries to stand outside of life and behold it as a spectator.

The second level, the *ethical stage*, requires that one abandon attitudes of selfishness and embrace universal standards, making commitments to others. Here moral standards and obligations are adopted as dictated by reason. The third and final stage, which Kierkegaard called the *religious stage*, entails a life of faith. This is final because it recognizes the existence of God and the need to relate oneself wholly to God.

In each stage, Kierkegaard selected a figure from literature or history as an example. For the model of the religious stage of life, the highest level through which humans go in their ascent toward God, he selected Abraham, whose trust of God and unwavering obedience led him to choose to sacrifice his only son Isaac, even in the face of absurdity, for to question God would be to place reason over faith. In selecting this example, Kierkegaard was not denying the validity of ethics. He stated that the individual who is called to break with the ethical must first be ethical, that is, must first have subordinated to universal morality. The break, when one is called to make it, is made in "fear and trembling" and not arrogantly or proudly. In this final stage, the ethical is not abolished but dethroned by a higher purpose or end, a phenomenon he described as the "teleological suspension of the ethical." The key to this final stage is not the commendable humanistic goal of universal duty to others, but the unqualified giving of oneself to God. For Kierkegaard, if one doesn't go beyond the ethical realm, beyond moral obligation, one cannot properly say that one is related to God, or obedient to God. Ethical duty, Kierkegaard believed, must ultimately lead to God, but since it usually leads to humanity (i.e. to humanism), then this stage must be transcended. An absolute relationship to an absolute (God) requires a relative relationship to relative ends. And for Kierkegaard, everything other than God is relative.

BECOMING A POSTCRITICAL BELIEVER

Most humans, ancient and modern alike, pattern their lives after some model, whether consciously or unconsciously. These models can be cultural, civic, intellectual, historical, cyclical, developmental, religious, or spiritual. Many people follow more than one pattern simultaneously. Most educated people in the West today have little trouble identifying with terms such as premodern, modern, or postmodern. They are also familiar with Karl Marx's adaptation of Hegel's thesis, antithesis, and synthesis as stages of social and economic development. This model has also been used to describe three stages of growth toward citizenship: claiming (thesis), doubting (antithesis), and redeeming (synthesis).

A similar model, consisting of precritical, critical, and postcritical stages, has been applied to theological, existential, and intellectual development. The *precritical phase*, also called precritical naiveté, first naiveté, or first simplicity, is an early state in which children accept whatever significant authority figures in their lives tell them to be true as indeed true. For some this state is short-lived; for others, it can last a lifetime.

In their early teens, some begin to question their beliefs, experiencing a collision between childhood beliefs and those of modernity. In late adolescence, college students often become exposed to the scholarly study of religion, to teachings of religions different from their own, to claims of science, and to atheistic or agnostic professors and points of view. Those who take these views seriously often enter the stage of *critical understanding*, from which there seems to be no way back. Some remain perplexed about God and conclude that there probably is no such reality. This second phase is a critical one, or possibly even an apathetic reaction to the first phase. In this phase, some abandon prayer and stop attending formal worship altogether, living as post-religious inhabitants of the secular city. For many "second phasers," critical reason becomes the object of their faith and secular humanism becomes their creed.

Those who persevere in their faith journey often discover that agnosticism and atheism are more like temporary stops than final destinations. Something happens to them—a mystical experience, something traumatic, a relationship, a sudden realization—and the word "God" becomes meaningful once again, only this time not as a reference to a supernatural being "out there" but to the sacred at the center of existence. God is no longer a mere idea or an article of belief external to oneself but rather an element of experience. Such persons have reached the state of *postcritical understanding* (also called postcritical naiveté, second naiveté, or second simplicity), a state where one participates in religious rituals because they are meaningful and not because they are required, where one hears ancient biblical stories as "true" while knowing them as not literally true.

Those who enter the third phase retain an appreciation of critical reason, but have moved beyond secular humanism in search of sacred ground. Third-phase believers understand their lives as open-ended journeys in which they seek, not an end to ambiguity and uncertainty, but rather breadth, depth, and meaning. They realize that life is a pilgrimage, and that the entire earth can become hallowed ground and therefore the locus of encounter with the living God.

When individuals view faith exclusively as dogma or belief, they impose upon themselves and others specific moral, theological, or doctrinal views to the detriment or exclusion of others, making religion rigid, intolerant, and increasingly confrontational. This form of thinking characterizes the religious approach biblical theologian Marcus Borg called the Precritical Paradigm. When polarities are embraced and the truth is sought through dialogue and in the area of overlap, this form of thinking characterizes the religious approach called the Postcritical Paradigm.

A TALE OF TWO PARADIGMS

It is no secret that we are living in a time of major change, resulting in monumental religious conflict, chiefly in North American mainline denominations. While there are many ways of being Christian in our day, two paradigms—two overarching interpretive frameworks—may be helpful to describe the current conflict in Christianity. The first, the Precritical Paradigm, has been a common form of Christianity for the past several hundred years. This approach should not be associated with Christianity as a whole, though it remains a major voice, perhaps the majority voice in global Christianity. Its adherents

1. View the Bible as a divine product, as the unique revelation of God.
2. Interpret the Bible literally.
3. Equate faith with belief, centering the Christian life on believing now for the sake of salvation.
4. View the afterlife as central, the Christian life being about requirements and rewards, with the main reward a blessed afterlife.
5. View Christianity as the only true religion, and belief in God, the Bible, and Jesus as the way to heaven.

This paradigm should not be equated with "the Christian tradition," as though it were the dominant or only way of being Christian throughout history. In actuality, it is the product of modernity, shaped by the birth of modern science and scientific ways of knowing. Since the Enlightenment of the seventeenth century, modernity has questioned both the divine origin and the literal-factual truth of many parts of the Bible, and the Precritical Paradigm is a response to that modern critique.

A second way of seeing Christianity, the Postcritical Paradigm, has been in existence for over a hundred years and has become an increasingly attractive movement within mainline Protestant denominations and in the Catholic Church. Like the earlier paradigm, its central features are a response to the Enlightenment, only in this case it embraces many Enlightenment ideals, including an appreciation of science, historical scholarship, religious pluralism, and cultural diversity. It also arose out of awareness of how Christianity had contributed to racism, sexism, nationalism, exclusivism, and other harmful ideologies. Its adherents

1. View the Bible as a human response to God.
2. Interpret the Bible historically and metaphorically.
3. View faith relationally rather than dogmatically—faith being the way of the heart, not the way of the head.
4. View the Christian life as one of relationship and transformation. Being Christian is not about meeting requirements for a future reward in an afterlife, and not very much about believing. Rather, the Christian life is about a relationship with God that transforms life in the present.

5. Affirm religious pluralism. This paradigm considers Christianity as one of the world's great enduring religions, as a particular response to the experience of God in the Western cultural stream.

From the perspective of the Postcritical Paradigm, the Precritical Paradigm seems anti-intellectual and rigidly (but selectively) moralistic. Its insistence on biblical literalism seems inadequate, as does its rejection of science whenever it conflicts with literalism. It seems to emphasize individual purity more than compassion and justice. And its exclusivism, its rejection of other religions as inadequate or worse, is objectionable. Can it be that God is known in only one religion—and perhaps only in the "right" form of that religion?[3]

THE FURTHER JOURNEY (SECOND HALF OF LIFE)

While many models—biological, social, psychological, cognitive, moral, ecological, religious, existential, mystical—exist to help conceptualize life's journey, one I find compelling is known as the "second half of life." Adult learning involves "second-half-of-life" thinking and living, a concept I have inserted into my books since the publication of *Dark Splendor* in 2015, my response to Richard Rohr's groundbreaking book *Falling Upward* in 2011. The reason I refer frequently to "second-half-of-life spirituality" is that the concept is transformative. In short, first-half-of-life living, thinking, and learning is characterized by the term "religion," a man-made system largely designed to keep human beings dependent and spiritually immature, using catechisms and creeds to raise and answer predesigned questions. This approach is no longer working, resulting in passivity, suspicion, and conformity for those who stay, and disdain and disinterest for those who leave. Fortunately, another option exists. Second-half-of-life living, thinking, and learning is characterized by the term "spirituality," a dynamic, organic, and unsystematic approach designed to promote wisdom, compassion, maturity, and independence, a transformational journey nourished by myth, metaphor, and mystery.

This "further journey" is not chronological, nor does one magically stumble upon it at midlife or in times of crisis, though these often serve as catalysts. While the second journey represents the culmination of one's faith journey, it is largely unknown today, even by people we consider deeply religious, since most individuals and institutions remain stymied in the preoccupations of the first half of life, establishing identity, creating boundary

---

3. Borg, *Heart of Christianity*, 16.

markers, and seeking security. The first-half-of-life task, while essential, is not the full journey. Furthermore, one cannot walk the second journey with first-journey tools. One needs a new toolkit.

While disagreements over matters such as the role of religion, the Christian life, the interpretation of scripture, the meaning of God, and doctrines such as belief in heaven and hell are attributable to upbringing, chronological age, social standing, and academic training, many disagreements are affected by our spiritual journeys, particularly by our place on that journey. This explains why some people are more open to growth, change, and transformation than others are. While intellect and background are factors, spiritual growth, curiosity, and development are often indicative of second-half-of-life spirituality.

The second-half-of-life journey has been likened to a second simplicity or a second naiveté. Whatever we call it, this condition is the very goal of mature adulthood and mature religion. First naiveté is the earnest and dangerous innocence we sometimes admire in young zealots, but it is also the reason we should not elect them or follow them as leaders. It is probably necessary to be impetuous when we are young, taking risks and eliminating most doubt. In the long run such approaches to life are not wise. Mature wisdom is content to live with mystery, doubt, and "unknowing," and in such living ironically resolves that very mystery to some degree. It takes a great deal of learning to finally "learn ignorance," as so many religious sages discovered. As T. S. Eliot puts it in the *Four Quartets*: "We had the experience but missed the meaning." Eliot's verse suggests that people in the second half of life need not expect to have the same experience as others; rather, simple meaning now suffices.

This new coherence, a unified field that embraces paradox, is precisely what characterizes second-half-of-life people. It feels like a return to simplicity after having learned from all the complexity. Finally, one understands that "everything belongs," even the sad, absurd, and futile parts. In the second half of life we can devote ourselves to integrating even the painful parts of our life into the now unified field, including people who are different or marginalized. If we can forgive ourselves for being imperfect and falling, we can now do it for others.

This talk of the first and second half of life is not new. It has been embodied for centuries in the scriptures, tales, and experiences of men and women who found themselves on the further journey. In this second half of life, people have less interest in judging or punishing others, or in harboring superiority complexes. Life is more spacious now, the boundaries of one's life having been enlarged by the addition of new experiences and relationships. Life is more participatory than assertive, and there is less need for self-assertion and self-definition. In the second half of life, people live in the presence of God. In that reality, the brightness comes from within, a reflection of the divine that is more than adequate.

The second half of life is transformative, producing individuals who are

- less fearful
- less hostile and combative
- less self-absorbed
- less assertive
- less self-concerned
- less dogmatic
- less possessive

Such transformation involves risk-taking in the following areas: (1) forgiveness (repudiating retaliation or "getting even"); (2) prayer (learning to listen in silence); (3) changing one's attitude ("unlearning"); (4) quiet persuasion (becoming an elder statesman); (5) becoming an agent of change (which starts with actively working for peace); and (6) influencing events (indirectly rather than directly, by modeling the transformative qualities of the second journey).

If unlearning is a way to deeper spirituality, the following attitudinal shifts represent pathways in the journey from the first to the second half of life:

- impatient to more patient
- critical to more accepting
- pessimistic to optimistic
- stoical to joyful
- independent to dependent
- aloof to affectionate
- self-centered to other-oriented
- frugal to generous

These observations do not represent precepts to be followed or new commandments to be obeyed. Second half of life is not about precepts or commandments, for there is only one guideline: to love the Lord your God with your entire mind, heart, soul, and strength, and your neighbor as yourself.

QUESTIONS FOR REFLECTION

1. After reading this chapter, what did you learn about the first and second half of life?
2. Which half of life characterizes your current lifestyle? Explain your answer.

Chapter 3

The Invisible Mountain

Promenade. A great many people in the world today think metaphors are facts. These we call theists. Many others think that metaphors are not facts. Those we call atheists. When we use the word "God," we are using a metaphor for a mystery that transcends all categories of thought, even the categories of being and nonbeing. The best things, mystics tells us, cannot be spoken; the second best are misunderstood; third best is conversation. If words are necessary but inferior forms of communicating truth, then mythology, though limited, is more effective. Yet it is penultimate rather than final truth—penultimate because the ultimate cannot be put into words. Ultimate truth is beyond words, beyond images. Hence, it is important to live life fully, yet not arrogantly or with finality, taking risks and recognizing the positive value in what appear to be negative moments and aspects of one's life. The big question in spirituality is whether one is able to embrace uncertainty and adventure simultaneously.

IN TELLING THE STORY of my parents and of my upbringing, I highlighted the importance of faith. The account is idyllic, for it reflects classic American evangelicalism, with its emphasis on the authority of scripture and the centrality of beliefs. In that respect, I cite again the account in the preface regarding my college friend's response to my comment about not being a biblical literalist: "I am very surprised, Bob, at how your belief system has changed. I have spent much of my life seeking God's face, and I have found God in my Bible, and in my heart. And I am quite content to remain securely rooted right there. Further, it seems to me that Jesus was strong on biblical literalism." Then she concluded, "At this point in my life, I am firmly set in my faith, which includes biblical literalism, or at the very least, biblical inerrancy."

Conservative believers, when confronted with new theological concepts or perspectives, often respond, like my friend, by affirming that they are set in their faith and unwilling to change. They often cite Hebrews 13:8, "Jesus Christ is the same yesterday and today and forever," or James 1, which discourages doubt (see Jas. 1:6–8), based on the unchangeability of God's nature (Jas. 1:17; see also Mal. 3:6). Having grown up in a conservative, evangelical, home, I, too, had every reason to be set in my faith. Why, then, did I change?

This chapter explores the meaning of faith and the importance of change. According to recent studies in the field of missiology, Christianity has changed dramatically over time, reinventing itself at least six times as the missionary movement advanced to different cultures and continents.[1] The truth of my friend's assessment is that my belief system has changed over the years, but my friend failed to recognize that the underlying faith has remained constant. Surprisingly, as my belief system has undergone transformation, receding and diminishing in importance, my faith has grown exponentially.

THE MEANINGS OF FAITH

Let us begin with the concept of faith. The misunderstanding arises over the meaning of the term "faith," for the term has various meanings. Acknowledging only one meaning, such as equating faith with belief alone, is the fly in the ointment, the elephant in the room, the invisible mountain, and the greatest impediment to Christian unity.

If someone asked you to identify the essence of Christianity, where would you start? Conventional Christians, focusing on dogma, begin with belief in Jesus, the atonement, and the authority of scripture and the church. This approach, however, is antithetical to spirituality. It is a byproduct of the Precritical Paradigm's vision of the Bible and the Christian tradition. Prior to the modern period, faith was not understood in this way. Faith was not about beliefs in one's head but about loyalty, allegiance, and trust in one's heart. Faith, of course, has always been central to Christianity, but an

---

1. See the award-winning essays by Walls in Missionary Movement, particularly chapter 2, "Culture and Coherence in Christian History," 16–25.

emphasis on faith as believing difficult things to be true is a relatively recent phenomenon in Christianity, the product of the last few hundred years.

Because religion by nature is primarily experiential, constructing religion on the foundation of belief leads to endless conflict, frustration, and unanswered questions. Children, of course, willingly accept belief, but as they go through adolescence and enter adulthood, many struggle with doubt and disbelief.

Faith, however, makes a better foundation and prepares one more adequately for life. Some readers may wonder about my distinction, because all through life they have equated faith with belief. But faith should not be equated with beliefs. It may reach conclusions about beliefs, but its foundation is experiential and relational rather than doctrinal. Based on experience, faith makes conscious choices that square with that experience.

As I mentioned previously, my childhood experience was essentially belief-based, and even though it was expressed in relational terms—such as "accepting Christ," acknowledging the Holy Spirit's guidance of my life, and speaking personally with God through prayer—it remained theoretical, based on a belief system that was in my head. Eventually my journey led me beyond belief to an understanding of the Christian life as a relationship of trust with a God to whom I am yoked and who participates in my journey of transformation. It is this understanding of the Christian life that I develop in the remainder of the book.

Faith and Belief: Ancient and Modern Meanings

Viewed anthropologically, faith is a universal human concern, not necessarily religious in content or context. Faith can be an ordinary part of relationships in general, as in placing trust in someone or confidence in something. Faith helps us get in touch with the dynamic, patterned process by which we find life meaningful. Faith is a way of giving meaning to the forces and relations that make up our lives, how humans see themselves against a background of shared meaning and purpose. Prior to our being religious or irreligious, we are already engaged with putting our lives together and with what makes life worth living, looking for something to love that loves us, something to value that gives us value, something to honor and respect that has the power to sustain our being. These are issues of faith.

Viewed theologically, the reorientation of life to accommodate the centrality of the supernatural virtues begins with faith because we must trust that there is a reality beyond ourselves in which our goals find fulfillment and where our efforts finally make a difference. Without that reality there is no point to worrying about anything except in terms of how it makes our own life better. Without faith, personal success is the highest kind of goodness we can achieve. Religious faith may involve a leap, but such a leap, as physicist (and now Anglican priest) John Polkinghorne reminds us, is a "leap into the light, not the dark."[2] The aim of the religious quest, like that of the scientific quest, is to seek motivated belief about what is actually true. Faith should not be equated with shutting one's eyes or whistling in the dark.

Reasonable faith seeks understanding. Faith is an essential ingredient in making religious claims, but it does not work alone. Theologians use reason, not only to examine the grounds for religious claims, but also to understand them better. Faith may be a distinctive way to gain access to God, but it is not separable from other ways of knowing; in fact, it is a way of knowing. As modern scholarship has identified multiple forms of intelligence, so it recognizes multiple ways of knowing, involving eight human faculties: sense perception, reasoning, emotion, intuition, language, memory, imagination, and—significantly—faith. For some, faith is considered a deterrent to knowledge, because it does not rely on proof. For others, however, faith is the most important way to know, particularly that part of reality that eludes reason or the senses. Surely Blaise Pascal, the celebrated French physicist, mathematician, and philosopher, had faith in mind when he wrote, "The heart has reasons that reason cannot know."

A Biblical Understanding of Faith

For the Bible, faith is the indispensable preliminary, without which true religious experience cannot develop. It involves a person's initial *awareness* of God, but also a continuing attitude of personal *trust* in God. The initiative is with God, but there must be the corresponding movement on the human side, and this is basically what is meant by faith. Religious and moral attainment is impossible without faith. As the New Testament affirms, all things are possible for the one who believes (Mark 9:23). And without faith, "it is impossible to please God" (Heb. 11:6).

In the Bible, faith is always relational, the object of faith being God, and the highest personalization is reached in the New Testament proclamation that God is best revealed in the life of Jesus. In this usage faith is a matter of personal relationship rather than abstract knowledge. In the Hebrew Bible the most important of the terms for faith is the root *amen*, meaning to trust someone. To say "Amen" to anyone is to trust that person, and in the Bible, nothing is as sure, permanent, or reliable as God.

2. Polkinghorne, Quarks, Chaos, & Christianity, 10.

Faith is essential to every religious, social, and political perspective, and it stands at the heart of Christianity. The concept is found throughout the New Testament, either as the noun "faith" (*pistis*) or the verb "believe" (*pisteuo*). When we examine the use of these words today, we discover that the common meaning of these words in modern English is very different from their premodern and ancient Christian meanings. When we speak of faith today, we usually have in mind "belief," which we take to mean holding a certain set of "beliefs," that is, "believing" certain doctrines or dogmas to be true. And that modern way of understanding "faith" leads to misreading key biblical texts. For instance, in the Gospels, we often get the impression that Jesus insisted that his followers acknowledge his divine status, almost as a condition of discipleship. Those who beg him for healing are required to have faith before he can work a miracle, and one is commended for calling out: "I believe; help my unbelief" (Mark 9:24–25).

We do not find preoccupation with belief in the other major religious traditions, however, so we wonder, why did Jesus place such an emphasis on it? The answer is that he did not. The Greek word translated as "faith" in the New Testament means "trust, loyalty, or commitment." Jesus was not asking people to "believe" in his divinity, but rather was asking for commitment. He wanted disciples who would engage with his mission to abandon their pride, laying aside their self-importance and sense of entitlement, trusting fully in the God who was their father. In this freedom they were to give what they had to the poor, feed the hungry, and spread the good news of God's kingdom everywhere, living compassionate lives. Such *pistis* could move mountains and unleash human potential (Mark 11:22–23).

When the New Testament was translated from Greek into Latin by Jerome early in the fifth century, *pistis* became *fides* ("loyalty"). Since *fides* had no verbal form, for *pisteuo* Jerome chose the Latin verb *credo* (from which we get the word "creed"), a word that derived from *cor do*, "I give my heart." In this context, "heart" does not refer primarily to feelings or emotions, though those are involved. Rather, "heart" is a metaphor for the self at its deepest level. When the Bible was translated into English, *credo* and *pisteuo* became "I believe" in the King James Version (1611). But the word "belief" has since changed its meaning. This English word, coming from the Middle English *bileven*, meant "to prize; to value; to hold dear." It was related to the German *belieben* ("to love"), *liebe* ("beloved"), and the Latin *libido*. So "belief" originally meant "loyalty to a person to whom one is bound in promise or duty."[3]

---

3. Armstrong, Case for God, 87; Fowler, Stages of Faith, 11–12. The seminal work on this topic was made by Wilfred Cantwell Smith, a comparative religionist with the linguistic competence to study most of the major religious traditions in the languages of

During the late seventeenth century, however, as our concept of knowledge became more theoretical, the word "belief" started to be used to describe an intellectual assent to a hypothetical proposition. Scientists and philosophers were the first to use it in this sense, but in religious contexts the Latin *credere* and the English "belief" both retained their original connotations well into the nineteenth century.

We commonly translate *credo* as "I believe," and we have been taught that saying "I believe" means giving mental assent to the literal truth of each statement in the creed or in the Bible. As we have seen, *credo* does not mean "I agree to the literal and factual truth of a statement," but rather "I give my heart to," "I commit my loyalty to." Thus, when we say "I believe" at the beginning of the creed, what we are really saying is, "I give my heart to God." And who is this God to whom we commit our allegiance? The rest of the creed tells the story of God as the One known through nature and in Jesus and as present in the Spirit.

The Four Faiths (Four Meanings of Faith)[4]

In the history of Christianity, faith has four primary meanings. The first of these sees faith primarily as a "matter of the head," whereas the remaining three understand faith as a "matter of the heart." Each meaning is described with a Latin term to show its antiquity, as well as how it is understood in English. For each term the opposite is given, for antonyms are often as illuminating as synonyms.

1. Faith as Assent (*assensus*). In this first sense faith means simply "belief," which we take to mean holding a certain set of "beliefs," that is, "believing" certain doctrines or dogmas to be true. This understanding of faith as belief is dominant today, both within the church and outside it. Its dominance in modern Western Christianity is due to the Protestant Reformation, which not only emphasized faith, but also produced numerous denominations, each defining itself by what it "believed," that is, by its distinctive doctrines or confessions.

This development also changed the meaning of the word "orthodoxy." Prior to the Protestant Reformation, orthodoxy referred to "right worship," meaning that those who practiced the liturgy correctly were orthodox.

---

their primary sources. In Belief and History and Faith and Belief, Smith argues persuasively that the classical writings of the major religious traditions never speak of faith in ways that can be translated by the modern meanings of belief or believing.

4. The material in this segment is adapted from Borg, Heart of Christianity, 28–41.

Following the Reformation, orthodoxy began to mean "right belief," and faith began to mean "believing the right things."

The birth of modern science and scientific ways of knowing in the Enlightenment also affected the meaning of "faith" and "believe." When Enlightenment thinkers began identifying truth with factuality, that is, as something verifiable, they began calling into question the reliability of the Bible and of many traditional Christian teachings. As a result, "faith" and "belief" came to be contrasted with knowledge and certainty. For skeptics, faith came to mean "opinion or conviction," something one turned to when knowledge ran out. For believers, faith is what one turned to when beliefs and knowledge conflict.

According to this understanding of faith, the opposite of faith as *assensus* is doubt or disbelief. In its fundamentalist permutation, those who doubt are said to lack faith, whereas those who disbelieve are said to have no faith. While this view is widespread, it puts the emphasis in the wrong place, for it suggests that what God really cares about is the beliefs in our heads, as if having "correct beliefs" is what will save us.

Faith starts with the willingness to recognize and question the core mysteries at the heart of existence: why we exist at all and how to make meaning out of our existence. As a result, it puts on our radar the yearning for the answers to these ultimate questions and the consequent intuition that draws us to the words, ideas, and rituals of the religious tradition that attempts to answer them. We can't know the answers to the ultimate questions like we can know scientific answers, which build bodies of knowledge over time. Religious answers are more like wisdom. With the habit of faith, we are willing to ponder such questions in our hearts and minds. Quoting Augustine, Aquinas says that belief is "giving assent to something one is still thinking about."

2. Faith as Trust (*fiducia*). In its second and higher sense, faith means "trust" in something or someone. In the Bible, it means radical trust in God. Significantly, it does not mean trusting in the truth of a set of statements about God, for that would simply be *assensus* under a different name. While our behavior is important, God seems to be less concerned with our actions than with our character, for our actions flow from our will: "For the Lord does not see as mortals see; they look on the outward appearance, but the Lord looks on the heart" (1 Sam. 16:7).

Faith is like floating in a deep ocean. If you struggle, if you tense up and thrash about, you will eventually sink. But if you relax and trust, you will float. Like the story of Peter walking on the water with Jesus, when he began to be afraid, he began to sink. According to this meaning, the opposite of *fiducia* is not doubt or disbelief, but mistrust, which results in worry and anxiety. Four times in the extended passage from Matthew's Sermon on the Mount, Jesus says to his hearers, "Do not worry," and then adds, "You of little faith" (Matt. 6:25-34). Lack of trust and anxiety go together; if you are anxious, you have little faith.

3. Faith as Faithfulness (*fidelitas*). In the Bible, faith is the trustful acceptance of God's promises, particularly of God's desire to bless all peoples and nations of the world. But faith is also trust in God's faithfulness to the promise, that is, in God's ability to deliver Good News to everyone, something that God accomplishes through Jesus Christ and his followers. Because God is steadfast and faithful, we too are called to faithfulness. *Fidelitas* does not mean faithfulness to beliefs about God, whether biblical, creedal, or doctrinal. Rather it refers to radical centering in the God to whom the Bible and creeds and doctrines point.

The English equivalent to *fidelitas* is "fidelity." Faith as fidelity means loyalty, allegiance, the commitment of the self at its deepest level. Its opposite is not doubt or disbelief. Rather, as in human relationships, its opposite is infidelity, being unfaithful to our relationship with God. To use a striking biblical metaphor, the opposite of this meaning of faith is adultery. Another vivid biblical term for infidelity to God is idolatry, meaning not so much the worship of idols as false gods, but centering in something finite rather than the sacred, which is infinite and beyond all images. As the opposite of idolatry, faith means being loyal to God "and not to the seductive would-be lords of our lives," whether one's nation, affluence, achievement, family, or desire.[5]

In the Hebrew Bible, faith as fidelity is the meaning of the first of the Ten Commandments: "You shall have no other gods before me." In the New Testament, it is the meaning of the Great Commandment: "You shall love the Lord your God with all your heart, soul, mind, and strength." This commandment is followed immediately by the exhortation to "love your neighbor as yourself." *Fidelitas* means being faithful to these two great relationships: God and your neighbor. And one's neighbor, as Jesus explains in the parable of the Good Samaritan, is first and foremost the person who is in need of help (Luke 10:29-37).

One is faithful to God, therefore, by being attentive to these two primary relationships. We are attentive to God through worship, prayer, and practice, and faithful to our neighbor through a life of compassion and justice. To be faithful to God also means to love that which God loves, which includes the whole of creation.

---

5. Ibid., 33.

4. Faith as Vision (*visio*). As the English word "vision" suggests, faith is a way of seeing reality, and how we view the whole affects how we respond to life. There are basically three ways we can see the whole:

- We can see reality as *hostile and threatening*, and therefore respond to life defensively, doing whatever we can to survive, for that is all that matters. Many forms of popular religion have viewed reality this way: God (or Life, or Nature) is going to get us, unless we behave the right way, practice the correct rituals, offer the right sacrifices, or believe the right things.

- We can see reality as *indifferent* to human purposes and ends. Although this response to life will be less anxious than that of the first way, we are still likely to be defensive and precautionary. We respond by building up whatever security we can, even enjoying and seeking to take care of the world, but ultimately we are likely to be concerned primarily for ourselves and those who are most important to us.

- We can see reality as *life-giving, nourishing, and full of promise*. To use a traditional theological term, to see reality as filled with wonder and beauty, and to nourish and spread this goodness, leads to radical trust. It frees us from the anxiety, self-preoccupation, and concern to protect the self with systems of security that mark the first two viewpoints. It leads to the ability to love and to be present to the moment. It generates a commitment to spend oneself for the sake of a vision that extends beyond ourselves. It leads to a life marked by the natural virtues, or to use Paul's words, it leads to a life marked by the "fruit of the Spirit": love, joy, peace, patience, kindness, generosity, faithfulness, gentleness, and self-control" (Gal. 5:22–23). These qualities are the result of a way of life that Paul characterizes as "freedom" (Gal. 5:1); freedom *from* evil and from allegiance to false authorities; freedom *for* love. For Paul, faith becomes active "through love" (Gal. 5:6).

To understanding faith as *visio* is to see reality as gracious; its opposite, un-faith, views reality as hostile and indifferent. This meaning of faith is closely related to *fiducia*, to faith as trust. Trust and vision go together; trust in God—the God of promise and faithfulness—and how we view God go together. In this way of life, radical centering in God leads to a deepening trust that transforms the way we view reality and live our lives. Seeing, living, trusting, and centering are all related in complex and salutary ways.

As we have noted, faith is relational, but this does not mean that beliefs do not matter. There are affirmations that are central to the Christian faith, affirmations such as the reality of God, the centrality of Jesus, and the significance of the Bible. These beliefs are essential, not only for Christians, but for people of all faiths, when properly understood. Faith as a way of seeing at the deepest level requires avoiding the human tendency toward excessive precision and certitude. Christian theology has often been plagued by both—the desire to know too much and to know it too precisely. Our minds tell us that such knowledge is not possible—perhaps not even desirable—and people cannot easily give their heart to something that their mind rejects.

While faith involves the mind, faith is primarily the way of the heart. Given the premodern meaning of "believe," to believe in God is to love God and to love that which God loves. The Christian life is as simple and as challenging as that.

THE CIRCLE AND THE ELLIPSE

When I teach a course on Christian theology, I draw an image of a circle and an image of an ellipse, and I explain how an elliptical approach to such concepts as the nature of God, an understanding of sin and salvation, and the relation between faith and reason, provides a more helpful result than approaches that rely on the model of a circle for theological understanding. A circle, of course, has a single center, and everything is determined by its relation to the center. The ellipse, by contrast, is a figure that can be described only in relation to two foci, which cannot be resolved into one.

Some people are unable to think elliptically (dialectically) about the question, "Where is God?" so they eliminate the tension between immanence and transcendence by deciding in favor of one polarity, that of supernatural theism—a model that conceptualizes God as "out there" and totally separate from nature. This understanding of God is reductionistic, for it allows for only one correct perspective on the presence of God; if God is "out there," God cannot be "here with us," or vice versa. The symbol of a circle is based on dualistic "either/or" thinking, a simplistic stance that settles on only one possibly correct answer.

The elliptical model, however, makes it possible to view God as simultaneously transcendent and immanent, for both views are biblical and both are essential to religion. The truth is in the polarity between the two foci; the truth is not one-dimensional but dialectical. When one polarity is emphasized to the detriment or exclusion of the other, religion becomes rigid, intolerant, and increasingly confrontational. This form of thinking characterizes the religious approach we have called the Precritical Paradigm.

The Postcritical Paradigm, guided by the holistic possibilities found in the dialectical model, places equal importance upon faith (as displayed in religious beliefs and practices, both corporate and private) and reason (as displayed in the disciplines of philosophy, science, religious studies, and other academic subjects) in the quest for knowledge and understanding of reality. It also values the antithetical anthropological perspectives suggested in the opening chapters of the book of Genesis—humans are made "in the image of God" in the first creation account (Genesis 1) and "from the dust of the ground" in the second creation account (Genesis 2)—and the tension created by these competing yet harmonizable views. Dialectical thought is simultaneously God-affirming and world-affirming. Advocates of the Postcritical Paradigm need not choose, indeed should not choose, one over the other.

If the transition from a circular to an elliptical model may be said to be characteristic of the Postcritical Paradigm in theology, there is a curious parallel with what occurred in modern astronomy. Until the time of Kepler, it was universally held that the planets moved in circular orbits—this was based not on observation but on the notion that, since the circle was considered to be the perfect figure, God, being perfect, could not have designed the orbits of the planets in any other way. When Kepler discovered that the planets move in elliptical orbits, he changed the shape of the astronomical universe, and, in the process, the course of future theology.[6]

BEFRIENDING CHANGE

Perhaps you have heard the expression, "The only constant is change." This saying comes from a statement by Heraclitus, the ancient Greek philosopher, who is quoted as saying, "No one ever steps into the same river twice," or, as one astute male student quipped, "No one ever kisses the same girl twice." An empiricist, Heraclitus's observations led him to conclude, "change is the only constant in life."

In his observations regarding change, Heraclitus is not alone. The Internet contains numerous lists of famous quotes about change in life, the universe, and ourselves. The first lesson these convey is the constancy of change. The next lesson is just as important, "Don't hang on; learn to let go." Perhaps that is what Denise McCluggage had in mind when she said, "Change is the only constant. Hanging on is the only sin." We fight the universe when we hold on to things whose nature is change. Whether it be a

---

6. Hendry, Theology of Nature, 128.

relationship, an ideology, or a way of life, to be healthy, happy, and wise, we must learn to let go. Not to do so is to be trapped, addicted to oneself.

This, I believe, is the meaning of Jesus' words to Mary Magdalene after his resurrection, "Do not hold on to me" (John 20:17). What Jesus is saying is, "Don't cling to the past, Mary, as if it were permanent. You and I are heading for something far better." Great love is both attachment and detachment. There is a spiritual art to attachment, but also to detachment.

The notion of detachment is also central to Buddhism. When asked the foremost principle in Buddhism, Bodhidharma, the founder of Zen Buddhism, famously replied, "Vast emptiness and nothing holy." To modern people in the West, who desire all life has to offer, and who want it immediately, this teaching sounds bleak and unappealing. However, when we note that to people in the East, "emptiness" is ultimately a positive rather than a negative concept, we become intrigued, particularly when we learn that "emptiness" is another word for "nirvana," which, incidentally, is also a negative word meaning "to extinguish," "to cease blowing," or "to cease striving." Buddhists speak of nirvana as Nothingness or an eternal Void, by which they mean a fullness without boundaries, from which all life emerges and to which all life returns. While most people think of nirvana as a possibility in the future, that is incorrect, for nirvana, at least according to Zen Buddhism, is forever present, always real here and now. To understand this is to experience liberation, that is, enlightenment.[7]

It is impossible to read Buddhist literature without catching the sense of the transitoriness of everything finite, its recognition of the impermanence of every natural object. The Buddha listed impermanence as the first of his "Three Marks of Existence"—characteristics that apply to everything in the natural order—the other two being suffering and the absence of permanent identity or a soul. In other words, nothing in nature is identical with what it was the moment before. Here, the Buddha was close to modern science, which has discovered that the relatively stable objects of the macro-world derive from particles that barely exist. The reason the Buddha belabored a point that seems obvious is because he believed we are freed from the pain of clinging to permanence only if the acceptance of continual change is driven into our very marrow.

This awareness, that at the center of everything there is nothingness, is said to result in liberation. How so? Because such knowledge frees us from clinging to ideas, people, or things as if they were permanent. This realization also frees us to become compassionate. Furthermore, it teaches

---

7. Liberation and enlightenment are the Buddhist equivalents of salvation in Christianity.

us always to remain open, considering no teaching or perspective in life as absolute truth. To explain these concepts, Buddhists, like Christianity, resort to parables.

One of my favorite such stories comes from Viet Nam. A father, whose wife had died, lived alone with his son. One day, when the father was away, robbers came to the home, burnt the hut, and kidnapped the son. When the father returned and saw the damage, his first thought was for his son. Nearby, he found a pile of ashes, and he assumed that they were the ashes of his son, burnt along with the hut. He took the ashes and placed them into a bag, which he carried around his neck.

One day, the boy escaped from the kidnappers and came home. He knocked on the door of the rebuilt hut, and the father called out, "Who's there?" And the son replied, "It is I, your son!" But the father said, "You aren't my son! He was killed by robbers. I have his ashes around my neck." Considering the boy an imposter or a robber, the father refused to let him in; so the boy had to leave.

The truth here is that when we accept something in life as the absolute truth and cling to it, we can no longer accept the idea of opening the door, even if truth itself is knocking. How often do we settle for a partial truth, thinking it is the final truth?

Like faith, the concept of change is controversial and feared by religious fundamentalists. Having attended Stony Brook School, a Christian college preparatory school near New York City, it was natural to continue my education at The King's College, a private evangelical college. While I thrived socially in this protected environment, I felt intellectually constrained.

The core curriculum, required of all students, included courses in Bible and theology. For one such class I proposed writing a term paper on the canonical process, wishing to investigate how the various books of the Bible had been selected as normative for Christians. The professor's response was unexpected: "Select another topic," he declared. "The topic you have chosen is unacceptable." That ended the discussion and I was forced to find another topic. In my professor's estimation, I had chosen to examine the human side of the Bible, a risky approach that might diminish my zeal, divert me from my spiritual goals, and compromise my faith. Rather than deter my progress, that "no" opened the door to graduate studies at Princeton Theological Seminary, an experience that exposed my adolescent spirituality, tested my faith, and equipped me for the journey ahead.

Adventures in Spirituality is grounded in the conviction that humans have the capacity to transcend conventional understanding of religion, dogma, and scripture, exhibiting a genuine and wholesome faith that is dynamic rather than static, future-oriented rather than past-oriented, and affirmed rather than passively acquired. This capacity is fueled by two principles: (1) that whatever does not grow dies (this principle encourages us to remain open to change and newness); and (2) that all truth is God's truth (this principle encourages us to remain open to truth wherever it may be found and wherever it leads).

From a neuroscientific perspective, it seems that the brain has two basic functions or goals: self-maintenance and self-transcendence. The self-maintenance function of the brain incorporates all of the things we associate with first-half-of-life concerns, everything that helps us survive. However, self-maintenance is only part of the story because an organism doesn't merely maintain one steady state throughout life. People change, and as a result, the brain must have the ability to change and adapt as well. To some extent, self-transcendence is part of self-maintenance because, presumably, an adaptable brain enables us to handle the vagaries of life more effectively. Thus there is a certain degree of stability within the brain and its connections. This allows us to be who we are throughout our lives. However, the brain also has flexibility, variability, and changeability. It has the ability to change by rewiring the connections between neurons, and possibly even changing the function of the neurons in a process referred to as neuroplasticity. Neuroscientists are now appreciating the role of religion in providing powerful mechanisms to accomplish these goals.[8]

A basic premise of this book is that the Bible, like religion in general, has both a conserving and liberating effect, providing perspective for both halves of life:

- perspective for *formation* (such first-half-of-life perspectives, while characterized as traditional, conventional, or conservative, are essential but not definitive or ultimate ways of reading and applying scripture);
- perspective for *transformation* (such second-half-of-life perspectives, characterized as progressive, radical, or liberal, are essential, definitive, and ultimate ways of reading and applying scripture).

Of course, it is quite possible for these approaches to overlap, due to the complexity of our intellectual, theological, and spiritual needs. It is equally possible that biblical passages convey messages appropriate to our varied abilities and needs. Scripture is multivalent, meaning that it's message allows for multiple interpretations. While one text might strike terror in the heart of an unrepentant person, the same passage might exhort devout believers to greater faithfulness and even greater freedom. As Paul

---

8. Newberg, The Spiritual Brain, 153–55.

shows in 1 Corinthians, the important thing is to keep growing spiritually. Paul's concern with the Corinthians is that they are in a state of spiritual immaturity, unable to eat solid food. It takes time—and conscious effort—to grow spiritually, from egocentrism (first-half-of-life spirituality) to soulcentrism (second-half-of-life spirituality). For Paul, how people hear and read scripture (eat spiritually) reflects their spiritual maturity.

After more than thirty years of teaching at Washington & Jefferson College, I value the college stance as independent and non-denominational, for it has provided me with unlimited opportunities for personal and intellectual growth. During this time I introduced over twenty different courses in world religions, spirituality, and biblical studies, in addition to studies in global Christianity, religion and ecology, and Christian theology. I spent summers at Chautauqua Institution in upstate New York, where I met world-class theologians and listened to some of America's most innovative thinkers. I have also remained active in my denomination, serving on various committees and preaching in numerous ecumenical settings.

The cumulative momentum of my experience at Washington & Jefferson led me to reevaluate my belief system. While teaching world religions and global spirituality at W&J, I uncovered numerous parallels between Christianity and other religions, including beliefs, practices, and historical development. This discovery convinced me that questioning beliefs, dogmas, and practices of other traditions but not one's own is inconsistent and biased. After all, had I been born Buddhist or Muslim, I would likely view everything from that perspective, so what makes my theological bias true but theirs false? In a pluralistic age, particularity is an invalid test for truth.

At W&J I became acquainted with The Outsider Test for Faith, formulated by former evangelical John W. Loftus. This approach encourages individuals of various faiths to assess their truth claims from the perspective of an outsider and with the same level of skepticism they use to evaluate other religious traditions. As The Outsider Test for Truth makes clear, no one religion can lay claim to ultimate truth, though most have done so with regularity, particularly when challenged by competing perspectives. In the absence of an absolute, objective vantage point whereby all religious truths can be judged, it seems best to acknowledge that none have more than a temporal or subjective value.

Applying this methodology to my own religious perspective, I subjected my religious beliefs to logical scrutiny, temporarily setting aside my faith presuppositions and replacing them with rational and scientifically verifiable premises. The short-term results of this deconstructive undertaking were disastrous; reason, it seemed, trumps faith every time. As I worked out the details of my worldview, it became evident that as long as one is constrained by the modern mentality, one cannot achieve "a sufficiently deep understanding of Christianity to find God, as revealed in Christ."[9] Other possibilities emerged, challenging the validity of my conclusions and commencing the reconstructive approach I describe as "postcritical understanding." Those possibilities could not be ignored.

Having begun with notions based upon or deduced from a literalistic understanding of the Christian scriptures, I reexamined them, applying critical thinking, intuition, and personal experience. Adopting pedagogical methods and topics compatible with current scholarship, I began challenging students to question the validity of inherited belief systems. The rationale came from the Outsider Test for Belief, which claims that beliefs based on unquestioned faith generally lead people to justify what they were raised to believe. Such reasoning is ultimately circular.

By way of support, I cite an insight gained during my qualifying exams at Princeton Theological Seminary, a battery of exams in the doctoral program that one must complete prior to commencing the dissertation phase of the PhD program. While preparing for an exam on Paul's letters, it became evident that my assumption about the authenticity or inauthenticity of those letters could always be confirmed by research. In other words, if I assumed that a disputed letter of Paul was actually written by Paul, it was not difficult to marshal sufficient argumentation for that assumption. Conversely, if I assumed that the disputed letter of Paul was not Pauline, I could present an equally convincing argument. However, if I started from a position of neutrality, I had to investigate all sides of the debate equally, and this became more challenging. Furthermore, such results were more compelling, since this approach forced me to examine all of the evidence and not simply argumentation that could be dismissed or filtered through my assumptive lens. Allowing the evidence to dictate the results required difficult evaluative work and exposed me to a wide range of methodologies, including conclusions not yet envisioned by scholars.

The same applies to all religious premises. If one begins with unexamined assumptions, one can easily arrive at foregone conclusions and overlook opportunities for learning, growth, or change of perspective.

A CRISIS OF MEANING

When I attended Princeton Theological Seminary in the late 1960s and 70s, society was in turmoil. I had recently graduated from college and completed a Master's in Latin American Studies. Uncertain of my future, I thought I

---

9. Allen, Christian Belief, 19.

might return to Latin America as a missionary, enter the ministry as a pastor, or become an academic. Princeton represented an ideal environment to pursue and advance those career options. Having always loved the study of scripture, biblical studies emerged as my best option.

Attending seminary to study scripture, theology, and church history, I was surprised to hear teachers say that the focal theological question was not primarily about God at all—not about God's nature, revelation, or will—but rather about what it means to be human. For the next three years, anthropology would be my bridge to theology. A divinity degree led to a doctorate in biblical studies, where my journey continued.

Eight years later, my PhD in hand, I embarked on a teaching career. I had gathered many facts and information, but I had not grown spiritually, for spirituality is not a school of thinking or a system of belief. Rather, it is the freedom to be present, which produces a different way of seeking and knowing facts and information. So much of religion involves accumulating facts and imperatives supposedly leading to salvation. However, as the great spiritual sages know, spirituality requires a change of perspective, a change in how one views the present moment. Presence is primary in life; presence is the prerequisite to divine Presence. Silence, listening, contemplation—these are not things I learned in seminary. Yet they remain the best way to grow spiritually, the best way to experience the Holy in our midst.

Presence is the one thing necessary for transformation, but in many ways, the hardest state to achieve. Why? Because presence is wisdom. Hence, presence is the practical, daily task of all mature religion and all spiritual disciplines. Like us, most of Jesus' contemporaries missed the Presence that was in their midst. Spiritually, they were focused on the afterlife, and he was focused on the Ultimate Reality around him, which he found in birds, lilies, infants, suffering, and the tasks of life. If we learn one thing from Jesus, it is that eternity is happening all around us, present all the time. Like Jesus, spiritual sages see continuity between time and eternity. Their assumption is unwavering: "if you have it now, you will have it then." If you examine the great accounts of spiritual breakthrough, the experiences of conversion, you will discover, as John Newton expressed in the famous lyrics of *Amazing Grace*, that they focus on *how* they see rather than on *what* they see: "T'was blind, but now I see."

Jesus used parables to subvert our unconscious worldview, unlocking it from within and thereby exposing its illusions. All religions have tried to do the same with riddles and koans and mythic stories. Our entire universe has to be rearranged truthfully before individual teachings can be heard correctly. Unfortunately, what religion has been doing in the West is give people new moral and doctrinal teaching without rearranging their mythic worldview. This approach does not work, for it leads nowhere new. It only creates legalists, specialists, ritualists, minimalists, and literalists, who always kill the spirit of a thing.

True spirituality is not a search for perfection, control, or the door to the next world; it is a search for divine union now. Union and perfection are two different journeys with very different strategies. Common religion seeks private perfection; mystics seek the foundation itself—divine union. Personal perfection insists on private knowing and certitude. Surprisingly, union is a much better way of knowing.

The most amazing fact about Jesus, unlike almost any other religious founder, is that he found God in disorder and imperfection—and told us that we must do the same or we would never be content on this earth. This is what makes Jesus so counterintuitive to most eras and cultures, and why most never perceive the good news in this shift of consciousness. That failure to understand his core message is at the center of our religious problem today. We look for hope where it was never promised, and no one gave us the proper software so that we could know hope for ourselves, least of all in disorder and imperfection. Worst of all, we did not know that hope and union are the same thing, that real hope has nothing to do with mental certitudes.

If you surrender to the fear of uncertainty, religious life can become a set of insurance policies. Your short time on earth becomes small and self-protective, circling around what you can be sure of and what you think you can control—even God. A second group tries a different approach. They choose to look the other way, or just keep busy, building "bigger barns." For them, life becomes a series of manufactured dramas, entertainment, and diversionary tactics intended to help them avoid the substantial questions. This avoidance is symbolized by what we call the consumer culture.

A third group seeks transcendence and spirituality, but often in immature ways. This characterizes so much religious seeking today, people dualistically split from any objective experience of union with God, self, others, or nature. Christianity, authentically experienced, is the overcoming of this split.

QUESTIONS FOR REFLECTION

1. What are the invisible mountains in your life?
2. After reading this chapter, what did you learn about overcoming obstacles in your way?

PART II
Truth Revealed

Chapter 4

Into Thin Places

> **Promenade.** The nondual (contemplative) mind holds truth humbly, knowing that if it is true, it is its own best argument, and any formulation is still partial and incomplete, as Paul states in 1 Corinthians 13:12, "Now I know only in part." Nonpolarity thinking teaches us how to hold creative tensions, how to live with paradox and contradiction, how not to run away from mystery, and therefore how to actually practice what all religions teach as necessary: compassion, mercy, patience, forgiveness, and humility.

HUSTON SMITH, IN HIS masterful introductory study, *The World's Religions*, writes that we are living at a time when world cultures are not simply meeting but colliding, "hurled with the force of atoms... The change that this new situation requires of us all—we who have been suddenly catapulted from town and country onto a world stage—is staggering." He tells of Diogenes, an exceptional individual who stated some twenty-five hundred years ago: "I am not an Athenian or a Greek but a citizen of the world." Today, Smith argues, we must all struggle to make these words our own. "We have come to the point in history when anyone who is only Japanese or American, only Oriental or Occidental, is only half human. The other half that beats with the pulse of all humanity has yet to be born."[1]

---

1. Smith, The World's Religions, 7.

From 1985 to 1995, I traveled extensively. Four times I headed toward a different compass point—west to the state of Washington for the start of a solo cross-country bicycle odyssey,[2] north to Scandinavia and other parts of northern Europe, south to Mexico, and twice to the Middle East. Each trip, in retrospect, was an adventure—a pilgrimage of sorts—and each experience yielded unique insights and spiritual benefits. Because these trips coincided with the start of my midlife years, life's most precarious yet promising transition, they came at a propitious time for personal growth and renewal.

Into Thin Places is the third and final volume in an autobiographical series that combines the adventure of life with the adventure of spirituality. *Love Never Fails*, the first in the trilogy, serves as a tribute to my parents, career missionaries in Latin America. That book introduces readers to my mother and father's spiritual and cultural legacy, imparted to me, their only child, during my childhood and early adolescent years: I remain grateful for this heritage and to these "unsung heroes."

The Invisible Mountain, the second book, focuses on a period of forty-two days in the summer of 1989 when I was able to translate my dream of a cross-country cycling trip into a trek on behalf of Habitat for Humanity, utilizing adventure as a means to help disadvantaged citizens. As I cycled across the "northern tier" of the North American continent, I matured as an individual and grew spiritually by going "Homeless for Habitat."

The lessons I learned through that trip prepared me for the two-month pilgrimage related in *Into Thin Places*, a journey that began a mere three weeks after the cycling trip. The adventures related in this book, a sabbatical trip that started in Amsterdam and ended in Cairo, were made possible by funds from a discretionary account administered by Dr. Howard J. Burnett, President of Washington & Jefferson College.

My journey—a quest for ancestral, cultural, and spiritual identity—was intentional. I mapped out an overland route, noting must-see cultural, archaeological, and religious sites along the way. My itinerary included four centers of Christianity: Geneva, known as "the Protestant Rome" and home of Reformed Christianity since 1536; Rome, the center of Catholicism; Istanbul, the historical center of Orthodoxy; and Jerusalem, spiritual home to Christians, Jews, and Muslims. Along the way I discovered additional spiritual centers, some quite by accident. And that sense of serendipity, of unexpected discovery, is part of every genuine pilgrimage.

As a professor of Religious Studies and an ordained college chaplain, I designed an itinerary through Europe, the Middle East, and Africa that

---

2. The account of this fund-raising adventure, undertaken on behalf of Habitat for Humanity, is told in The Invisible Mountain.

would enable me to appreciate and better understand my roots. My objectives included (a) visiting religious and cultural centers in the region, (b) exploring archaeological sites and museums, (c) conversing with Israelis and Palestinians on matters of mutual concern, (d) gaining a perspective not ordinarily achieved in guided tours, and (e) exploring my identity to better understand its spiritual core or center.

At times I mingled with tourists and listened to tour guides. On other occasions I was accompanied by college students and other travelers who viewed me as a resource. But most of the time I traveled alone. Being on a tight budget, I arranged my own lodging in pensions or youth hostels, traveling by train, bus, and ferry instead of by plane. My two-month sojourn took me to eleven countries, where I explored hundreds of cultural and historical sites and dozens of museums. I experienced places of stunning beauty and objects of such magnetism that devout believers over time revered them as sacred. I also met some remarkable human beings. Touching history—or rather being touched by history—I recognized my place in the Great Story and affirmed my role in the ongoing metanarrative.

THIN PLACES

"Thin places," a metaphor taken from Celtic spirituality, refers to places, objects, events, persons, and other phenomena that are understood as being transparent to the divine. The concept has its home in an understanding of reality that affirms at least two layers or dimensions of reality: (a) the visible world of ordinary experience and (b) the sacred, understood as the source of all things but also as a presence interpenetrating everything. In "thin places," the boundary between the two levels becomes diaphanous and permeable.[3]

As "places" of beauty, fascination, and intrigue, thin places stir the imagination; as "places" of honesty and courage, where truth and justice prevail, they call us to action and selfless service; as "places" of conviction, inspiration, and empowerment, they challenge us to transformation; as "places" of insight, wisdom, and discernment, they call us to spiritual renewal.

Thin places are paradoxical: they are places of power and weakness; they provide weal and woe, bliss and pain; they are found in crosses and cancers but also in resurrection and remission; they may be ordinary, or extraordinary; sometimes they delight us, other times they perplex us; they are places of wonder but also of terror. When they surround us, we are

3. Borg, "A Vision of the Christian Life," in The Meaning of Jesus: Two Visions, 250.

enraptured, and when they fade, we experience despair. Thin places fuel the imagination, foster risk-taking, feed the spirit, and foment human transformation. They have the ability to alter our way of thinking, transform our character, and renew our souls.

Why do they intrigue us? Why do they grip us like a vice? In his influential study, *The Idea of the Holy*, Rudolph Otto put forth the view that religious experience relies upon a deep sense of the "numinous." Coined from the Latin *numen* (holy, sacred), the term expresses a natural human response to the experience of the sacred developed prior to rational and moral notions about it. Experiencing the numinous as ultimate mystery, people feel a strong sense of awe and reverence. The holy is also *fascinans* (fascinating); it exerts an irresistible attraction because it is recognized as profoundly familiar and essential to humanity. The experience of the sacred has always involved wonder and fascination.

Thin places are liminal spaces—in-between spaces, windows, doorways, thresholds, intersections, portals, transitions—that usher us from one state or space to another. They signify boundaries, beginnings, and becomings that open the way to something new, expanding our awareness and providing unity to our reality. For Christians they encompass activities, events, persons, objects, and experiences by which the Father speaks, in which Christ is present, and through which the breath of the Spirit blows freest. Thin places are transparent to the divine because God is there: through-and-around-and-over-and-under-and-behind-and-before-and-within them.

C. S. Lewis, one of the twentieth century's foremost Christian authors, knew about "thin places." He wrote about them in the *Chronicles of Narnia*, a set of seven children's classics in which he created a land of wonder and enchantment called Narnia. Following this publication, Lewis rigorously defended the fairy tale against those who claimed that it gives a false conception of life. The fairy tale, he argued, like the myth, arouses longing for more ideal worlds but at the same time gives the real world a new depth. While Lewis's Narnia Chronicles remind us of other works, such as the Alice-in-Wonderland-like opening of *The Lion, the Witch and the Wardrobe* or the voyage made by the *Dawn Treader*, which is akin to the voyage of Odysseus, Lewis blends Christian themes with events created from the rich world of fantasy. A dominant idea in his stories is that of an earlier time when reality was more harmonious and unified. It was Lewis's hope that upon reading these stories, children (and adults) would return to the "real world" with a new perspective, their minds opened to the possibilities of an unseen spiritual world and to the limits of merely human intellect and undeveloped imagination.

Lewis was referring to "thin places" without using the term. He knew, as children of all ages discover when they read his Narnia Chronicles or J. K. Rowling's Harry Potter books, that our world is alive with liminalities (threshold spaces between the sacred and the mundane); pictures, closets, fireplaces, train stations—any object, event, or person can open our minds to the possibilities and transport us to an unseen spiritual world. Matter is, and has always been, the hiding place for Spirit, forever offering itself to be discovered anew.

THE CENTER

"Searching for the Center" refers to a phenomenon that is said to be universal, for it is the subject of myths and rituals found across the globe in all time periods. Joseph Campbell, the world's foremost authority on mythology until his death in 1987, labeled it the myth of the human quest. The concept can be described culturally, psychologically, and spiritually, but at its minimum, it embodies three pursuits: (1) the quest for adventure, (2) the quest for meaning, and (3) the quest for wholeness.

Into Thin Places encourages readers to quest for the Center, to find thin places in their own journeys of discovery that are filled with extraordinary potential for insight, growth, and transformation. Chapter 1 examines questing in general, exploring the notion of the labyrinth as a unique path to the sacred. Here readers are urged to rediscover the sense of the sacred and the sanctity of space (thin places) that their predecessors found indispensable for the human quest, and that pilgrims of all time utilize as requisite in their encounters with the divine.

The final segment (chapter 22), labeled "Living in the Center," concludes the work and provides a practical dimension. Here readers can gain deeper insights into their own sacred journeys and explore how faith journeys can impact and energize them for life.

Sacred journeys should not be confused with more commonplace trips and adventures such as expeditions, tours, and vacations. As important as the latter may be for one's emotional health and wellbeing, they are primarily outward by nature. They generally have predetermined geographical destinations, as well as distinct beginnings and endings. Sacred journeys may have geographical and temporal associations, but they are largely inward journeys, and as such are not limited by space or time. They commonly result in changes of perspective and in transformations of character and emotional state. In many ways sacred journeys are atemporal because they have no discernible endings. By nature, they are beginnings. Sacred journeys prepare us for destinations that lie in eternity. The best one can hope for is to be on the way.

I believe my sabbatical trip was more than a geographical or intellectual adventure because it produced a change of perspective. I returned a citizen of the world, no longer searching for the Center but awakened to the realization that the Center lies within, that it goes wherever I go, and that it needs to be nurtured. The book's conclusion charts out the responsibilities that come with this awareness.

In narrating the account of my journey from Amsterdam to Cairo, I utilize the three classic stages that constitute every life-transforming adventure. The first stage, separation or *departure*, is described in Part I. This section narrates the journey through Holland, Switzerland, Italy, Greece, and Turkey. The middle stage—the trials and fulfillment of *illumination*—appears in Part II. This section narrates regions of the eastern and southern Mediterranean known in biblical times as Canaan. It includes my travels through Syria, Jordan, the Sinai, and Israel. The final section, the *return*, comprises Part III. This section narrates my departure from Israel and my journey through the Sinai to Egypt and back home.

THE QUEST FOR ADVENTURE

In *The Hero with a Thousand Faces*, Joseph Campbell dwells on a particular type of myth from all times and found across the globe: the myth of the human quest. This classical endeavor, titled "The Hero's Adventure," symbolically addresses the stages of human realization, the trials of the transition from childhood to maturity, and the meaning of maturity. The various mythologies, whether they depict the hero as going in quest of a boon or in quest of a vision, present the same essential undertaking: individuals leave their everyday lives and travel a distance, sometimes into a depth, and sometimes up to a height. The hero leaves the ordinary world, sometimes by choice and other times by force, and undertakes a journey to the center, into a region of supernatural wonder, where he[4] encounters fabulous forces and wins a decisive victory. Then comes a greater challenge: should the protagonist remain in his enchanted setting, thereby forsaking his former world, or should he return with a boon to benefit others? The hero does come back from this mysterious adventure, returning with the power to bestow blessings on fellow humans.

---

4. In traditional quests, the hero is typically male. Today, heroes are equally male and female.

The hero's adventure, we are told, is about one's character and its potential for transformation. The path of the mythological adventure, and of all successful quests, involves a twofold venture: an inward journey to a spiritual center—a place of healing, vision, and transformation—and an outward journey toward others.

The messages of the world's great teachers—Moses, the Buddha, Jesus, Muhammad—differ greatly. But their visionary journeys are much the same. All are heroes, for they leave the predictable in search of the unknown, resisting temptation to find a liberating truth. Moses is such a hero, for he ascends the mountain, meets with Yahweh on the summit of the mountain, and comes back with Torah, a constitution for the formation of a new society. That's a typical hero act—departure, illumination (fulfillment), and return.

One might also declare that the founding of a life—your life or mine, if we live authentically instead of imitating the lives of those around us—comes from a quest as well. At birth, a lifetime of adventure beckons. A hero lies dormant within each person, awaiting a spiritual awakening, a call to departure. In order to affirm something new, one must leave the old and go in quest of the germinal idea, a seed that contains the potentiality of bringing forth that new thing.

Opportunities for transformation are present all around us. When they arise at critical moments in our lives, they are called rites of passage, conversions, revivals, or moments of awakening. What we call them is not important, but how we envision them. Not all transformational opportunities arise dramatically. Some are manifested subtly, through solitary endeavors such as meditation, fasting, confession, prayer, and Bible reading; others emerge publicly and corporately, through disciplines like worship, receiving a sacrament, or through sacrificial service to the poor and needy. The deepest opportunities arise unexpectedly, however, through the twists and turns of everyday life, including suffering, loss, and events that we think of as accidents and tragedies. Such experiences can rob us of our vitality or they can fuel the growth of our spirit and provide a powerful transformative impetus for our character.

THE QUEST FOR MEANING

Humans quest for meaning. Meaning, understood as vitality of purpose, leads to fulfillment, and the prospect of fulfillment makes life worth living. When Abraham Maslow outlined his hierarchy of needs, represented as a pyramid consisting of five levels, he placed "self-actualization" (by which he meant working toward fulfilling one's fullest potential) at the top. In Maslow's scheme, the final stage of psychological development comes when the individual feels assured that lower levels of needs—both physiological and emotional—have been satisfied. Once these are met, self-actualization drives the personality.

Mythology and ritual traditionally supplied the symbols that carry the human spirit forward, energizing individuals to navigate successfully the necessary passages of their adulthood. Think of the rites of passage, those rituals associated with the vital transitions of human life, especially birth, puberty, marriage, and death. Each of these passage points frames the individual within the context of the community, serving to transform the person into the new stage of life and to integrate her or him into the community at that new spiritual level. Because passages of life are liminal—that is, they involve crossing a threshold from one state of existence to another—they are critical to the full human development of the person and to the welfare of the community.

In the past, people quested for meaning through rites of passage; their quest was intentional, predictable, and patterned. Society demanded it, clans promoted it, and families made it happen. Although similar rites are enacted today, particularly in traditional families, modern (and postmodern) people tend to quest spontaneously, often doing so unintentionally.

To find meaning, or to connect with something deeper, some people quest through adventure, visiting exotic locations or engaging in enterprising ventures. Others quest through careers of service and devotion to others. Some apply for the Peace Corps; others participate in humanitarian efforts or campaigns to eradicate poverty or disease. Some quest through lifestyle choices such as fasting, celibacy, or vegetarianism. Others quest hedonistically, seeking meaning through pleasure, drugs, power, wealth, and materialism. Some seek meaning through disciplined acts of devotion such as prayer, Bible study, and inspirational reading. When human beings stop questing, they abdicate their identity.

THE QUEST FOR WHOLENESS

Humans—indeed most living creatures—desire good health, safety, and security; taken together, these vital qualities contribute to the wholeness and wellbeing that make life supremely special. In traditional societies, the ability to apprehend the sacred was regarded as of crucial importance to health, wholeness, and wellbeing. Indeed, without this sense of the divine, people often felt that life was not worth living. Like other aesthetic experiences, the sense of the sacred needs to be cultivated. In our modern secular society, the sacred has diminished in value and in priority; left unused, it has tended to wither away.

In the past, when people tried to speak about the sacred or about their inner life, they did not express their experience in logical, discursive terms. Rather they had recourse to symbols and myths. Freud and Jung, who were the first to chart the so-called scientific quest for the soul, turned to the myths of the classical world or of religion when they tried to describe interior events. Mythology, they realized, was never designed to describe historically verifiable events. Mythology was an attempt to express inner significance or to draw attention to realities that were too elusive to be discussed in logically coherent ways. Mythology, religion scholar Karen Armstrong indicates, was an ancient form of psychology.

Western religions are often focused on the past, on what happened long ago. The accent is on the historical understanding of images. By contrast, the focus on Eastern religions is on what is happening to you now, how the symbol is affecting you now. Eschatology works for those who think in historical terms. Those who see eternity in all the forms of time think mythologically—living and thinking in ways that transcend time. Mythologically speaking, the Christ idea and the Buddha idea are equivalent symbolically. To live out of that center, out of that immanence, becomes the way of salvation—to do so is to accept nature as beneficent and harmonious, not as fallen or corrupted.

QUESTIONS TO PONDER

1. After reading this chapter, what did you learn about living adventurously?
2. How are you open to risk and change? Explain your answer.

Chapter 5

Beyond Belief

Promenade. The great enemy of both mystery and perennial wisdom is dualistic thinking, which uses either/or questions to arrive at truth, generally associated with certainty. The problem with either/or questions is that they promote either/or answers. Such dichotomous forms of thinking set a trap, for the structure of either/or thinking implies that the options presented exhaust all other alternatives: either the Bible is divine or it is human; either one believes there are proofs for God's existence or one is an atheist; if one religion is true, others are false; and so on. Either/or thinking is intolerant of religious pluralism, impatient with both/and resolutions, and dissatisfied with anything less than all-or-nothing answers. It accepts only absolute answers and dismisses uncertainty as a sign of unbelief. I am fond of the question, "What is the opposite of faith?" Either/or thinking answers, "Disbelief!" Both/and thinking answers: "Certainty!"

EXPANDING ONE'S RELIGIOUS OUTLOOK, deepening one's relation to the sacred and infinite, is essential for persons to age creatively. Carl Jung, the prominent Swiss psychiatrist, emphasized that gaining a religious attitude, the kind that allows us to see our own personal lives as moving toward wholeness and our own stories as related to a larger story, is the psychological/spiritual task for one's later years: "Among all my patients in the second half of life—that is to say, over thirty-five—there has not been one whose problem in the last resort was not that of finding a religious outlook on life." If Jung was correct, then discovering one's personal way to relate to God and to speak about ultimate concerns may well be the most significant task of life.

Beyond Belief, published in 2012, is my fifth book. It describes one of life's greatest adventures: the quest for God and for authentic faith in a postmodern age. The target audience includes (1) those who may have reached a "critical place" in their faith journey—prompted by academia, science, reason, culture, and their own experience—and feel compelled to choose between two alternatives, their faith or the claims of science and reason, and (2) progressive Christians who might find in this book a framework that addresses their current theological understanding and provides impetus for their spiritual journey.

Beyond Belief forms a sequel to my "Adventures in Spirituality" trilogy. *Beyond Belief* describes an inward adventure—my search for an understanding of God in an age of science. Despite the multitude of topics addressed in that book, there is one overriding concern: my experience and understanding of God. My colleague Dan Stinson made this abundantly clear when, after reading the manuscript, he declared, "This work is written by a man who has experienced God in so many ways that he is discovering he can never experience all of God." Upon hearing that statement I was honored, for no words, then or since, better capture what is in my heart.

From time immemorial, in every age, a set of questions has persisted, perplexing human beings. What's going on in the universe? Is there any point to it all? Why are we here? Is there any purpose to our lives? How should we live? Does God exist? Where did the universe come from? Why does anything exist at all? Why is there so much suffering? Why do we die? Do we live on after death? How can we find release from suffering and sadness? What can we hope for? These have been called life's "big questions"; philosophers speak of them as "ultimate questions." They are the ones that never go away.

It is the main business of religion to answer the big questions. And this is why, even when we try to distance ourselves from it, we remain intrigued by religion. Religion responds to the preoccupations that arise when life comes up against barriers beyond which ordinary—including scientific—ways of coping cannot take us. For our purposes, therefore, religions may be understood very simply as pathways or "route-findings" through the ultimate limits on our lives. These limits include not only death and meaninglessness but anything that threatens our wellbeing, anything that stands between us and lasting peace or happiness.

To accomplish this task, every generation of believers benefits by reexamining its theology, thereby providing society with vision. A theology that is stagnant reflects a religion that is limited in both usefulness and in effectiveness. The Reformation project has done its work, as has much of nineteenth-century liberalism and twentieth-century modernism, and there are more critical issues now at stake. Fundamentalist claims (inerrancy, young earth, literalism, dispensationalism, premillenial rapture eschatology) have set themselves up for attack by critical scholars, producing individuals bent on discarding the baby with the bath water when they encounter evidence that their strict upbringing may not be up to the task of explaining itself in the post-reformation, postmodern world. We can do better than that.

Spiritual and theological understanding, particularly in Western Christianity, can be said to have evolved or progressed through various stages:

1. Primal spirituality (primarily focused on cosmic and holistic spiritual experience, corporately and individually applied). This stage is pre-Christian.

2. Organized religion (primarily focused on scriptures, rituals, dogmas, and clerical intermediaries and on the spiritual experiences they engender). This stage includes classical Judaism and Christianity.

3. Enlightened religious movements (primarily focused on individuals who value rationality and the scientific method). This phase occurred to some extent in medieval scholasticism and flourished during the Enlightenment.

4. Fundamentalist religious movements (primarily a reactionary approach to the rationalistic and scientific advances of the Enlightenment, while valuing its own perceived rationality). This phase flourished in the nineteenth and twentieth centuries.

5. Postmodern spirituality (primarily focused on holistic spiritual experience, corporately and individually applied, based on global and pluralistic values). This stage began in the twentieth century and will be a predominant Western form of spirituality in the twenty-first century.

This progression can be summarized in the following manner: In the beginning a form of spirituality existed that was natural, holistic, and focused on achieving harmony with the universe. That primal spirituality became formalized in religious traditions, under the guidance of prophets, priests and other religious intermediaries. Religious authorities established scriptures and rituals, using rational principles and insights currently in vogue to formulate dogmas and creeds, which became part of the ongoing tradition. Scripture, creeds, and doctrine further shaped spiritual experience. Over time, free-thinking individuals and their followers questioned the methodology and conclusions of organized religion. They began to embrace new spiritual principles valued by progressive people of their time. In the twenty-first century, such values came to include freedom of conscience, reverence for nature, respect for life, compassion for all, nonviolence, equality under the law, appreciation of spiritual diversity, openness to new revelation, and the abolition of discrimination based on race, color, sex, religion, age, class, or nationality.

Such spirituality, reinforced by organized religion, has the potential to lead humanity into spiritual enlightenment. While not all evolution, spiritual or psychological, biological or political, is progressive, authentic spirituality seeks the trajectory of an upward spiral.

It is easy in our day to drive a wedge between spirituality and religion, to declare that organized religion is the source of many of the world's ills, and that to solve the world's problems we must eliminate religion. Such is the view of zoologist Richard Dawkins, who views religion as a cancer, as the enemy of humanity and the progenitor of endless violence. He is quick to cite remarks by some of America's most illustrious Founding Fathers, such as Thomas Jefferson's "Christianity is the most perverted system that ever shone on man," and John Adams's ringing critique, "This would be the best of all possible worlds, if there were no religion in it."[1]

Neale Donald Walsch, in his celebrated *Conversations with God*, asks the question, "Do we need to return to religion? Is that the missing link?" To which his God replies: "Return to spirituality. Forget about religion." When Walsch asks for clarification, "God" responds: "[Religion] is not good for you. Understand that in order for organized religion to succeed, it has to make people believe they *need* it. In order for people to put faith in something else, they must first lose faith in themselves. So the first task of organized religion is to make you lose faith in yourself. The second task is to make you see that *it* has the answers you do not. And the third and most important task is to make you accept its answers without question."[2]

Walsch attempts to clarify this point by addressing the differences between "spirituality" (what we might call "natural or authentic religion") and "religion" (what we might call "authoritarian or fundamentalist religion"), contrasting their views in the following manner:

- Religion fills the hearts of humans with *fear of God*, where once individuals loved That Which Is (God) in all its splendor.

---

1. Dawkins, God Delusion, 43.
2. Walsch, Conversations with God, 2:247.

- Religion ordered humans to *bow down before God*, where once individuals rose up in joyful outreach.

- Religion has burdened humans with *worries about God's wrath*, where once individuals sought God to lighten their burden.

- Religion told humans to be *ashamed of their bodies* and their most natural functions, where once individuals celebrated those functions as the greatest gifts of life.

- Religion taught us that we must have an *intermediary in order to reach God*, where once we thought ourselves to be reaching God by the simple living of our lives in goodness and in truth.

- Religion *commanded humans to adore God*, where once humans adored God because it was impossible not to.

Despite Walsch's penetrating insights, I find an alternative approach more realistic and much more hopeful. According to world religions scholar Huston Smith, the contrast between spirituality and religion is both unnecessary and unwise. Using the analogy that religion is to spirituality as institutions of learning are to education, Smith maintains that while it is possible to become educated without schools, universities, and books, to do so is like reinventing the wheel in every generation. Just as institutions of learning are the way education gets traction in history, so also religion is the way spirituality gains traction in history.[3] While there are perversions and extremes in religious beliefs and behavior, religion's external forms should be regarded as vessels of spirituality rather than as virulent cancers or useless vestiges, as some suggest.

THE PHILOSOPHER'S DISEASE

During the modern period, the Western world experienced a massive loss of hope, due, in part, to a crisis in theology and cosmology. As views of God narrowed, the impact of the physical cosmos grew exponentially, in increasingly fragmented and threatening ways. From time immemorial, theology and cosmology had mirrored one another. As our understanding of the universe expanded, our views of God narrowed, making God more vindictive and punitive. For this equation to change, we need a vision of God bigger and more glorious than someone to fear, and a vision of the cosmos as grand, coherent, and benevolent. Whereas insecurity increases fear and isolation, reverence fosters confidence and relationship.

3. Smith, Why Religion Matters.

Does God exist? Is there a deity somewhere within or beyond the known universe? The only true answer is nobody knows for sure. No ordinary human being, whether in the past or in the present, has been able to offer conclusive evidence either for the existence or the nonexistence of a deity, however defined, envisioned, or experienced. With regard to the existence or nonexistence of God, all of us are agnostic. Some of us lean toward theism, others toward atheism, but beyond we cannot go.

As we know, all God language and God experience is faith based. This means that whatever we believe or disbelieve is only an extension of our faith orientation, presuppositional base, or intuitive worldview. As we learn from modern philosophy, all so-called proofs for the existence or nonexistence of God are but footnotes to one's assumptive stance. Meaningful human discourse or reflection on the existence or nonexistence of God requires acknowledgement of assumptive premises and starting points.

The next concern when speaking about the existence or nonexistence of God involves identifying the specific understanding or view of God being affirmed or denied. Quite frequently thoughtful theists and atheists find themselves agreeing on caricatures or stereotypes of God they mutually reject, such as God's supposed omnipotence and omnibenevolence, contradictory concepts at best. Unless one upholds extreme or untenable views such as biblical inerrancy or doctrinal infallibility, all God-talk is figurative in nature and all Christian theology provisional. If you find a statement about God helpful or relevant, adopt it with caution and examine it carefully. Conversely, if you find a statement about God problematic or irrelevant, approach it with an open and inquisitive mind before you modify or reject it.

Perhaps your spiritual experience is similar to mine. You have known about God since your childhood, having been taught that God is loving, gracious, just, forgiving, almighty, and omnipresent. You believe in God, and you would even say you love God. At times your love of God may have been passionate and intense, but overall more lukewarm or cold than hot. You consider yourself spiritual, and you have practiced the disciplines of devotion such as attending church, reading scripture, meditation, and giving of your time and money to church and to those in need. Your prayer life has been habitual, though mostly limited to mealtime or to situations of anxiety, uncertainty, or perplexity. Although there have been times when you prayed regularly and faithfully, even then God seemed silent and remote.

You long for God, desiring intimacy with this source and ground of your being, yet you feel you do not know God directly. Your religious upbringing taught you a great deal about God, and perhaps you had a conversion experience. There may have been times when you felt God communicating with you or through you—perhaps through a vision, a dream, an insight, or in ways that had no other explanation—yet your desire for intimacy with God went unfulfilled. In the end, however, all of these seem somehow unconvincing, for the impulse, initiative, and motivation appeared more human than divine. You desire something more, and are unsure that all this spiritual activity is but a human contrivance, a way of meeting some human need for meaning and transcendence.

The apostle Paul was commenting on human spirituality in general when he noted that "we see through a glass, darkly" (1 Cor. 13:12, KJV). Yet inadequate vision of the divine need not prevent us from occasional glimpses of light in the darkness. While the human experience often takes us into great deserts of doubt, dryness, and lostness, we need not remain there. How often we see only our failures and forget those times when we have been channels of divine love.

My spiritual journey—described in detail in the opening chapters of *Beyond Belief* (2012) and in the introduction to *Iron Sharpens Iron* (2013)—follows the religious paradigm outlined in chapter 2, which views one's faith story as a journey through three stages: precritical understanding, critical understanding, and postcritical understanding. While many individuals experience all three stages fully and chronologically, as I did, some remain in the precritical phase—a state in which they accept without question those values and beliefs they received from parents and other significant authority figures in their lives. For others, this state is short-lived, abandoned in their adolescent years or during college or early adulthood, a time in life when they began questioning the existence of God and other inherited religious beliefs.

While many seekers today choose to remain in this critical phase, perplexed by the competing views promoted by multicultural traditions, world religions, and by secular worldviews, those who persevere in their faith journey discover that agnosticism and atheism are not final destinations but rather temporary stops. That has been my experience. Though my engagement with the critical perspective began seriously during my graduate and postgraduate studies at Princeton Theological Seminary, I did not fully commit to that phase until the final years of midlife, well into the second half of my teaching career at Washington & Jefferson College. Then, for a two-week period, I became an atheist. During that brief period I became convinced that God, however conceived, did not exist. Strangely, despite a sense of deep loss, I found the awareness exhilarating, for I had based this conclusion on my own experience. For a year I had immersed myself in scientific and philosophical literature, searching for an understanding of God in these academic disciplines. I took seriously the conclusions of Richard Dawkins and other "new atheists" and found convincing the methodology outlined in The Outsider Test for Faith. Applying this methodology to my own religious perspective, I spent a year subjecting my religious beliefs to logical scrutiny, temporarily replacing faith presuppositions with rational and scientifically verifiable premises. This undertaking infected me with rational thinking, labeled "the philosopher's disease" by a Zen Buddhist sage. While the critical phase brings euphoria, closure, and a sense of freedom to some, my experience left me scarred, emotionally and intellectually, a condition exacerbated by my religious upbringing, my vocation, and my ordination vows.

Beyond Belief reflects my thinking during this stage, short-lived in my case. Subsequent writings, including my biblical commentaries and works on theology and spirituality published since 2013, represent postcritical reflections. Whereas critical thinking leads to religious skepticism and withdrawal from religious activity, postcritical believers participate in religious rituals as meaningful but optional. They hear ancient biblical stories as "true" and recite the creeds sincerely while knowing them as not literally true. That distinction is what separates postcritical from precritical understanding. While practitioners in both phases exhibit similarities, speaking and even worshiping alike, the differences are profound, making it virtually impossible for someone who has embraced critical and then postcritical thinking to revert to precritical understanding.

Speaking as a postcritical Christian, I am heartened by the words of Morton Kelsey, a spiritual counselor and therapist who reflected on his own agnostic phase when he wrote: "To help the questioning, the agnostic and the atheist, [spiritual counselors] need to be people who have struggled with doubt themselves and have come out on the other side with a meaningful faith. . . . The trouble with most people is that they are not agnostic enough; they are not consistent in their agnosticism and do not go into it far enough to see its darkness and agony."[4]

I recall reading Bishop John A. T. Robinson's best-seller, *Honest to God*, during my first year at Princeton Theological Seminary. The book, published four years earlier, sent shock waves around the Christian world. Robinson, the English Bishop of Woolwich, had taken the writings of three seminal Christian thinkers—Rudolph Bultmann, the leading New Testament scholar in his generation; Dietrich Bonhoeffer, the German Lutheran pastor who had participated in the underground anti-Nazi resistance movement and who had been hanged at a German prison camp in 1945; and Paul Tillich, the most widely read theologian in the twentieth century—and made their thought accessible to the population at large. Bultmann referred

---

4. Kelsey, Companions on the Inner Way, 61.

to the biblical scripture as "mythology" that needed to be "demythologized," since its message had been framed in the presuppositions of an ancient world that no longer existed. Tillich, who suggested that God could no longer be conceptualized through the analogy of a person, developed a transpersonal theology in which God was perceived as "the Ground of All Being." Bonhoeffer called for the development of "religionless Christianity," arguing that just as Christianity in the first century could not be contained within Judaism, so in our day Christianity could no longer be contained within religion. *Honest to God* sold more copies than any religious book since John Bunyan's *Pilgrim's Progress*, for the masses of people recognized in Robinson's words the articulation of things which they had long felt, but did not know how to express.

Like other seminarians, I studied Bultmann, Bonhoeffer, and Tillich and found their ideas intriguing and perceptive. Although Robinson's book and others like it were conceptually exciting, they did not square with my Christian upbringing or current "belief system." I eventually set them aside as contextual to my divinity training and continued preparing for ministry within the church. Such thinking was "modern" and I remained guarded.

Later, at Chautauqua Institution, I heard lectures by cutting-edge scholar Karen Armstrong and "Jesus scholars" Marcus Borg and John Dominic Crossan. I purchased their books and read them thoroughly, incorporating some of their ideas into my lectures. I read books on comparative religions and grappled with John Hick's notion of "religious pluralism" and Brian McLaren's concepts of "a new kind of Christian" and "a generous orthodoxy." Although these writers tilled the soil of my spirit and sowed transformative seeds, none prompted the wake-up call that I experienced during the first week of the 2010 Chautauqua season, when I attended a weeklong series of lectures delivered by Episcopal Bishop John Shelby Spong.

For that series of talks, which included a panel discussion and five public lectures, a crowd of over one thousand people gathered to listen, to question, and to interact with key concepts from Spong's controversial writings. In keeping with my customary response to such presentations, I took copious notes, purchasing and then reading several of the speaker's books. During the ensuing academic year, while transcribing notes from that experience, I recognized the effect cosmic and human evolution had upon Spong's theology, and my outlook changed dramatically. Watching a videotaped lecture series by evolutionary biologist Richard Dawkins titled *Growing Up in the Universe*,[5] I accepted the evolutionary teachings of

5. Growing Up in the Universe was a series of lectures given by Richard Dawkins as part of the Royal Institution Christmas Lectures, in which he discussed the evolution of life in the universe. The lectures were first broadcast by the BBC in 1991, in the form

Charles Darwin as foundational for my worldview. That decision forced me to re-examine my belief system and its assumptions. No concept, however sacred, was exempt from scrutiny.

SCIENCE AND RELIGION: THREE MODELS

In many ways, a sharp and ever-widening gulf characterizes the relationship between Christian scholars and traditional lay persons. The chasm is attributed to several factors, including the assumptions and conclusions of modern scholarship as well as the convictions and needs of parishioners. Scholars seek factual knowledge, whereas laypersons seek inspiration and reassurance. Not all parishioners, of course, are traditionalists, and not all scholars are progressive or open to new ways of thinking about their faith.

Economist E. F. Schumacher, author of *Small Is Beautiful*, believed there are two places to find wisdom: in nature and in religious traditions. To seek wisdom in nature one should look to science, to those who love nature enough to study it. Because science explores nature, it can be a powerful source of wisdom. In most developed cultures, religion and science have teamed to offer a cosmic story that allows people to understand their universe, find meaning in it, and live out their lives with purpose. In the West, however, religion and science have been at odds since the seventeenth century. This split has been disastrous: religion has become privatized and science a tool of technology. As English philosopher Alfred North Whitehead (1861–1947) wrote: "Religion is tending to degenerate into a decent formula wherewith to embellish a comfortable life . . . Religion will not regain its old power until it can face change in the same spirit as does science."[6] To recover the wisdom embedded in religious traditions, we must abandon unhelpful religious traditions. In the words of Meister Eckhart, the profound mystical theologian of the West: "Only those who dare to let go can dare to reenter."

Many Christians today find it difficult to accept the notion that creation and evolution belong together. The belief that such concepts are opposing and conflicting has become so ingrained in the minds of many that it is hard to conceptualize how the God of the Bible may work out his creative purposes through an evolutionary process. Believers have been taught that they must choose between creation and evolution. However, many distinguished

---

of five one-hour episodes. The Richard Dawkins Foundation for Reason and Science was granted the rights to the televised lectures, and a DVD version was released by the foundation in 2007.

6. Whitehead, *Science and the Modern World*, 188–89.

scientists and theologians are inviting us to see that this is a false choice and asking us to consider instead a both/and alternative.

The eminent biologist Theodosius Dobzhansky (1900–1975), who immigrated to the United States from the Soviet Union, did important work in the field of population genetics and was instrumental in the development of the Modern Synthesis of evolutionary theory. He was also a practicing Russian Orthodox Christian. "It is wrong," he wrote, "to hold creation and evolution as mutually exclusive alternatives. I am a creationist *and* an evolutionist." In his writings he presented a tribute to paleontologist Pierre Teilhard de Chardin, another Christian who embraced evolution and who influenced him spiritually: "There is no doubt at all that Teilhard was a truly and deeply religious man and that Christianity was the cornerstone of his worldview. Moreover, in his worldview science and faith were not segregated in watertight compartments, as they are with so many people. They were harmoniously fitting parts of his worldview. Teilhard was a creationist, but one who understood that the Creation is realized in this world by means of evolution."[7]

Were Dobzhansky and Teilhard the only Christians in the sciences who brought evolution and creation together, one might choose to dismiss them, but in fact they are among many scientists, in the United States and elsewhere, who have done so, including many evangelical Christians. What these men and women are doing is hardly new. Beginning in the thirteenth century, theologians adapted their understanding of creation to the Aristotelian-Ptolemaic model of an earth-centered circular cosmos, so different from the ancient Hebraic model. Later, after struggling with the Copernican and the Newtonian models, theologians eventually found ways to accommodate their thinking to that cosmology as well. The current reflections on God's action in an evolving creation—the universe of Darwin and Einstein—stand very much in this tradition of faith seeking understanding.[8]

What Alfred North Whitehead stated in 1925 still holds true today: "When we consider what religion is for mankind, and what science is, it is no exaggeration to say that the future course of history depends upon the decision of this generation as to the relations between them. We have here the two strongest general forces . . . which influence men, and they seem to be set one against the other—the force of our religious institutions, and the force of our own impulse to accurate observation and logical deduction."[9]

---

7. Dobzhansky, "Biology Makes Sense," 125–29.
8. Schneider, Science and Faith, Essay VII: "Theologies of an Evolving Creation."
9. Whitehead, Science and the Modern World, 181–82.

Examining the spectrum of contemporary views, Roman Catholic theologian John Haught identified three distinct ways in which science and religion can be related to each other:
opposition (conflict), separation (contrast), and engagement (contact).[10]

1. Within the Opposition camp there are several viewpoints, unanimous in their claim that religion and science are irreconcilable and mutually antagonistic in their assessment of which option provides an ultimate explanation of reality. They can be examined under two broad categories: *scientific materialism*, also known as "scientism" (characterized by a mindset in which the scientific method is the only reliable path to knowledge), and *biblical literalism* (characterized by a mindset in which religious faith and scripture always trump evidence). While both represent the opposite ends of the theological spectrum, they share various characteristics in common. Both believe that there are serious conflicts between contemporary science and classical religious beliefs. Both seek knowledge with a sure foundation—that of logic and sense data, on the one hand, that of infallible scripture, on the other. They both claim that science and theology make rival literal statements about the same domain—the history of nature—so that one must choose between them. Both represent a misuse of science. The scientific materialist starts from science but ends up making broad philosophical claims. The biblical literalist moves from theology to make claims about scientific matters. Both fail to respect the differences between the two disciplines. The idea that science is locked in eternal combat with religion is an understandable reaction to the common practice of confusing their respective roles.

2. One way to avoid conflicts between science and religion is to view the two realms as independent and autonomous. Each has its own domain and its characteristic methods. Proponents of the Separation view say there are two jurisdictions and each must tend to its own business and not meddle in the affairs of the other. The task of science is *descriptive*, answering "what," "how," and "what is" questions, whereas the task of religion is *prescriptive*, dealing with questions of value, purpose, destiny, and ultimate origin; in other words, answering "who," "why," and "what ought to be" questions.

Because it keeps distinctions clean, the separatist approach appeals to theologians and scientists alike. On the surface, at least, it allows the substance of theism to remain untouched by evolution, while at the same time it forbids religion and theology to intrude into the business of science. The distinction, however, appears shallow. Can religious thought remain utterly unaffected by evolution? Do not the randomness, struggle, and

---

10. Haught, God After Darwin, 24.

impersonality of the evolutionary process decisively refute theism, as the scientific skeptics have argued? Can we separate our theological convictions from what seem to be the spiritually devastating implications of evolutionary science?[11]

3. If science and religion were totally independent, the possibility of conflict would be avoided, but the possibility of constructive dialogue and mutual enrichment would also be ruled out. Life, on the whole, cannot be so neatly divided into separate compartments, since it is experienced in wholeness and interconnectedness. In the end, any adequate treatment of science and religion requires that, without giving in to temptations to conflate them anew, as occurred in the West during premodern times, we focus on ways in which they concretely affect each other.

This third, more harmonious option, views science and religion as interdependent; both are needed, and both are here to stay. The Engagement option builds on commonalities between science and religion, understanding that science needs to harness the faith, passion, and commitment of religion and that religion must learn to embrace the contributions of science and consider Darwin's "idea" not so much a danger as a great gift. Evolution, according to this third approach, can awaken in theology a fresh way of thinking about the central claims of traditional theistic faith.

GOD'S "TWO BOOKS"

In the past four centuries, remarkable changes have occurred in the field of science, including what is known about cosmology, elementary substances, and origins of the cosmos and of the human race. New conceptions of the cosmos led to new views concerning God and God's relation with the world. Modern Christians essentially regard science as a good gift and appreciate its benefits. Yet when science addresses religious concerns such as human origins or divine sovereignty, many Christians feel they need to choose between the competing claims of religion and science. In such situations, conventional Christians favor the claims of religion.

Twenty-first-century cosmogonies present several alternatives, namely the choice between a universe closed to influences from God and a universe open to influences from God.[12] If the universe is held to be closed in the sense proposed by scientific materialists, then what is observable is

---

11. Ibid., 28.

12. A cosmogony is an account of the generation of the universe; it represents a model of history, a hypothesis about the past that cannot be tested by experiment and therefore remains a conjecture.

solely the result of "natural laws" upon pre-existent matter and/or energy. No guidance or design is needed. The other major alternative is that the universe is open to God's influences, which may be overt or subtle.

From the early years of the Christian church until the beginning of the seventeenth century, respected theologians held a common position on the relationship between the Bible and science. In the early seventeenth century Cardinal Baronius expressed this principle succinctly: "The intention of the Holy Spirit is to teach us how to go to heaven, not how the heavens go."[13] In uttering this statement, Baronius had Copernicus in mind, who challenged the theory of geocentrism and was condemned for disbelieving the biblical teaching that the sun moves, not the earth (Josh. 10:13, Ps. 19:6; 96:10). Baronius's statement was in accord with the perspective of Augustine, Thomas Aquinas, and John Calvin, who developed the classic Christian theology of creation and who were united in their conviction that Christ is the center of scripture and not science, meaning that what the scripture teaches is the message of salvation through Christ.

In the centuries following the Reformation, as the conflicts intensified between Catholics and Protestants, persons on both sides began to emphasize the literal sense of the Bible. Some argued that the Bible is without error not only in what it teaches about God, Christ, salvation, and the Christian life, but that it is also infallible in whatever statements it makes about any area of human knowledge, including science. This position gathered strength during the nineteenth century, when scientific discoveries and theories about the age of the earth and evolution as well as the development of modern biblical criticism seemed to call the authority and trustworthiness of the Bible into question. While influential conservative scholars such as T. M. Lindsay and James Orr rejected inerrancy as a necessary defense of the Bible's inspiration and trustworthiness, conservative theologians such as Charles Hodge and Benjamin B. Warfield argued with great force that the Bible is free from error in every respect. Thus, conservative Christians were themselves divided over the extent to which they ascribe inerrancy to scripture, disagreeing over the extent to which the Bible should be considered authoritative in matters of science, history, economics, and other areas of human knowledge and practice.

Any discussion of the Bible requires an additional important qualification: the distinction between revelation and interpretation. Whereas revelation pertains to the communication of divine truth, interpretation is the human effort to understand it. Since there is no such thing as an objective

---

13. The material in this segment is adapted from Schneider, Science and Faith, Essay III: "Does the Bible Teach Science?" The quotation is cited by Schneider.

reading of scripture—for interpretation involves meaning, which is clearly subjective—one cannot say: "I believe exactly what Genesis 1 says and I don't need any theory of reconciliation with science." Such an assertion confuses revelation with interpretation. Simply accepting the truth of the biblical writings does not specify their meaning. The problem still remains: what does Genesis 1 mean for twenty-first-century Christians? Just as our observations of the natural world must be interpreted within some explanatory framework, scripture also must be interpreted. The question for the Christian becomes: what interpretive framework can offer the most fruitful way to understand the meaning of biblical cosmology in the light of modern scientific knowledge?

One such framework is provided by the concept of the Two Books, the Book of Nature and the Book of Scripture. This influential notion was articulated by Tertullian (c. 160–c. 230), an early Christian theologian, whom Galileo cited approvingly in his 1615 treatise on the use of biblical quotations in matters of science. Galileo agreed with Tertullian that both nature and scripture proceed alike from the creative Word of God. Therefore, when properly read and interpreted, the truths revealed at each level cannot contradict one another. Sir Francis Bacon (1561–1626), who promoted the scientific method of induction, agreed with Galileo that if one establishes by assured empirical and logical processes the truth of something in nature that appears to be in conflict with a biblical passage, then the problem is not with what the biblical text *says* but with the *interpretation* placed upon its words.[14]

The notion of God's "Two Books" became a commonplace in Christian thought and is still cited by those writing about the relationship between religion and science. Even the great nineteenth-century champion of inerrancy, Charles Hodge, agreed with Galileo and Bacon, but he put the matter even more bluntly. He insisted "in common with the whole Church, that this infallible Bible must be interpreted by science," a proposition he considered "all but self-evident." Hodge used the Copernican revolution as the classic example of this view: "For five thousand years [sic] the Church understood the Bible to teach that the earth stood still in space, and that the sun and stars revolved around it. Science has demonstrated that this is not true. Shall we go on to interpret the Bible so as to make it teach the falsehood that the sun moves round the earth, or shall we interpret it by science and make the two harmonize?"[15]

---

14. Ibid.
15. Cited by Schneider, ibid.

Throughout history, those who promoted the "Two Books" concept were concerned to defend the integrity of both the study of nature and the study of scripture, but when the language of the latter seems to contradict the former, as in the classic example Hodge used, they encouraged readers of scripture to invoke another important element in their interpretive framework, the principle of accommodation. Accommodation is the notion that the biblical writers describe phenomena of nature in a way that was understandable and accessible to ordinary and unlearned people.

Augustine utilized the principle of accommodation in his interpretation of the "six days" of Genesis; Thomas Aquinas likewise used it when he interpreted Genesis 1 in light of Aristotelian science. John Calvin, in his commentaries on Genesis and Psalms, was quite clear in stating that the sacred writers described nature simply as it appeared to their senses: "The Holy Spirit," he wrote, "had no intention to teach astronomy; and in proposing instruction meant to be common to the simplest and most uneducated person he made use by Moses and other prophets of the popular language."[16] Noting that the author of Genesis 1 "did not treat scientifically of the stars" but referred to them "in a popular manner," he invited readers interested in learning science to come not to Genesis 1, but "to go elsewhere." Galileo was thoroughly orthodox when he wrote: "These propositions [regarding the phenomena of the heavens] uttered by the Holy Ghost were set down in that manner by the sacred scribes in order to accommodate them to the capacities of the common people."[17] Thanks to this widely accepted principle, theologians could hold that the biblical writers accurately and truthfully described the creation as they perceived and understood it. But they were describing natural phenomena within their ordinary human understanding, using the common language of everyday speech; they were not being guided to make revelatory statements about the nature of the universe. The "Two Books" concept remains for many theologians and scientists a fruitful metaphor for understanding the relationship between biblical and scientific knowledge.

One insight that historians and philosophers of science have given to our generation is that the theories and models that scientists construct to make sense of natural phenomena are always provisional. Such are true so long as scholars continue to offer the best account of the operations of nature; their superior explanatory power and the fruitful results of scientific research make them convincing. Yet, even though these theories may be so compelling as to be accepted as true for hundreds of years, they may still be

16. Cited by Schneider, ibid.
17. Cited by Schneider, ibid.

replaced or modified whenever new knowledge provides the impetus and necessity to construct new theories to explain nature and its operations. Our knowledge of the universe remains incomplete, for the sum of human knowledge about the natural world is always increasing. The final description of the universe has yet to be devised, the full potential of science yet to be realized.

Thus, as meaningful a model as the ancient Near Eastern peoples had constructed to account for the phenomena they observed in the heavens and upon the earth, it was bound to be superseded, just as every subsequent model of the universe has been replaced or significantly modified to the present day. It is here that our contemporary understanding of scientific truth joins hands with the principle of accommodation. Ancient biblical cosmology needs to be understood as a time-bound conception of human knowledge and understanding that provided a context for the biblical writers' revelations about God, rather than as a timeless statement about the nature of the universe.

Such thinking, however, leads some believers to ask, "If I can't believe the Bible when it talks about science (or creation), then how can I believe it when it talks about Jesus Christ and my salvation?" This question, however, and the "all-or-nothing" thinking that lies behind it, is simply wrong-headed. First, this line of thinking confuses priorities. If the purpose of the Bible is to point to Jesus Christ, as theologians have taught for centuries, then one's belief in the Bible needs to be based on the message proclaimed about Christ and the effect those words have on one's life. All else is secondary, and no interpretations regarding other topics, including those having to do with nature, should be held up as criteria for believing in its inspiration and authority. Furthermore, this way of thinking confuses the Bible's theological proclamations about creation with the cosmological model of the creation that forms the backdrop to these teachings. It assumes wrongly that what biblical texts state about the nature of the heavens and the earth are timeless scientific descriptions, implicitly confusing interpretation with revelation.

This mindset has done a great disservice to believers and to the Bible itself because of the false dilemma it creates. Having been taught that what the Bible teaches about creation is valid scientific truth today and is opposed to certain theories of modern science, and having become convinced that the latter are true, many go where intellectual integrity leads, even if this means abandoning the biblical message altogether. The other unfortunate outcome is that some believers feel forced to reject modern scientific theories or models such as Big Bang cosmology or human evolution, which conflict, not with what the Bible says about God, but with a human interpretation that is confused with revelation. The operations of nature as modern science depicts them, then, are perceived as threats to belief, and science is treated as an enemy of faith.

Both of these outcomes can be tragic. They set up an unnecessary conflict between science and the Bible, perpetuating a dissonance between the kinds of knowledge revealed in each of "God's Two Books." While science and religion both presuppose the reality of depth in the universe, they do not read it in the same way. Science does not—indeed should not—formally address the dimension of depth. In fact, science employs methods that seemingly push aside, at least currently, religion's tacit awareness of the inexhaustibility of the world.

It has long been recognized that the sciences can be organized into a hierarchy, with physics at the bottom, then chemistry, then biology, psychology, and the social sciences. Since physics studies the smallest, most basic constituents of reality, it appears at the base of the hierarchy. Higher sciences permit study of more complex organizations or systems of the entities at the next level down. Adopting this model, the Anglican theologian and biochemist Arthur Peacocke proposes that theology be considered a science and then places it at the top of the entire hierarchy, since theology involves the study of the most encompassing system of all: God in relation to both the natural world and human society. This model reconciles the best insights of the Opposition and Separatism viewpoints. In addition, it also affirms the Engagement model, since it recognizes that theology cannot be isolated from the rest of knowledge.

The relation between theology and the sciences is much like the relation between one science and another. Each science employs its own proper language and subject matter and provides a relatively autonomous description of reality. Yet each science can learn from its neighbors. Thus theology provides a relatively autonomous description of reality, yet has some things to learn from the sciences and some things to teach them as well. While some may object that classing theology among the sciences is a mistake, theology operates much like a science. It has its own proper data—from history, revelation, and the cumulative experience of the church—and its doctrines are comparable to theories in the sciences, rationally justified by their ongoing ability to explain the data.

Each science abstracts in its own unique way from the rich dimensionality of the universe, contemplating from its vantage point what it considers its subject matter. However, as we discern from the hierarchical model of the sciences, explanation is an abstraction begging to be complemented by yet other kinds of explanation. No given scientific field can legitimately claim to read the entire text of nature. It is reductionism that brings scientists into conflict with religion, just as biblical literalism inevitably leads religious people to reject aspects of science.

Whenever it takes its founding metaphors and symbols too literally, religion also loses its own depth. For example, Judaism, Christianity, and Islam represent the depth of nature in personal or anthropomorphic terms. They do so in order to render vivid their intuition that the universe is grounded in an all-encompassing love and promise. However, the sense of nature's infinite depth can sometimes be pushed aside by religious fixation on certain images of a personal God. The danger here is that the deity may then come to seem smaller than the universe itself. Such a "God" becomes too small to command the response of genuine worship. And when our sacred traditions become too literalist in their understanding of a personal God, the universe of science may seem to open up a deeper and more enticing context for spiritual adventure than that provided by religion.

Living in a post-Darwinian universe, where evolution is factual, does not demand that we give up the idea of God. Rather it asks that we think about God in a fresh way. Evolutionary knowledge, accepted and rightly viewed, can help blunt centuries of world-fleeing mystical spirituality and align our religious existence with the natural zest for life that links us biologically to our evolutionary past. For a growing number of Christians today, evolution is a helpful and even a necessary ingredient in our thinking about God. As the Roman Catholic theologian Hans Küng put it, evolutionary theory makes possible (1) a deeper understanding of God—not above or outside the world but in the midst of evolution; (2) a deeper understanding of creation—not as contrary to but as making evolution possible; and (3) a deeper understanding of humans as organically related to the entire cosmos.[18]

QUESTIONS FOR REFLECTION

1. After reading this chapter, what did you learn about the relation between religion (scripture) and science?
2. What role does biological evolution play in your faith journey?
3. Are you a person of faith or belief? Explain your answer.

---

18. Küng, Does God Exist?, 347.

Chapter 6

Refined by Fire

Promenade. Much of religion is a search for order, group cohesion, personal worthiness, or a way of escaping into the next world, which unfortunately destroys much of its transformative power. For many traditional people of faith, hope is centered on the afterlife—going to heaven and not to hell. However, as many theologians are discovering, heaven and hell are primarily "states of consciousness," and the "kingdom of God" is the Reality we experience when we have moved through duality to nonduality. Heaven is now and forever for those who are willing to keep changing, for those who practice "letting go" into love. Those who are in communion with Ultimate Reality are already in heaven. As Catherine of Siena put it, "It is heaven all the way to heaven, and it is hell all the way to hell."

IN 2018 I PUBLISHED my fifteenth book, *Refined by Fire*, a discussion guide containing an amalgam of theological comments and questions found in my previously published writings. My passion for learning, based on a forty-year teaching career, resulted in the conviction that the best teachers—certainly the most effective—are committed to the *process* of education, a task that revolves around two priorities: (1) commitment to the pupil—as person and as learner—and (2) commitment to the joy of learning, to ever-fresh insights and possibilities. An effective teacher in the field of religious studies provides students with tools for inquiry and keeps the conversation going, not arriving at conclusions too quickly or using authority to clinch an argument. I tried to follow this advice in that workbook, wondering whether a small group, centered on biblical study and committed to honest and intelligent dialogue, could move society one step closer to a more hopeful future. Here, I introduce the topic of truth and continue the discussion on religion and science begun in chapter 5.

A DEFINING MOMENT

Several years ago, nine students, all seniors, joined me around a large old table in a seminar room for a course titled "The Development of Western Christianity." The topic was "The Sources of Authority for Modern Christians." The assigned reading featured the well-known epistemological approach called the Wesleyan Quadrilateral, which enumerates four sources of theology within the Christian tradition—scripture, tradition, reason, and religious experience—and the students were asked to prioritize them.

One fellow, preparing for the Christian ministry, began the discussion by suggesting that scripture should be given top priority. The books of the Bible, he stated, are the basis of all Christian belief and practice, since all were inspired directly by God and therefore provide the highest degree of authority. All sources of authority should defer to biblical revelation.

The next student questioned that conclusion. Admitting that scripture is central to Christianity, she noted that the biblical canon was produced by the church and therefore should be included under the category of tradition. In her estimation, tradition, understood as comprising scripture, should have priority for Christian belief and practice.

Another person brought up an equally valid point: tradition, including scripture, comes bound in cultural and historical context and requires interpretation in order to be applied meaningfully to contemporary life. Since interpretation must be filtered through a variety of lenses, including human reason, one could argue that reason stands as the final and foremost source of authority for modern Christians. Several students found this to be persuasive, while recognizing that not all aspects of faith derive from human reason or can be subjected to the authority of reason.

The last person to speak, while agreeing that reason should be held in high esteem, particularly where theological beliefs might be shown to contradict logic or scientific conclusions, noted that logic and reason are not exclusively objective phenomena. Rational people, after all, disagree, and in a global and pluralistic world, it is increasingly conceded that there are—and always have been—many different "rationalities." So, while affirming the centrality of reason, she concluded that reason cannot claim the final word. In all cases, experience has the first and final word.

We left class pondering that final insight. Does reason, together with scripture and tradition, derive ultimately from experience? Our exercise seemed to support that conclusion, for none of the students had prioritized or substantiated their organization of the four categories in the same way. Subjective experience, it seems, lies at the heart of human consciousness and fashions reality as we know it. What we experience, we are. What we are, we think. What we think, we create. What we create, we become. What we become, we express. And what we express, we experience.

THE NATURE OF TRUTH

For a society to work, rules and laws are necessary, with consequences for their violation. When we were children, most of us followed a code of conduct, explicit or implicit, such as obey your parents, get along with your siblings, and treat your elders with respect. Our parents gave us these rules, understood to be absolute, assuming that they passed the test of time because they worked, and that they worked because they were rooted in reality. The implication of such an assumption was that reality was essentially singular and uniform. According to this way of thinking, truth cannot be arbitrary or relative, because there is no continuum between right and wrong. Some things are naturally right, and others naturally wrong, with very few degrees of overlap or confusion.

This is how many of us think, because that is how our parents indoctrinated us from our youth, and rightly so. For their own safety and wellbeing, children need absolutes. They need to obey their parents and those in authority, and the best way to elicit obedience in children is to teach them to embrace values based upon the principle that right and wrong are polarities, distinct and without overlap, not to be breached or questioned. For that reason, most children grow up having a sense of right and wrong, of what is fair and unfair. This does not mean they always follow their conscience or conform their behavior to that code, but they seem to acknowledge the difference between right and wrong, knowing when they have crossed the line.

As we grow up, many of us begin to question the "life commandments" we received as children, and that can be good, necessary, and valid for becoming healthy adults. As Paul reminds us in his poetic masterpiece on love: "When I was a child, I spoke like a child, I thought like a child, I reasoned like a child; when I became an adult, I put an end to childish ways.

For now we see in a mirror, dimly [lit. in a riddle], but then we will see face to face. *Now* I know only in part; *then* I will know fully..." (1 Cor. 13:11–12).

While interpreters tend to view Paul's face-to-face clarity as his longing for an eternal meeting with God in a future afterlife, I would like to suggest a different interpretation. When I hear these words, I envision a scenario in the present rather than in the distant future, empowered by God but occasioned by the hopeful results of collaborative encounters between adults who are spiritually, morally, and intellectually mature and open to newness and change. If, as Christian theologian Dietrich Bonhoeffer suggested, contemporary humanity has "come of age," can this mean that we humans already possess the capacity and the resources necessary to attain the future of which Paul spoke? I submit that such potential is present here and now, to those who approach truth dialectically, that is, who view truth as composed of elements varied and diverse, seemingly incongruous with one another. As the philosopher Hegel (1770–1831) famously noted, progress (social, moral, and even spiritual) occurs dialectically rather than linearly, through a process of struggle and interaction between polarities dubbed "thesis" and "antithesis." The resultant "synthesis" requires listening, appreciating, and learning from perspectives at variance from one's own. According to this scenario, Christians need no longer live out of the resources of Paul's first-century "now," but rather out of the potential of his twenty-first-century "then." If we humans can be said to have "come of age," spiritually, intellectually, and scientifically, isn't it time for those who follow Christ to unpack the implications of that shift?

While most authorities would agree that science and religion are still evolving, these disciplines have developed significantly since the first century. As contemporary physics reveals, nature is neither predictable nor uniform, and as contemporary philosophy reveals, truth is neither objective nor absolute. History is not guided by divine or human forces, as people of the West once believed, but by a process more random and circular than purposeful or progressive. We humans are caught in this vast evolutionary web of trial and error, our survival dependent upon adaptation and harmony rather than upon coercion and control. As even a casual conversation with people of different faiths, cultures, races, or social class reveals, relativity rules.

The nineteenth-century Christian existentialist Søren Kierkegaard (1813–1855) famously argued that spiritual truth is neither objective nor certain. Kierkegaard wrote to free people from illusion, and the greatest illusion, he believed, was the view that truth was objective, meaning that one could compress it into creeds or doctrines for all to hold equally and without question. By arguing that truth was subjective, he did not mean to suggest that truth did not exist. However, unlike ethical principles, which can be expressed rationally and categorically, and unlike mathematical principles, which are universally binding yet ultimately impersonal, spiritual truths are by nature passional, subjective, and radically individual. By necessity, such truth is objectively uncertain.

Unlike objective truths, which tend to make us observers, subjective truth makes us participants. Viewed objectively, truth is something humans possess and therefore define. Viewed subjectively, however, truth is something that possesses us and therefore that defines us. For Kierkegaard, religious faith (truth) is not a universal "given" that can be passed on to others or inherited. Such faith is active, not passive, and is paradoxical by nature, for it is characterized by objective uncertainty. Active truth entails "a leap of faith," for it requires trust and commitment before it can be known. To be valid, religious truth must penetrate one's personal existence, for if it does not become one's own, it is meaningless.

Intuitively, we know that Kierkegaard was right, and if truth is essentially subjective, there must be degrees of rightness and wrongness, depending on circumstances and points of view. In our contemporary world, this perspective seems to have much in common with the mindset known as postmodernism, a way of thinking that builds on the assumption that what we call reality is constructed by the mind, and that human understanding is interpretation rather than acquisition of accurate, objective information. From this assumption it follows that knowledge is relative, subjective, and fallible rather than certain and absolute, and that truth is open-ended and inherently ambiguous.

To be clear, I am not denying the validity of facts or particular truths. The realms of science and mathematics rely on probabilities and certainties—on truths—and the realms of ethics and philosophy on absolutes and universals. But when we speak of religious truth, we are in the realm of subjective rather than objective reality.

GOD-TALK

A person's view of God is vital because it serves as a lens through which people view reality, influencing their perspective of life, the cosmos, others, and of themselves. As one's view of self provides a microcosm of reality, so one's view of God serves as a macrocosm of that reality. If one's view of God is positive—such as lover or friend—then the universe seems benevolent, others are valued, and the self is considered good. However, if one's view of God is negative—such as angry antagonist or vindictive judge—then the universe seems harsh, others are devalued, and the self is considered evil or sinful.

Theology is "talk about God." The majority of people who use the term "God," particularly in the Western world, have in mind a theistic concept of God, meaning an all-powerful and supreme ruler of the universe. Supernatural theism, by implication, includes the view that all finite things are dependent in some way on this ultimate reality, a reality generally described in personal terms. After all, imaging God as a personal being is very common in the Bible. It is also the natural language of worship and prayer, and there is nothing wrong with it in such contexts. A transcendent reality that does not possess at the very least those qualities that constitute the dignity of human beings, qualities such as intelligence, feeling, freedom, power, initiative, and creativity, could not adequately inspire trust or reverence in human beings. In this sense, God would have to be "personal" to be God. It is doubtful whether believers could worship something that does not have at least the stature of personality.

While the idea of a "personal God" is beneficial in that it makes God relational and accessible to humanity, the extremes of this position, such as presented in the Hebrew scriptures, raise insuperable problems for people in the modern era. This God fights wars and defeats enemies, chooses people and works through them, sends storms, heals the sick, spares the dying, rewards goodness, and punishes evil. Many people have trouble intellectually with these anthropomorphic renderings of God and with the seeming irrationality of belief in a personal God. While only the most traditional believers and the most literal readers of scripture believe such things anymore, this deity remains the primary object and substance of the Christian church's faith. It is this understanding of God that is becoming meaningless to increasing numbers in the modern world.

While it is attractive to speak of intimacy with God and accessibility to God, religious philosophers have long warned against ascribing human qualities and attributing human feelings to God. Still, the joy of familiarity with God and the need to recognize and be recognized by God override the philosopher's critique. There is, however, a critical flaw in this perspective: Once we conceive of God as a person like ourselves, God becomes open to criticism.

To protect God, apologists and theologians urge us to discard this way of thinking. God is not like us, says twentieth-century theologian Karl Barth; God is "Totally Other." This understanding views God as different not only in degree but also in kind. Humans can only speak of God indirectly, says thirteenth-century theologian Thomas Aquinas, for they cannot "know" God directly. Humans can only speak of God or "know" God indirectly, by saying what God is not (the *via negativa*), or by saying what God is like, thereby resorting to analogies or metaphors (the *via analogia*).

In using models of transcendence, whereby God is said to be all knowing, all powerful, and all good, we instinctively know that we are not referring to the same kind of qualities we understand when speaking of attributes in humans. Does this mean, then, that God cannot be said to be moral in the manner that we are said to be moral? If so, that raises deep resentments. We hear it in the outburst of the philosopher John Stuart Mill: "I will call no being good who is not what I mean when I apply the epithet to my fellow creatures, and if such a being can sentence me to hell, to hell I will go."[1] In his publication, *The Sins of Scripture*, Bishop Spong examines biblical moral principles attributed to the will of God and concludes that those who wish to base their morality literally on the Bible have either not read it or not understood it. Spong spoke forcefully and shockingly when he wrote:

> There is no supernatural God who lives above the sky or beyond the universe. There is no supernatural God who can be understood as animating spirit, Earth Mother, masculine tribal deity or external monotheistic being. There is no parental deity watching over us from whom we can expect help. There is no deity whom we can flatter into acting favorably or manipulate by being good. There are no record books and no heavenly judge keeping them to serve as the basis on which human beings will be rewarded or punished. There is also no way that life can be made to be fair or that a divine figure can be blamed for its unfairness. Heaven and hell are human constructs designed to make fair in some ultimate way the unfairness of life. The idea that in an afterlife the unfairness of this world will be rectified is a pious dream, a toe dip into unreality. Life is lived at the whim of luck and chance, and no one can earn the good fortune of luck and chance.[2]

With Spong, I too recoil at these words, for the traditional understanding of God has been my guide from the beginning. Unlike some who have concluded that God is no more, Spong does not mean to say that God once existed but has since died. Nor does he mean to say that there is no God. What he calls "God" is real, only not as popularly conceived.[3]

1. Cited by Schulweis, Those Who Can't Believe, 132.
2. Spong, Eternal Life, 121–22.
3. The conventional understanding of God, based in part on medieval debates and the language of certain classical theologians, attributes to deity such qualities as impassibility (that God cannot experience pain and suffering), transcendence (that God is eternal and unchanging and largely unrelated to this world), and omnipotence

But what are the alternatives? Is atheism (a-theism) the only alternative to theism? Technically, of course, there are numerous options, including polytheism (the belief that there are numerous deities), pantheism (the belief that God is in everything for everything is divine), henotheism (the notion of worshipping a territorial god, conceived as one god among many), animism (the belief that nature is filled with spirits or souls, which must be worshipped or appeased), and panentheism.

Many people today are finding the case for panentheism increasingly attractive in an age of science and reason. One can find historical traces of panentheism in both Western and Eastern Christian theology, though the word itself was popularized by Alfred North Whitehead. Panentheism is not the same as pantheism, the concept that "all things are God." Rather, panentheism is the concept that "all things are *in* God." Panentheism views God not as a supernatural being separate from the universe, beyond nature and history, but as the encompassing Spirit around us and within us. According to this conception, God is more than the universe, yet the universe is in God. Viewed spatially, God is not "out there" but "right here." Whereas supernatural theism emphasizes God's transcendence—God's otherness, God as more than the universe—panentheism affirms both the transcendence and immanence of God. It does not deny or subordinate one in order to affirm the other. For panentheism, God is both more than the universe and yet everywhere present in the universe.

In this regard, panentheism is located between traditional theism and pantheism. As David Ray Griffin describes it, panentheism "combines features of both pantheism, which regards God as 'essentially immanent and in no way transcendent,' and traditional theism, which regards God 'as essentially transcendent and only accidentally immanent.'"[4] Griffin's work helps to explain why panentheism isn't just pantheism with a new name: "Panentheism is crucially different from pantheism because God transcends the universe in the sense that God has God's own creative power, distinct from that of the universe of finite actualities. Hence, each finite actual entity has its own creativity with which to exercise some degree of self-determination, so that it transcends the divine influence upon it."[5]

(unlimited in power and capable of doing all things). Overall, such views are unbiblical and, with regard to the concept of "omnipotence," philosophically indefensible.

4. Griffin, Reenchantment, 141.
5. Ibid., 142.

THE VULNERABLE GOD AND COSMIC PROMISE

Whitehead characterized God's relationship to the world as that of a "Persuasive Lover;" and Haught, Peacocke, and others have offered variations on Whitehead's theme. The love relationship is an apt metaphor, for love is the fundamental and most intimate of relationships. Two qualities make this analogy particularly attractive: (1) that the essence of love is persuasive rather than coercive, and (2) that the experience of the beloved is to flourish and grow and emerge into fullness of life as a result of being loved. If this is so in human experience, then in a much more profound way God's unconditional love for the creation must be such as to invite the creation into ever more complex levels of being. To accomplish this, the God of infinite love freely accepts the integrity of nature, its processes and its laws, thereby inviting the world through the complex interplay of all of its elements to emerge into more novel forms and greater beauty through the evolutionary process.

A significant number of scientists from many religious faiths, including Christian traditions, are among those who promote the research that every year more firmly points to evolution as a valid scientific way of understanding the history of life. They earnestly desire that all Christians understand what evolution actually is and why one can accept it without giving up belief in God, the doctrine of creation, and other wonders of the Bible. To those who approach this assertion with skepticism, I ask that they try to set aside their negative views or feelings and listen to the voices of scientists, including their fellow Christians, as they explain evolution.

When *scientists* describe the universe today, eventually they tell a story because they understand the universe far differently than did Sir Isaac Newton and his eighteenth-century successors. Newton understood the universe to be static: space is infinite, time marches onward, and in the three dimensions of space, the solid matter making up the stars and planets of our galaxy ceaselessly follows the law of universal gravitation. Newton and his contemporaries believed that their universe was created, and that God was responsible for setting it in motion. How differently scientists understand the universe today! Scientists now know that we live in an *unfinished* universe, with a beginning and probably an end, though that end is not yet in sight.

Before Darwin, many religious thinkers had argued that laws and patterns in nature could not have come about by chance, but only by intelligent design. And, of course, the intelligent designer had to be "God." Darwin, however, gave us a drastically different explanation of the design in living beings. He did not deny that nature is intricately ordered, but his theory implied that the complex patterning in living beings is the natural product of an enormously lengthy process of trial, error, and adaptation. During the course of evolution, because most organisms had been too crudely "designed" to survive in their habitats, they died out, leaving no offspring. Only relatively few, the best adapted, were able to survive and reproduce. However, if we look closely even at the survivors we can see that none of them, including ourselves, can be said to be "perfectly" designed either. Evolutionary biology calls our attention to the ample evidence of imperfect adaptation, and to the clumsy and even "wasteful" history of experiments that lies buried beneath the surface of extant life forms.[6]

Darwin, along with many of his followers, concluded that the theory of evolution undermines the time-honored belief that the order or "design" in living organisms requires a divine designer. And so, if God is thought of primarily as an intelligent designer, evolution does appear to challenge religious belief. However, if God is thought of not simply as the ultimate source of order (or design), but also as the source of novelty (as the biblical God "who makes all things new"), then evolution is consonant with biblical faith in the God of new creation.

If we are going to speak honestly and intelligently about God after Darwin we must do much better than simply polishing up old design arguments. There must be a better way to account for living complexity than either a pure naturalism that rejects the notion of God altogether, or a supernaturalism that must occasionally and arbitrarily appeal to the miraculous.

Theologian John Haught offers a wonderful solution.[7] He starts with the Augustinian suggestion that a creator has richly endowed the universe, from its opening moments, with the potential for evolving toward the kind of complexity we see in the cell and genetic DNA. Having done so, there is no need for God to tinker with the cosmic process. The universe is given an internal capacity for self-organization that removes the need for special divine manipulation. The sprouting of life and mind in the universe is analogous to the blossoming of an oak tree from the inauspicious beginnings of a simple acorn.

From that starting premise, Haught moves to a second possibility, that God "seeds" the universe not with design but with the promise of novelty and a complexity that eventually becomes alive and conscious, at least here on earth, but quite possibly elsewhere in the universe as well. The "word of God," which according to Genesis hovers over creation in the beginning, is a word of promise. The self-organizing universe, inseparable from God's promise of a future, may be seen as continuously moving through a "field of

---

6. Haught, Responses to 101 Questions, 85.
7. Ibid., 92–93.

promise," consisting of all the possibilities offered at the start. For Haught, in some sense God (or "the Spirit of God") is this field of promise. "Ultimately it is the world's moving more fully into God, and God's quietly coming into the world in the mode of promise, that allows nature to evolve and self-organize in the direction of life and mind. Such intimate involvement with the world on God's part remains, however, completely outside of the range of scientific detection."[8]

Haught's thesis is that cosmic purpose lies deeper than either Darwin or design. The idea of "design" is too brittle to represent the richness, subtlety, and depth of the life-process and its raw openness to the future. Life is more than "order." Life requires the continual admittance of disruptive "novelty," and so the idea of "promise" serves more suitably than "design" to indicate life's and the universe's inherent meaning. This way of "reading" evolution seems consistent both with science but also with religious hope.

The key point is that evolutionary biology, now supported and widened by cosmology, has made us realize that we live in an unfinished universe. Scientific and religious systems, together with living species and all of the cosmos, are part of a process still coming into being. The history of religion, like that of science, is a long series of partially successful but mostly inadequate human attempts to adapt to the inexhaustible depths of the cosmos (which, in part, we label "God"). Religion tries to adapt humans to the world's depth through various symbols, myths, and creeds. But the infinite elusiveness of this depth forever evades exhaustive depiction. And so, the religious quest, like that of science, is always frustratingly incomplete.

The fact that the universe is even now perhaps in the early phases of its full emergence helps us understand why, religiously speaking, we remain always somewhat in the dark, why our answers to the biggest of our questions will always be frustratingly opaque, why we must walk by faith as well as by sight, and also why it makes more sense to hope than to yield to despair. The physical universe is a work in progress, and religions, firmly embedded within nature itself, are continuous with this evolutionary responsiveness. This process of adaptation can by definition never reach a static point of completion. Hence the enormous amount of time involved in cosmic, biological, cultural, and religious evolution should come as no surprise, theologically speaking. Theology after Darwin can now suggest that the universe, understood as an adaptive process, evolves at all only because in the remote reaches of its endless depth there beckons something like a promise (this is akin to what theologians call "providence"). Promise (providence) is

---

8. Ibid., 93.

not manipulation of nature, but is instead a reservoir of possibilities offered to the world throughout its creative spread.

GOD AS SPIRIT

In his accessible book titled *The God We Never Knew* (1998), biblical scholar Marcus Borg examined the variety of images of God in the biblical and Christian traditions and discerned therein two primary "models":

1. The "*monarchical model*," which clusters images of God as king, lord, and father. This approach leads to what Borg calls a "performance model" of the Christian life.

2. The "*Spirit model*," which clusters images of God that point to intimate relationship and belonging. This model leads to a "relational model" of the Christian life.

Both models, Borg discovered, are found throughout all periods of Christian history, though the first is more common. From roughly the fourth century—when Christianity became the dominant religion of Western culture—through the present, the monarchical model has dominated. But alongside it, as an alternative voice, the Spirit model has also persisted. These models reflect two different voices within the Christian tradition.

The monarchical model portrays God as male, as all-powerful, as lawgiver, and as judge. Images of God in this model suggest that God is distant. Within this model, humans have offended divine majesty and deserve judgment. But because God loves his subjects, God creates a way for his people to escape the punishment they deserve: through appropriate sacrifice and true repentance. In the royal theology of ancient Israel, atonement was institutionalized in temple rituals. In the Christian version of the monarchical model, the king's (Lord's) love is seen especially in Jesus. Because God loves us, he sends his son into the world to die on a cross as the sacrifice that makes our forgiveness possible.[9]

The Spirit model, as used in the Bible, is broader than the specific Christian doctrine of "the Holy Spirit," which sees the Spirit as one aspect of God. In the Bible, Spirit is used comprehensively to refer to God's presence in creation, in the history of Israel, and in the life of Jesus and the early church. While the monarchical model also affirms that God is Spirit, of course, and that affirmation can be a source of confusion that limits our understanding of God, there is a difference. When Spirit is assimilated to the monarchical

---

9. Borg, *God We Never Knew*, 63–64.

model, God is not Spirit but a spirit—that is, a spiritual being out there, not here. But when Spirit is set free from the monarchical understanding, Spirit retains the suggestive meanings associated with breath and wind: God is the encompassing Spirit both within and outside us.[10]

In addition to wind and breath, the Bible provides other non-anthropomorphic images, such as rock (meaning a place of refuge and safety). Additional non-masculine images include mother, wisdom, lover, and shepherd. These metaphors for the Spirit affect our root image of God in quite obvious ways: (1) they emphasize *the nearness of God* rather than the distance implied by the monarchical model, thereby suggesting the language of relationship; (2) they utilize *both male and female metaphors* (as well as some that are neuter), rather than the exclusively male images of the monarchical model; and (3) they include *both anthropomorphic and nonathropomorphic images*. Taken together, both models suggest that the relationship to God is personal, even as God is more than a person. The sacred is not simply an inanimate mystery but a presence. Using an ancient biblical analogy, these metaphors lead to a covenantal understanding of the divine-human relationship, which emphasizes belonging and connectedness. This model is intrinsically dialogical.[11]

The Spirit model of God affects the meaning of a number of central Christian teachings. It does so by changing the framework in which things are seen. Borg provides four examples:

1. *Creation looks different.* According to the monarchical model, God's creation of the world is understood as an event in the distant past involving the creation of a universe separate from God. The Spirit model depicts God's creation as an ongoing activity: in every moment God as Spirit (as the nonmaterial "ground" of all that is) is bringing the universe into existence.

2. *The human condition looks different.* Our central problem is not sin and guilt, as it is within the monarchical model, but "estrangement," meaning that humans are separated from that to which they belong. Our problem is blindness to the presence of God, separation from the Spirit that is all around us and within us and to which we belong.

3. *Sin looks different.* For the monarchical model, sin is primarily disloyalty to the king, seen especially as disobedience to his laws. The Spirit model addresses "sin" in more profound ways: for the metaphor of God as lover, sin is unfaithfulness; for the metaphor of God as the compassionate one who cares for all her children, sin is failure in compassion. Thus sin remains, but as betrayal of relationship and absence of compassion.

---

10. Ibid., 72.
11. Ibid., 75–76.

Repentance also remains, only now it does not require sacrifice and contrition but a turning and returning to that to which we belong. Judgment also remains, only now not as the threat of eternal judgment but rather as living with the consequences of our choices. To remain estranged from God is to remain unsatisfied and unfulfilled.

4. *God as king and lord looks different.* God as Spirit is glorious, radiant, and splendid, like the splendor of a king. In the Spirit model, God as king and lord is the subverter of systems of domination, not the legitimator of domination systems.[12]

The images of God associated with the Spirit model dramatically affect how we think of the Christian life. Rather than God as a distant being with whom we might spend eternity, Spirit—the sacred—is right here. Rather than sin and guilt being the central dynamic of the Christian life, the central dynamic becomes relationship—with God, the world, and each other.

The mystics of every religious tradition, following the Spirit model rather than the monarchical model, have always spoken out against specific definitions of God. Augustine, the great fifth-century theologian, articulated that very idea when he declared, "*Si comprehenderis, non est Deus*" (If you understand, then what you understand is not God). God, it seems, cannot really be known, but only related to.

Such teaching, central to scripture, is regularly overlooked by people committed to religious uniqueness or denominational distinctives. Due to scripture's narrative nature, essential teachings about God are not dealt with abstractly, dogmatically, or systematically, but rather in pastoral or social settings, such as by caring for the poor and needy (Jer. 22:16) and by loving fellow human beings in general (1 John 4:20; see also Jas. 1:27).

Alternatively, as mystics assert, we know God by loving God, by trusting God, by placing our hope in God. Such relating is always non-possessive, a non-objectified way of knowing. It is always I-thou and never I-it, to use Martin Buber's insightful perspective. God, for the mystics, is found at the depths of life, working in and through the being of this world, calling all nature to its deepest potential.

THE DOCTRINE OF SALVATION: FROM WHAT ARE WE SAVED?

Many Christians have been reared with the sin and salvation paradigm, a view prominently upheld in evangelical preaching and teaching. This view compresses the overarching storyline of the Bible into a conversionist

---

12. Ibid., 77–78.

template. It begins with absolute perfection in the Garden of Eden, followed by a Fall into original sin. (It is important to note that terms such as "Fall" and "original sin," while essential to the fall/redemption paradigm, are not found in the Bible. This view, dualistic and patriarchal, has proven unfriendly to artists, prophets, science, women, and minorities).[13] As a consequence of the sin of Adam and Eve, all humans find themselves in a state of condemnation. Unable to save themselves (that is, to be restored to proper relationship with God, others, themselves, and nature), they are dependent upon God's grace to provide a way of redemption. Because of God's great love for humanity, God sent Jesus to die in our place. God's gift, however, must be accepted by faith, and those who accept Christ as Savior are assured of eternity in heaven with God. Those who remain unrepentant or in a fallen state—which represents the vast majority of humans, according to some versions of this conventional view—face damnation to hell, defined traditionally as banishment from God and eternal torment.

Traditional Christians sometimes modify this storyline, but rarely do they question its trajectory as a whole, its morality, or even whether it is biblical. If it is biblical, did Abraham hold it, or Moses, or Isaiah, or Jesus? Is it explicitly taught in scripture? Was it held in the first three centuries of Christian history? Surprisingly, the answer to each question is "no."

While the Christian tradition tends to present the doctrine of salvation in terms of the ultimate destiny of the individual, this is not accurate, for as the etymology of the word demonstrates, "salvation" comes from the Latin words *salutas*, meaning "security, safety, or wholeness" and *salvus*, meaning something "whole, intact, or in good working order." In biblical times, as today, a viable religion must keep its social system intact, meaning it has to provide salvation at the social level. The majority of current Christian scholars are convinced that the modern evangelical emphasis on "being saved," which views salvation primarily as an assurance of entrance to heaven, is at best a rather recent emphasis in Christian tradition, going back no earlier than the nineteenth century.

In the Bible the concept of salvation had an essentially this-worldly orientation, meaning that the concept was used to assure believers of security from physical and external threats and to guarantee their place in

---

13. In his seminal work Original Blessing, Dominican scholar Matthew Fox calls for a paradigm shift in religious thinking about human origins and the nature and destiny of human beings, from the fall/redemption paradigm to creation spirituality. The creation-centered tradition, which is more ancient than the fall-redemption tradition, emphasizes goodness, blessing, joy, creativity, play, innocence, and pleasure rather than sin and guilt. Unlike fall-redemption spirituality, creation spirituality supports compassion and justice-making. Creation spirituality does not ignore sin, but views it differently. Evil is neither original nor eternal, but rather something good gone bad.

the coming kingdom of God on earth. The paradigmatic model for salvation is the exodus from bondage in Egypt. The Song of Moses, a hymnic passage about the exodus, proclaims God as the "salvation" of the Israelites (Exod. 15:2; see Ps. 106:21) because God was instrumental in their deliverance from oppression. They were later saved from various other oppressors, sometimes through a human being sent for that purpose: "The Lord gave Israel a savior, so that they escaped from the hand of the Arameans" (2 Kgs. 12:5). During the Babylonian exile, God is said to have prepared Cyrus of Persia to carry divine salvation to the Israelites yet again (Isa. 44:28—45:7). Thus the prophet Jeremiah could call God the "hope of Israel, its savior in time of trouble" (Jer. 14:8).

Christianity holds that the created order, particularly humanity, has fallen into disorder. Things are not what they were meant to be, and something needs to be done about this. The same God who made the created order must act to reorder it, something God accomplished through the life, death, and resurrection of Jesus Christ. In his widely used text *Christian Theology*, Alistair McGrath provides answers given by Christians throughout their history to the question, "*from* what are we saved?" In each case, the doctrine of sin provides an answer. Each model, in turn, also points to the doctrine of salvation, with its hopeful answers.[14]

From what, then, are we saved? McGrath provides six answers: Christians are saved from (1) their human condition, (2) their guilt, (3) their lack of holiness, (4) their inauthentic human existence (characterized by faith in the transient material world), (5) oppression, and (6) from forces that enslave humanity—such as satanic forces, evil spirits, fear of death, or the power of sin. In summary, the Christian doctrine of salvation deals with the restoration of all things, including humanity, to its proper relationship to God.

THE DOCTRINE OF SALVATION: FOR WHAT ARE WE SAVED?

Salvation, consequently, represents new possibilities, a new state of being. McGrath provides models of salvation that correspond to the six models of sin. Together, they answer the question, "*for* what are we saved?" Christians are saved for (1) relationship with God, (2) righteousness in the sight of God, (3) personal holiness, (4) authentic human existence, (5) social and political liberation, and (6) spiritual freedom.

---

14. McGrath, Christian Theology, 339–42.

The doctrine of salvation is complex, and different aspects of the Christian understanding of sin and salvation have been emphasized by theologians, teachers, or by different sects and denominations during different periods of church history or for specific situations. Recent studies of the biblical notion of salvation emphasize the importance of contextualization, meaning that because the Christian gospel always addresses specific situations, the doctrine of salvation should be contextualized in those circumstances. For example, to the oppressed—whether spiritually, economically, or politically—the gospel message is that of liberation; to those burdened by personal guilt, the message is one of forgiveness; to the despondent, the message is one of hope.

The understanding of salvation presented above exhibits a radical this-worldly orientation. The reason is clear: traditional Christians followed their Jewish counterparts in placing their faith into a historical context. The basic conviction of the Greeks was that truth was changeless and hence not tied to events. The earliest Christian creeds, such as the Apostles' Creed, were composed to counter such views, which tended to overspiritualize Jesus and detach Christianity from history.

QUESTIONS FOR REFLECTION

1. How do you prioritize the roles of scripture, tradition, reason, and religious experience in your thinking and living? Explain your answer.
2. After reading this chapter, what did you learn about God's nature?
3. After reading this chapter, what did you learn about cosmic promise?
4. After reading this chapter, what did you learn about sin and salvation?

PART III
Wisdom Revealed

Chapter 7

Securing Life

> **Promenade.** As is well known, we humans tend to see things not as *they* are, but rather as *we* are, through our own level of development and consciousness. This affects not only how we view Reality, but also how we read scripture. We see the text through our available eyes. Punitive people love punitive texts; loving people hear in the same text calls to discernment, clarity, choice, and decision. In the world of spirituality, nondualists are the only experts.

WHEN MY FUNDAMENTALIST COLLEGE friend noted, "Although I read various books and Bible studies, the Bible wins out every time," I want to shout "hallelujah," for I agree. Having studied world literature and read and taught the world's major scriptures—the Greek Iliad and Odyssey; Indian classics such as the Vedas, the Upanishads, and the Mahabharata, including the Bhagavad Gita; the Buddhist Sutras; the Tao Te Ching; the Qur'an, and the Book of Mormon, among others—in my estimation, the Bible wins out. While Hindus, Buddhists, and Muslims view their scriptures as inspired, reading them with passion, devotion, and delight, the Bible—with its legal, wisdom, and prophetic writings, its psalms, gospels, epistles, historical tales, and apocalyptic visions—is incomparable. The all-time best-selling book, the Bible is the most read, best known, most published, and most widely disseminated book in the world. It contains the most fascinating and inspiring of stories, told with wit, wisdom, and artistic acumen, hence, its inspirational nature. It is inspired because it inspires, its spiritual and literary quality unparalleled. The Bible's value is inestimable, for it has single-handedly changed the course of world history, guiding empires, influencing legal systems, and impacting the lives of untold millions around the globe.

For two thousand years this book, in part or in whole, has been viewed as sacred by generations of believers, its sacredness related not to the origin of the Bible but rather to its status within the Christian community. At the time of their composition, the books of the Bible were not considered to be part of scripture. Rather, the various parts of the Bible became sacred through canonization, a process that took several centuries. For Christians, the status of the Bible as sacred scripture means it is the primary collection of writings they know, definitive for faith and practice. The sacredness of scripture is validated by its ability to inspire believers in every age, thereby authenticating its enduring message.

BIBLICAL INSPIRATION

Christians have always affirmed a close relationship between the Bible and God, just as other religions affirm a close connection between the sacred and their holy scriptures. Foundational to reading the Bible is a decision about how to view its origin. Is it a divine product, a human product, or somehow both?

Building on the conviction that divine revelation and manmade religion are fundamentally irreconcilable, many Christians believe that the only choice a person can make about the Bible is to view it either as the infallible, inerrant word of God or as a collection of fairy tales with little or no value for modern people. Since the latter is what unbelievers think, fundamentalist Christians believe they must view the Bible as God's very word of truth, defending it in all respects, even on historical and scientific matters. For many, the Bible's reliability is so critical that they will argue, "If I can't believe the Bible when it speaks about creation or history, then how can I believe it about Jesus Christ and salvation?" That position, adopted by my fundamentalist college friend, also typified two students in one of my college Bible classes some years ago.

Sitting next to one another in my class "The Hebrew Bible in Context," these students were clearly a couple. They knew one another from home, probably having attended the same high school and church. They did not speak out in class, so I had little context when they submitted responses to the assigned reading of Richard Friedman's book *Who Wrote the Bible?*

The authorship of the Bible—particularly of the Pentateuch—remains one of the Western world's oldest puzzles. For centuries, the question of human authorship rarely arose, and when it did, it was quickly suppressed. The Bible was understood to be divinely inspired, and whether that happened through dictation or some other form of divine direction seemed irrelevant. The task of Christians was to live according to its principles, not to question its authority. To frame the question of the inspiration and authority of the Bible in this manner, however, is to do an injustice to the traditional doctrines of the inspiration and authority of scripture.

The story of the composition of the Bible begins with the Pentateuch, five books traditionally attributed to Moses but written at least three hundred years after his death. Once we have a clear idea of the compositional history of the Pentateuch, our understanding of the composition of the rest of the Old Testament follows naturally.

There are two basic theories regarding the authorship and composition of the Pentateuch. The traditional view is that the primary author was Moses, who incorporated both written and oral material into the Pentateuch. This view affirms the basis unity of the Pentateuch. This view is maintained by many Jewish and Christian readers, particularly those who assert the divine inspiration of this material. The second view, known as the Documentary Hypothesis, states that the Pentateuch is a compilation of at least four different sources, none of which predates 950 BCE. Each of these sources is said to preserve oral matter that may go back to the original time of the events. However, this oral material has been altered by the sources for political and theological reasons.

Modern, liberally trained biblical scholars like Friedman espouse this second, contextualist approach. It is Friedman's approach that I asked students to read and evaluate in a five- to eight-page paper. Requesting a summary and evaluation of Friedman's thesis, the assignment asked students to end their paper by addressing two topics, (1) whether they found the Documentary Hypothesis convincing, and (2) whether Friedman's thesis challenged their views of the Bible and biblical authority.

To my surprise, after reading and grading the papers by the two students, I found their response unacceptable, both in length (the papers were slightly over two pages long) and in content (the papers failed to address the concluding topics). Rather than give the students a failing grade, I spoke to them after class, asking if they had read the book. When they replied that they had not, I gave them another chance to complete the assignment. The second draft, however, was no better than the first. As they later admitted, they were simply afraid to read the book, fearing it might somehow corrupt their beliefs and bring them spiritual condemnation. They represent traditional believers who view the role of religion as assuring conformity and submission, rather than as stimulus to healthy doubt and risk-taking, essential for growth and maturity. Fundamentalists believe the Bible should be read and accepted, not challenged or questioned. Such perspectives, shallow, superficial, and stagnant, are obviously alien to liberal education.

Acknowledging the obvious human element in the Bible, modern Christians generally take a both/and stance regarding biblical authorship: The Bible is both divine and human. However, this approach is also problematic. Viewing the Bible as both divine and human leaves us two options. One option is to say that it is all divine and all human. That may sound good, but no one maintains such an unworkable tension. The other, more typical option is to attempt to separate the divine parts from the human parts—as if some come from God and others are human. The parts that come from God are then given greater authority. However, who is to say which parts are divine and which human? The Bible does not come with footnotes that say, "This passage reflects the will of God; the next passage does not." Therefore, those who take the entire Bible as divine are consistent, but they might be consistently wrong.

How, for instance, does one understand the Ten Commandments? Most Christians who think of the Bible as both divine and human would say that the commandments come from God. Does that mean that they are equally authoritative? If so, all Christians should worship God on Saturday, since that is the day clearly in mind as the day of worship. There is biblical evidence that the sanctity of the sabbath was in effect among the Israelites prior to the revelation of the commandments to Moses on Mount Sinai (cf. Exod. 16:22–30). And if the Ten Commandments are divinely inspired, why are they written from a male point of view (for instance, they prohibit coveting your neighbor's wife but say nothing about coveting your neighbor's husband)? Furthermore, the commandments against stealing, adultery, murder, bearing false witness, and so forth are simply rules that make it possible for humans to live together in community. Biblical scholarship affirms that the pattern upon which these commandments are based is a treaty pattern devised by the Hittites, a powerful empire that predated Moses and came to an end prior to the time of Moses. Divine genius is not required to come up with rules like these. This is not to say that the Ten Commandments are unimportant, but rather that their origin is human.[1]

Modern scholars view the Bible as the product of two faith communities, each responding uniquely to divine revelation. The Bible, therefore, contains ancient Israel's perceptions and misperceptions, just as it contains

---

1. Borg, Reading the Bible, 26–27.

the early Christian movement's perceptions and misperceptions. Likewise, the Gospels, which record the account of Jesus, reflect not static truths but rather changing theological perspectives. Moreover, these texts are not the words of eyewitnesses, as is often claimed, but were shaped by the events of the second half of the first century, perhaps even more dramatically than by the events of the time in which Jesus actually lived.

Christians who look to the Bible as a source of religious teaching or for guidance concerning how to live, bring to their reading presuppositions that affect interpretation. These presuppositions influence their understanding of inspiration and the authority of the Bible. Some church traditions say that God is the author of the Bible in the sense that God actually dictated the words of the Bible to human writers who recorded the words verbatim. This approach is called a *literalist view* of inspiration. Other church traditions hold that the human authors of the Bible are real authors in every sense, but that the words of scripture are still somehow what God wanted to communicate to humanity. This approach, called a *contextualist view* of inspiration, allows that God is the author of the Bible without specifying how the Bible is inspired, except to emphasize that the freedom, individuality, and creativity of the human authors are preserved. Of course, actual understandings of inspiration are often subtler and more complex than these approaches might suggest. This approach is called contextualist because it emphasizes that to understand scripture readers need to take into account the historical, political, cultural, literary, and religious contexts in which the documents were written. This approach is compatible with contemporary historical and literary methods of studying the Bible.

Concerning the authority of the Bible, communities and individuals that hold a contextualist approach to inspiration might say that the Bible is best described as compelling and persuasive. This means that the Bible has authority insofar as it compels us to respond with faith, hope, and love. Further, it does not legislate a particular moral action in response to specific situations, but it provides a series of guidelines upon which Christians can reflect on modern issues and concerns. William Countryman, a theologian and professor of the New Testament, explains the authority of scripture in this way: While the church participated in creating the Bible and acts as its interpreter, the Bible functions as the church's judge, constantly calling it to conversion.[2] Therefore, the authority of the Bible is closely connected to its power to transform.

Biblical scholars suggest three broad possibilities regarding the inspiration of the Bible, to which we add a fourth as corollary:

---

2. Countryman, Biblical Authority or Biblical Tyranny?, 52–57.

- *Verbal inspiration*—the view that every word of the Bible is divinely inspired and therefore inerrant.
- *Human response to inspiration*—the view that biblical writers were witnesses to divine revelation; their words and experiences may be human but they serve as vehicles to a higher voice and a deeper reality.
- *Inspired imagination*—the view that the Bible is great literature, designed to capture the imagination; though the books of the Bible contain heightened insight, their message is conditioned by historical, sociological, and cultural factors. When the Bible is studied academically, it is this view that scholars espouse.

Corollary:
- *Inspired process*—the view that scripture requires ongoing interpretation. This assertion, flowing naturally from the preceding options, recognizes that the sacredness of scripture is validated by its ability to inspire Christians in every age. Scripture, defined and finalized by the canonical process, has an open-ended quality both dynamic and alive, thereby extending the revelatory process to the present. Viewing scripture as "inspired process" safeguards the original revelation while authenticating its ongoing meaning.

The earliest Christians had no Bibles to study or read individually. It was the church, and more specifically the religious leaders of that community, that interpreted the scriptures. This was so not only because it had been the church and its leaders that had defined which texts were "scriptural," but also because the texts themselves were not intended as much for private reading as for their suitability for liturgical use. If a document was not considered revelatory, it was not to be read in church. Since most Christians were illiterate and copies of the scriptures were rare, the majority of the faithful could only hear scripture read to them in church, almost always as part of the ritual celebration of the Eucharist. It was principally through the mediation of the clergy and in the restricted context of worship that early Christians could approach scripture.

From the earliest days, Christian leaders formulated theories of biblical interpretation. By the fourth century, clearly defined interpretive theories were already widely accepted by Christian leaders, including that scripture contained four levels of meaning: literal (historical and literal level), allegorical (hidden mystical and spiritual truths), tropological (moral lessons), and anagogical (eschatological level, revealing secrets concerning the afterlife and Christ's future kingdom). While allegorical and other levels of interpretation provided Christian theology with flexibility, giving it the capacity to intertwine written and oral traditions and the ability to adapt to ever-changing situations, in the wrong hands it could be abused, leading to heterodox beliefs and practices. From the fifth through sixteenth centuries, scripture remained firmly in the hands of the church elites who had mastered the accepted exegetical methods. Major controversies were addressed by bishops through synods or councils.

The Protestant Reformers of the sixteenth century declared that the church had become corrupt because it had buried the truths of scripture beneath layers of humanly devised traditions. Claiming to base their reforms on scripture, the Reformers encouraged the translation of scripture into the vernacular, a process aided by the invention of the printing press. Martin Luther (1485–1546), a first-generation Reformer, believed that faith and the Holy Spirit's illumination were prerequisites for an interpreter of the Bible. He laid down the foundational premise of the Reformation, the principle of *sola scriptura* (scripture alone), the primacy of scripture above all other authorities. Asserting that the Bible should be viewed differently from other literature, he downplayed dependence on church authorities to understand the Bible. Luther also challenged the prevailing "rule of faith," maintaining that rather than the church determining what the scriptures teach, scripture should determine what the church teaches. He also believed that the Bible is a clear book (the "perspicuity" of scripture), in opposition to medieval dogma that the scriptures are so obscure that only the church can uncover their true meaning. He favored a literal understanding of the text, rather than the allegorical method of interpreting scripture, stressing that the interpreter should consider historical conditions, grammar, and context in the process of exegesis.

Probably the greatest exegete of the Reformation was John Calvin (1509–1564), a second-generation Reformer. Agreeing in general with the principles articulated by Luther, he too believed that spiritual illumination is necessary and regarded allegorical interpretation as a deceptive device that distorted the clear sense of scripture. Assuming the divine authorship of scripture, he adhered strictly to the principle of harmony, meaning that scripture is its own best interpreter. No passage of scripture should be set up against another; secondary and obscure passages in scripture should always be subject to primary and plain passages. He placed importance on studying the context, grammar, words, and parallel passages, stating that the primary task of an interpreter is to allow the author to speak, rather than to import one's own meaning into the text.

Espousing the priesthood of all believers, the Reformers believed every Christian capable of reading scripture, as guided individually by the Holy Spirit. Rather than leading to unanimity, however, that impetus resulted in further disagreement and fragmentation. Despite their emphasis on scripture as sole authority, the Reformers could not agree with one another on the application of scripture to polity, social issues, and sacramental practices such as baptism or the Eucharist. The unraveling of Christian unity in the sixteenth century led to the emergence of rival communities, each claiming to be the "true" church and to have the correct understanding of scripture.

The Renaissance and the Enlightenment gave rise to ideologies such as humanism, rationalism, skepticism, scientism, and existentialism, each to varying degrees undermining the authority of scripture while simultaneously unleashing a monumental critical effort to ascertain truth in scripture. Searching for truth in scripture, biblical scholars increasingly detected the humanity of the authors who wrote the documents that together constituted the Bible. As Johann Gottfried von Herder argued in the late eighteenth century, the Bible was religious literature, a composite of fact and fiction that was to be analyzed just as one would study any ancient literature. This approach to the Bible came to be known as higher criticism.

During the nineteenth and twentieth centuries, various patterns of response countered biblical criticism. One response was the resurgence of *pietism*, a concerted effort to retreat from the chaos and complexity of modernity to a simpler, less rational approach, where scripture was encountered primarily through one's heart. A second response was that of Protestant *fundamentalism*, which countered modernism by reiterating supernaturalism and the inerrancy of scripture. Fundamentalism was joined by Pentecostalism and evangelicalism, movements that likewise embraced conservative biblicism. A third response, *liberalism*, stressed morality in religion and gave precedence to reason over supernaturalism. Liberalism attempted to redefine Christian tradition in such a way as to engage modernity directly. Embracing the discoveries of higher criticism, liberals replaced literalistic approaches to scripture with moral ones. A fourth response, that of *Roman Catholicism*, accepted religious pluralism and modern biblical criticism while encouraging Catholic laity to engage more directly with scripture, arguing that the Catholic Church was the ultimate interpreter of scripture, with the help of the Holy Spirit.

Literature invites interpretation; significant literature demands it. This is particularly true of scripture, its truth claims fraught with meaning and therefore open to investigation. There is no such thing as a noninterpretive reading of the Bible. Reading the stories of creation or the stories of Jesus' birth literally involves an interpretive decision equally as much as does the decision to read them metaphorically. When we speak of meaning in relation to a biblical text, five levels come to mind: (1) what the Spirit of God intended and intends; (2) what the human author intended (this concern should be important to all readers, conservative, moderate, and liberal alike); (3) how biblical scholars and theologians interpret a particular passage or verse (their views, both ancient and modern, are readily available in commentaries, handbooks, Study Bibles, and other interpretive aids. Those interested in breadth of insight should consult works from across the denominational and theological spectrum); (4) how leaders in one's church or denomination interpret a particular passage or verse; and finally, (5) what the text means to you. This final level, while indispensable, should not be arrived at quickly. Without the corrective of the other levels, this approach to the Bible can result in as many meanings as it has readers. This postmodern approach, based on the belief that "the meaning of a text is what it means to me," lacks hermeneutical validity.

STORY THEOLOGY

In *Securing Life*, my text on the Bible, I addressed the seemingly perplexing question about why the Bible seems to be interpreted and applied so differently by its readers, often due to cultural, sexual, racial, social, and geographical factors. I also pondered why the Bible seems to have a conserving effect on conservative readers, a tempering effect on moderate readers, and a liberating effect on liberal readers. The answer, I suggested, was attributable to four factors, including (1) the tendency to read into the text one's own interests, bias, or meaning (what scholars call "eisegesis"); (2) selective reading of passages that support one's point of view while avoiding passages that challenge cherished beliefs; (3) the polyvalence of scripture (namely, that biblical texts bear multiple layers of meaning); and (4) the nature and depth of one's faith journey and perspective. To these we need to add another reason, (5) the centrality of "story" in Jewish and Christian scriptures.

In our effort to see the significance of scripture, we are greatly aided by this relatively recent emphasis in biblical and theological scholarship. In the 1970s and 1980s, story theology called attention to the centrality of "story" in Jewish and Christian scriptures. This theme can be seen in three features of the Bible: (1) the narrative framework of the Bible as a whole, which on a grand scale can be considered as a single story beginning with paradise lost in the opening chapters of Genesis and concluding with the vision of paradise restored in the book of Revelation; (2) the presence of literally hundreds of individual stories in the Bible; and (3) finally, the centrality in scripture of a small number of "macro-stories"—the primary sources of the religious imagination and life of ancient Israel and the early Christian community.[3]

3. The following is adapted from Borg, Meeting Jesus Again, 119–37.

Story theology not only emphasizes the centrality of story in the biblical tradition, but also criticizes much of Christian theology and modern historical scholarship for having obscured this feature. Theology has typically focused on extracting a core of meaning from a story, which is then expressed conceptually. The story as story is lost. Modern historical study of the Bible has also deemphasized the story, either by searching for the underlying history or by an analytical approach that often loses the story by focusing on its fragments. In both cases, the story as story disappears.

Story theology seeks to recapture the narrative character of scripture. Though it is a recent movement, its approach is very ancient, for the Bible largely originated in story. The story of Israel originated in and was carried by storytelling, as were the Gospels, their traditions about Jesus having been transmitted as stories long before they became texts.

As a genre, religious stories function in a particular way. Unlike religious laws, which address behavior, and unlike theology and doctrine, which address understanding and belief, stories appeal to the imagination. The great stories of the Bible model the religious life. And it is with life, rather than belief, that we are here concerned.

At the heart of scripture lie three macro-stories that have shaped the Old Testament as a whole and have imaged our understanding of Jesus and the religious life in a particular way. Two of the stories are grounded in the history of ancient Israel: the story of the exodus from Egypt and the story of the exile and return from Babylon. The third, the priestly story, is grounded in an institution, namely, the temple, priesthood, and sacrifice. As the three formational stories of the Hebrew Bible, they shaped the religious imagination and understanding of both ancient Israel and the early Christian movement.

1. The *exodus story* is essentially a story of bondage, liberation, journey, and destination. For the slaves, life in Egypt is marked by oppression. The story moves through the plagues and the liberation itself, but does not end with leaving Egypt. Liberation frees the people from the lordship of Pharaoh by transporting them to a transitional phase in their journey: the wilderness sojourn. That phase lasts forty years, but the destination is the Promised Land.

2. Like the exodus story, the *story of exile and return* is grounded in a historical experience, when, after Jerusalem was destroyed by Babylon in 587 BCE, many of the Jewish survivors were forced into exile in Babylon. There they lived as refugees for some fifty years, separated from their homeland and under oppression. Next to the exodus, this experience was the most important historical event shaping the life and religious imagination of the Jewish people.

3. The third story, the *priestly story*, is grounded in an institution. Within this story, the priest is the mediator who makes us right with God by offering sacrifice on our behalf. Unlike the previous stories, this one leads to a different image of the religious life. It is not primarily a story of bondage, exile, and journey, but a story of sin, guilt, sacrifice, and forgiveness.

All three stories shape the message of Jesus, the New Testament, and subsequent Christian theology, but only one of them—the priestly story—came to dominate the popular understanding of Jesus and the Christian life to the present day. Despite the power and positive meaning in this model, suggestive of Jesus' love and forgiveness, this image, when it becomes isolated from the others or the dominant understanding of religious life, can produce severe distortions: (1) it leads to a static understanding of the Christian life, making it into a repeated vicious cycle of sin, guilt, and forgiveness; (2) it creates a passive understanding of culture and of the Christian life, thereby losing the sense of life as a process of spiritual transformation; (3) it leads to an understanding of Christianity as primarily a religion of the afterlife, emphasizing belief now for the sake of salvation later; (4) it presents God primarily as lawgiver and judge, picturing God's love as conditional and placing grace within a system of requirements; (5) this story has merit when understood metaphorically, but taken literally, it seems nonsensical; (6) this story works only when people feel guilt, which should not be the central issue in our lives.[4]

The macro-stories, when taken together, are holistic. They share four powerful elements:

- All understand something profound about the human condition, that life involves suffering and alienation.
- All make powerful affirmations about God, portraying God as intimately involved with human life.
- All are stories of hope, new beginnings, and new possibilities.
- All are stories of a journey. This includes the priestly story, for taken in context with the others, the priestly story means that God accepts us just as we are, whatever our place on the journey.

These stories, taken from the Hebrew scriptures, have powerful application in Christianity as well. In addition, the New Testament has a journey story of its own, that of discipleship. The initial clue is the meaning of the word "disciple," which does not mean to be "a pupil of a teacher," but rather a "follower after somebody." Discipleship in the New Testament, of course, is

4. Ibid., 130–31.

a journeying with Jesus. To follow Jesus means being on the road with him; it means undertaking the journey from the life of conventional wisdom to the alternative wisdom of life in the Spirit. Journeying with Jesus can involve denying him, even betraying him. Journeying with Jesus also means to be in a community, to become part of the alternative community of Jesus. And discipleship involves becoming compassionate, compassion being the defining mark of the follower of Jesus. Compassion is the fruit of life in the Spirit and the ethos of the community of Jesus. This understanding, unlike the conventional moralistic images of the Christian life, presents a transformist, dynamic understanding of the Christian life, where everything old passes away and where everything new becomes better (2 Cor. 5:17).

THE BIBLE IN THE POSTCRITICAL PARADIGM

The Bible represents the heart of the Christian tradition, providing Christians their identity, their sacred story. Despite its formational nature, the Bible has become a stumbling block for many Christians today. In particular, many are leaving the church because the Precritical Paradigm's way of reading the Bible—with its emphasis on biblical infallibility, historical factuality, and moral and doctrinal absolutes—ceases to make sense to them.

The Postcritical Paradigm provides an alternative to biblical literalism. Utilizing three adjectives—*historical, metaphorical,* and *sacramental*—it describes how scripture should be understood. These three approaches apply as well to the creeds and other normative Christian teachings.[5]

1. To speak of *the Bible as a historical product* is to see that it is a human product, not a divine product. Not "absolute truth" but relatively and culturally conditioned, the Bible uses the language and concepts of the cultures in which it took shape. It tells us how our spiritual ancestors saw things, not how God sees things. The Bible is not verbally inspired, since the emphasis is not upon words inspired by God but on people moved by their experience of God.

For the Postcritical Paradigm, describing the Bible as sacred scripture and therefore as "holy" is to value the historical process known as canonization. The documents that make up the Bible were not "sacred" when they were written, but over time were declared sacred, meaning that they became the most important documents for that community, providing its foundation and shaping its identity.

2. Much of the language of the Bible is metaphorical: one-third of the Old Testament is poetry or semi-poetical literature. To speak of *the Bible*

---

5. The following points are adapted from Borg, ibid., 43–60.

as metaphor is to emphasize that this language should not be interpreted literally. Metaphor does not mean that the Bible is not true, but rather that it is not primarily concerned with facticity. The Bible does contain history, but even when a text contains historical memory, its meaning is more than (not less than) literal. For example, although the exile in Babylon in the sixth century BCE really happened, the way the story is told gives it a more than historical meaning. As we noted earlier, it became a metaphorical narrative of exile and return, providing images of the human condition and its remedy. In other cases, as the Genesis stories of creation, there may be little or no historical factuality. Though these stories are not literally factual, they are profoundly true.

Because the Gospels combine memory and metaphor, some of these accounts, when literalized, become literally incredible. The story of Jesus changing water into wine at the wedding in Cana (John 2:1–11) illustrates the point. A literal reading of the story emphasizes the spectacular event as a sign of Jesus's identity, "proof" that he was divine. A metaphorical reading of this story yields a different meaning. It notes the story's literary context in John's Gospel as the opening scene of the public activity of Jesus. It seems to be John's way of saying: "Here in a nutshell is what the story of Jesus is about."

The story begins: "On the third day, there was a wedding." The phrase "on the third day" evokes the Easter story at the end of the Gospel. The imagery of a wedding banquet helps us view the ministry of Jesus as a celebration at which the wine never runs out and the best is saved for last. Here we have a pointer to the sacramental nature of the Christian life and to the belief that Jesus is God's best.

A metaphorical reading of the Gospels provides rich meaning for Christians in all times and places; a literal reading misses all of this, emphasizing belief in the miraculous elements rather than on its meaning for a life of faith. Metaphorical language is *a way of seeing*. To apply this to the Bible means that in addition to its metaphorical language and metaphorical narratives, the Bible as a whole may be thought of as a "giant" metaphor. "Thus the point is not to believe in the Bible—but to see our lives with God through it."[6]

3. To speak of *the Bible as sacrament* is to say that it mediates the sacred. If a sacrament is a physical vehicle or vessel for the Spirit, the Bible is sacrament in the sense that it is a visible human product whereby God becomes present to us.

---

6. Ibid., 57.

For the Postcritical Paradigm, "the Bible—human in origin, sacred in status and function—is both metaphor and sacrament. As metaphor, it is a way of seeing—a way of seeing God and our life with God. As sacrament, it is a way that God speaks to us and comes to us."[7] The Bible is a two-way bridge, a path to the divine and a way to connect to our deepest self. Like a backboard in the game of basketball, scripture is a means to an end, not an end in itself.

QUESTIONS FOR REFLECTION

1. After reading this chapter, what did you learn about reading and interpreting scripture?
2. What role does scripture play in your living and thinking?

---

7. Ibid., 59.

Chapter 8

The Scandal of Divine Love

Promenade. Western Judeo-Christians are often uncomfortable with the word "nonduality." They often associate it with Eastern religions. In some cases, of course, this is true. But in other respects, it is central to the teachings of Jesus. As Richard Rohr reminds us, "Jesus was the first nondual religious teacher of the West,[1] and one reason we have failed to understand so much of his teaching, much less follow it, is because we tried to understand it with a dualistic [a Platonic or Greek philosophical] mind."[2] Even after two thousand years, it is hard to realize what a revolutionary teacher Jesus was. He turned theology upside down. He said, in effect, "Who you think God is, God isn't." He learned this not only through the crucible of his life, but primarily in his death and resurrection. This may explain why people who encounter the risen Christ are humble people. In Christ they find a humble God, a God who is not triumphant and overwhelming, with all the answers and all perfection, but a God who is somehow in this with us; a God who is infinite, yet somehow finite; who is in charge, yet chooses not to be in control at all. The most amazing fact about Jesus, unlike almost any other religious founder, is that he found God in disorder

---

1. See, for example, Matthew 5:45 ("[God] sends rain on the righteous and on the unrighteous") and 13:30 ("Let [the weeds and the wheat] grow together"). However, Jesus is dualistic about wealth, caring for the poor, and allegiance to God (see Luke 4:18; 6:24; 14:13–14; and 16:13), for he knows we are wired to care for ourselves and to focus on profit and personal gain.

2. Rohr, Naked Now, 34–35.

and imperfection—and told us that we must do the same or we would never be content on this earth. This is what makes Jesus so counterintuitive to most eras and cultures, and why so many followers fail to perceive the good news in this shift of consciousness. That failure to understand his core message is at the center of our religious problem today.

THE CENTRAL THEME OF the New Testament is a person, Jesus of Nazareth, a wandering preacher of the first century who has changed the course of history. Whether Christian or not, all who live in the Western world have been influenced by the teachings and life of this individual. Early disciples envisioned Jesus as the climactic historical figure, the Messiah who brought the long-awaited messianic kingdom of God, a rule that by ending evil and suffering would usher in an age of bliss. Later followers and even unbelievers would view Jesus' historical role as pivotal, representing its midpoint. Ernst Renan, famous nineteenth-century scholar, maintained this view when he wrote: "All history is incomprehensible without Christ"; also Napoleon, who confessed toward the end of his life: "This man, Jesus, vanished for eighteen hundred years, still holds the character of men as in a vise"; and H. G. Wells, who once declared: "I am an historian. I am not a believer. But I must confess, as an historian, that this penniless preacher from Galilee is irresistibly the center of history."

The message of the New Testament is reducible to two claims: (1) that Jesus' appearance and career came at the climax of a series of historical events of which the Old Testament is witness, and (2) that God was in Christ, confronting humanity with reconciling power and transforming truth. The paradoxical emphasis upon both Jesus' humanity and deity is evident not just in his message but in his life, his actions, and his person.

UNDERSTANDING JESUS THROUGH JEWISH EYES

The whole of the New Testament—every book, chapter, and verse—is theology: all is written from faith for faith (Rom. 1:17), by believers for the edification of other believers, or for the conviction of unbelievers, that they might be brought to faith. All twenty-seven books are written to explain and promote faith in Jesus Christ.

Biblical scholars famously distinguish between the "Jesus of history" and the "Christ of faith." While the New Testament writers spoke eloquently about the latter, what did they say about the former? Who was Jesus of Nazareth?

Although we cannot be precise about the length of his life or even the duration of his ministry, scholars maintain that Jesus was born around 5 BCE, shortly before the death of Herod in 4 BCE, and that he died by crucifixion around 30 CE. The New Testament is a response to Jesus of Nazareth, whom Christians call Christ, and to a cluster of events scholars call the "Christ event," centered on his birth, death, and resurrection.

Like other great religious teachers, Jesus left nothing in writing. While he may have been familiar with some Greek words, throughout his ministry he seems to have spoken Aramaic, a form of Semitic speech akin to Hebrew and Syriac that became a lingua franca over a large part of the Middle East. This means that every saying attributed to him in the Greek New Testament has come to us through translation. Even his teachings and the traditions concerning Jesus were passed on orally, so little, if anything, was written down. During the oral period (30–50 CE, the years between the date of the crucifixion and the first letter written by Paul), the sayings of Jesus circulated mostly as isolated units, detached from their original context, and preserved in connection with the preaching and teaching activities of early Christians. The famous missionary doctor Albert Schweitzer, at the end of his survey of scholarly attempts to write the life of Jesus, concluded that such a task cannot be accomplished: "He comes to us as One unknown, without a name, as of old by the lake-side He came to those who knew Him not."[3] Jesus, he declared, could only be known by faith. Many current biblical scholars are less pessimistic, recognizing that in the Gospels, particularly in the Synoptic Gospels, there is a great deal of material that can be accepted as genuinely historical and therefore as going back to Jesus himself.

It is clear that the human Jesus must have been a figure of great power and originality. In him a force of immeasurable magnitude began to operate in this world, unleashing a movement that has lasted through twenty centuries and is yet on the rise globally. When a person of such eminence appears, who can apprehend that person totally? One observer will see one aspect, another a different aspect; and even the collection of their observations cannot yield the whole person. Of course, no one can know another person completely. Even after years of marriage, husbands and wives often discover aspects of one another's being of which, up to that moment, they had been ignorant. This being so, it is not surprising that, when Jesus of Nazareth appeared, no single mind could encompass the whole of him, no single artist could paint the definitive portrait. What we have in the New Testament is a collection of fragments of memory and interpretation concerning Jesus,

---

3. Schweitzer, Quest of the Historical Jesus, 403.

extruded through longstanding Jewish hermeneutical processes.[4] Early Christians, believing that in Jesus all of God's promises were fulfilled (2 Cor. 1:20), added to this tradition, searching the Hebrew scriptures for passages that could be interpreted christologically.

At quite an early period in their corporate existence, before they called themselves Christians, the fellowship of disciples of Jesus in Jerusalem followed what they called the Way—the way of faith and life initiated by Jesus (see Acts 9:2; 19:9; also 18:25). This expression was not unprecedented in Judaism; it is found, for example, in the ancient Jewish writings known as the Dead Sea Scrolls as a designation for the Qumran community's faith and life, and may be understood as a shortened version of "the true way" or "the right way." As companions of the Way, the followers of Jesus found themselves assessing the place of Jesus in God's unfolding purpose for humanity. With increasing clarity they saw his identity and role foreshadowed in the Jewish scriptures, especially as he had taught them how to understand those scriptures.

JESUS AS LORD

At the heart of Christianity stands an affirmation that is without parallel in the monotheistic tradition: "Jesus is Lord." This statement, believed by scholars to be an early Christian creed, contains a striking confession, indicating that the first followers of Jesus viewed him as an extraordinary human, one whose influence exceeded that of human rulers (the imperial Ceasars) as the power and authority of God exceeds that of humans.

C. S. Lewis, a former atheist who converted to evangelical Christianity and gained fame as an apologist for traditional Christianity in the mid-twentieth century, famously argued that three options—and three alone—are available for people in thinking about Jesus Christ: either he was a liar, a self-deceived lunatic, or else he was what Christians have traditionally affirmed, Son of God, Lord of all, and therefore God in human flesh. Despite my appreciation for Lewis and his distinctive writings, I find these options inadequately narrow and woefully misguided, for Jesus does not literally fit any of these categories. They emerge from the perspective of the Precritical Paradigm, from reading the Gospels as if they were straightforward historical documents.

Lewis's conclusion distorts the image of Jesus, for it focuses exclusively on his deity, emphasizing the miraculous—especially the virgin birth and

---

4. For information on testimonia, pesher, typology, midrash, and other Jewish interpretive techniques, see my discussion in Securing Life, 176–79.

the physical bodily resurrection. Concentrating on the saving significance of Jesus' death (that he died for our sins), this approach concludes that Jesus and Christianity are the only way of salvation. Furthermore, it places head knowledge—belief—at the center of Christianity, stressing that to be a Christian requires affirmation that all of the above are factually true.

Modern scholarship discounts such narrow understanding of Jesus and views literalistic interpretations of scripture as misleading. In our attempts to rethink our understanding of Jesus, it is vital that we start with the humanity of Jesus (what scholars call "christology from below")[5] rather that with his preexistence and deity (what scholars call "christology from above"). It is possible to move from the humanity of Jesus to his divinity, but not from his divinity to his humanity. That was the path available to the first believers, and the only path available to us. The key is to begin where the first Christians began, with their relationship with Jesus of Nazareth, the teacher and role model they knew, trusted, and loved, and then to press forward with the development of that understanding in understanding the church's experience of Christ. If we start with Jesus, we understand better who we are as humans and what we can become. If we start with Christ, we stand to lose our present and our future, our human actuality as well as our human potentiality.

As Martin Luther noted: The "humanity [of Jesus] is our holy ladder, by which we ascend to the knowledge of God. . . . Who wishes safely to ascend to the love and knowledge of God . . . let him first exercise himself in the humanity of Christ."[6] For Luther, "The scriptures begin very gently, and lead us on to Christ as a man, and then to one who is Lord over all creatures, and after that to one who is God. So do I enter delightfully, and learn to know God. But the [church] philosophers and doctors have insisted on beginning from above, and so they have become fools. We must begin from below, and after that come upwards."[7]

There are, as Luther indicates, two types of christology, "from below" and "from above." Both types can be expressed in orthodox or in heterodox ways, and both are present in the New Testament. The earliest heretical movements in Christianity, however, tended to overspiritualize Jesus, dissociating the spiritual Christ from the physical Jesus and thereby attempting to detach Christianity from history. Such views, gnostic in nature, found

---

5. The term christology refers to the Christian doctrine of the person and significance of Christ.

6. Luther, Weimarer Ausgabe 57.99.3; cited in Hamilton, New Essence of Christianity, 88.

7. Luther, Weimarer Ausgabe 10/I 2.297.5; English translation taken from Mackintosh, Person of Jesus Christ, 232.

agreement in docetic views of Christ, denying he was ever a true human being. A basic conviction of the Greco-Roman world was that truth, eternal and supernatural, was changeless, and that it could not (or should not) be tied to ephemeral phenomena or transitory events. By inserting the name "Pontius Pilate," the Roman procurator who authorized the crucifixion of Jesus, into the second article of the Apostles' Creed, orthodox Christians were emphasizing the historicity of the Christian faith as grounded in a series of historical events while counteracting dualistic views of reality.

Traditional Christianity has had a large stake in historicity. From the start, much of classical christology—particularly the doctrine of the two natures—has depended on being able to regard the words and deeds of Jesus in the Gospels as actual and reliable, and the resurrection, equated with the empty tomb as historical fact, has been seen as the hinge of the Christian faith. Yet modern Christians cannot escape the evaluation of critical biblical scholarship, which asserts that there is no certainty that Jesus did or said most of the things attributed to him in scripture.

The skepticism of the postmodern ethos, which questions traditional language about the mystery of Christ, has shattered the beliefs of the past, reducing universal religious, metaphysical, and moral truths to tentative, private, and subjective claims and opinions. The classic way of expressing ultimate reality had been to use the vocabulary of uniqueness, of finality, of timeless perfection. That Christian theology presented Jesus Christ as *the* Son of God and *the* Son of Man, *the* Alpha and *the* Omega, in whom all lines meet uniquely, perfectly, and finally. Our world, however, relativistic, pluralistic, and diverse, compels us to be more modest about our claims. For many today, to go on saying the same things in the old terms is to be in danger of rendering Christ meaningless, the answer to questions few are asking.

Thankfully, as we are discovering, the static model of reality is largely unbiblical, the imposition of a later and alien culture. The Bible is much more at home with God as active and dynamic, who confronts humans in and through the particularities and peculiarities of the here and now. The Bible does not portray God as one who is unmoved by human need, who lags behind social and biological change, but as one who is characteristically found on the shifting frontiers of such change and need, incarnated in mundane and timely events rather than in a timeless absolute beyond them all.

With regard to the historical Jesus, two closely connected questions arise: "What *can* we know of him?" and "What do we *need* to know?" The latter question, of course, is significantly more important. Our intent is not to reduce God or Christ to our level, but to relocate "the beyond" and "the ancient," the absolute and the metaphysical, to our midst. This does not mean denying the dimension of transcendence or the supernatural, but it does mean starting where modern skeptics and postmodern seekers might have the best chance of encounter. It means beginning with the familiar and the contingent. In this process, the claims of honesty and integrity, of justice and freedom, of solidarity with universal suffering may be taken seriously and without reserve. One may not see how it all adds up or discern any final truths or laws that cannot be broken, but in the particular, concrete situation, one knows that persons matter more than procedures, principles more than precepts.

Today, in our cultural milieu, the place of theology in general and of christology and soteriology in particular, is the servants' quarters, not, as in the period of Christendom, the throne. Its style will be more modest, more broken. Yet at its center is a figure, as the author of Hebrews insists he always is, who is "suited to our need" (Heb. 7:26, NEB), and whom in all his humiliation Christians still rightly call "Teacher" and "Master" (John 13:13).

Whatever more he is—or was—he must be one of us. If Jesus is to be our Person, our Man, he must be a human being in every sense of the word. This is what we find in the New Testament. The early Christians began with a view of Christ that was uncomplicated and relatable. They certainly did not see Jesus to be of *merely* human significance, since he embodied what God was doing in their midst. But their earliest memory was fashioned into a simplistic christology, perhaps the earliest, of "a man," Jesus of Nazareth, singled out by God, crucified and raised from the dead, as Peter's speech on the day of Pentecost recalls (Acts 2:22–24). "This Jesus God raised up, and of that all of us are witnesses. Being therefore exalted at the right hand of God, and having received from the Father the promise of the Holy Spirit, he has poured out this that you both see and hear" (Acts 2:32–33).

John Knox has made the point that as long as this primitive "adoptionist" or "exaltationist" christology prevailed, "the simple actuality of the humanity was in no sense or degree compromised. Not only could it be whole and intact, but it was also subject to no theological or mythological pressure of any kind."[8] But the pressure began soon thereafter, when the idea that the death of Jesus was according to "the definite plan and foreknowledge of God" (Acts 2:23) became translated as the preexistence of Christ. As soon as Jesus Christ was, or could be, represented as a preexistent being who had come down from heaven, then the genuineness of his humanity while he was on earth was open to question. Not that his followers actually questioned his humanity, for the memory was too strong. From the beginning of theological reflection on the significance of Jesus there was the insistence on his solidarity with humanity; otherwise his relevance for us would be

---

8. Knox, Humanity and Divinity of Christ, 6–7.

undercut. Nevertheless, the threat to his humanity was there, precisely because of the story told about him to bring out the significance of his humanity for our salvation.

Who, then, was Jesus, and what, from the historical records, can we infer about him? Despite belonging to the Jewish peasant class, he was minimally literate, in that he undoubtedly went to school in the synagogue in Nazareth, where the emphasis would have been on reading and writing, with the Torah as the primary text. He became a woodworker, which, in terms of social standing, placed him at the lower end of the peasant class, more marginalized than a peasant who still owned a small piece of land.

At some point in his life Jesus embarked upon a religious quest. He probably underwent what William James calls a "conversion experience," not, of course, from paganism to Judaism, for he grew up Jewish. Conversion, as James defines it, need not infer a change from one religion to another, or from being nonreligious to being religious. It can refer to a process of internal transformation, whether sudden or gradual, which led him to undertake his ministry. Influenced by a fiery preacher known as John the Baptist, in his late twenties or around the age of thirty he embarked on his career. Mark dates the beginning of Jesus' ministry to John's arrest, which suggests that, with his mentor in prison, Jesus stepped in to carry on.

What was the adult Jesus like, and what did he come to understand about himself and his mission? All understandings of Christianity rely ultimately on two assessments: Jesus' self-understanding and the early church's conceptualizing of that self-understanding. Let us start with the obvious: Jesus was deeply Jewish. Not only was he Jewish by birth and socialization, but he remained a Jew all of his life. His scripture was the Jewish Bible. He did not intend to establish a new religion, but saw himself as having a mission within Judaism. He spoke as a Jew to other Jews. His early followers were Jewish.

Jesus became a gifted teacher. His verbal gifts were remarkable. His language was most often metaphorical, poetic, and imaginative, filled with memorable short sayings and compelling short stories we call parables. He was clearly exceptionally intelligent. Like the classical prophets of ancient Israel, he performed symbolic actions: on one occasion he staged a demonstration in the temple, overturning the tables of the money changers and driving out the sellers of sacrificial animals. There was a radical social and political edge to his message and activity, as he challenged the social order of his day and indicted the elites who dominated it. He must have been remarkably courageous, willing to continue what he was doing even when in lethal danger. He was a remarkable healer: more healing stories are told about him than about anybody else in the Jewish tradition. He attracted a following, which means he was quite compelling. He also attracted enemies, especially among the rich and powerful. Unlike the founders of the world's other major religious traditions, his public ministry was brief, lasting at most three or four years. Living only into his early thirties, he was then crucified on charges of sedition. At his crucifixion the Romans placed an inscription on his cross that read, "Jesus of Nazareth, King of the Jews," thereby issuing a warning to his followers that Roman rule would not tolerate insurrection.

Though it is hard to believe, some Christians are unaware of the Jewishness of Jesus, or, if they are aware, either downplay it or obscure that reality with later Christian anti-Semitism. The separation of Jesus from Judaism has had tragic consequences for Jews throughout the centuries, and any faithful image of Jesus must take with utmost seriousness his rootedness in Judaism. If we fail to understand Jesus as a Jewish figure teaching and acting within Judaism, we will misunderstand his mission.

As a result of reading the New Testament, filtered through the creeds of later Christendom, Christians have arrived at an understanding of Jesus that is quite different from the sketch presented above. That understanding might be summarized under the phrase "Christian messiah," an exalted status that includes such titles of Jesus as "Son of God," "Word of God," "Wisdom of God," "Lamb of God," "Light of the World," "Bread of Life," "Alpha and Omega," and "firstborn of all creation." These may not convey what Jesus of Nazareth thought or taught about himself, but they came to summarize what New Testament Christians believed Jesus to be.

The Gospels, as the rest of the New Testament, are products of developing traditions of the early Christian communities in which they were written. As such, they contain two types of information: *history remembered*, meaning some of the things reported in the Gospels really happened and reliably represent Jesus as a figure of history, and *history metaphorized*, meaning some of the tradition is not literally true but represents the revised understanding of the communities themselves following Easter. Biblical scholarship distinguishes between these two understandings of Jesus by speaking of "the Jesus of history" and "the Christ of faith." Marcus Borg, in his writings, substitutes the phrase "the pre-Easter Jesus" for the historical Jesus and "post-Easter Jesus" for the "Jesus" of Christian tradition and experience. The latter includes both "the canonical Jesus" we meet on the surface level of the New Testament and "the creedal Jesus" we encounter in the classic Christian creeds of the fourth and fifth centuries. For Borg both pre- and post-Easter understandings of Jesus are valid, the first as the community's memory of the historical Jesus and the second as the community's testimony of Jesus. In other words, after his death, Jesus the Galilean Jew became in the experience and language of his followers "the face of God" and ultimately the second person of the Trinity.

This conceptual transformation may be viewed as a three-fold process; early Christian thinking about Jesus began with (1) experience, and then moved through (2) metaphorical expression to (3) conceptual formulation. In the beginning was experience, that of the disciples and others of Jesus. The primary cause of the transition from the pre-Easter to the post-Easter Jesus was the Easter experience, expressed by the early Christian conviction that "God raised Jesus from the dead." Though the gospel stories portray this as occurring literally, "the core meaning of Easter is that Jesus continued to be experienced after his death, but in a radically new way: as a spiritual and divine reality."[9]

The Easter experience led to a transformed perception of Jesus among his followers. In the sixty or seventy years after Jesus' death, when the traditions found in the New Testament took shape, Jewish Christian communities searched the Hebrew scriptures, finding a large number of metaphors or images that related to Jesus and his significance, images such as servant of God, lamb of God, light of the world, bread of life, Lord, door, vine, shepherd, messiah, savior, great high priest, sacrifice, Son of God, Son of Man, Wisdom of God, and Word of God. Over time, these metaphors became the subject of intellectual reflection and conceptualization. Some, ultimately, became doctrine. This process produced the post-Easter Jesus—the "Christ of faith"—of Christian tradition.

THE HUMAN BRIDGE TO GOD

As noted in my earlier publication on biblical christology,[10] there is no more important topic for inquiry today than the meaning and message of Jesus, no more important concern than one's answer to Jesus' perennial question, "Who do you say that I am?" (Mark 8:29), for in this quest, I believe, lies the solution to individual malaise and humanity's woes.

If, as some theologians suggest, humans cannot know God directly, how then can we know God? The biblical answer is through Jesus, for he is the bridge that connects the profane and the sacred, the human with the divine. If humans wish to grasp the character and will of God, the New Testament writers affirm, they need only look to Jesus, "the pioneer and perfecter of our faith" (Heb. 12:2), for Jesus is the best picture ever taken of God. The fundamental affirmation of Christianity is that Jesus is the clue to

9. Borg, God We Never Knew, 93.
10. Vande Kappelle, Scandal of Divine Love.

the mystery of Christ, just as Christ is the clue to the mystery of God and the meaning of human existence. For those who call themselves Christians, the human Jesus is decisive for interpreting Christ, just as Christ is decisive for understanding God.

One of the central teachings of Christian anthropology is that humans are made in the "image of God." In the first chapter of Genesis we read these words: "Let us make humankind in our image, according to our likeness; and let them have dominion over . . . the earth" (Gen. 1:26). While it is not clear what it means to say that humans are made in the "image" of God—that idea is never systematically explained in the Bible—it cannot refer to physical likeness, for the writer of Genesis 1 takes pains to stress the holiness and transcendence of God. Nevertheless, that concept clearly is central to what it means to be human. Concerning the phrase "image of God" (often referred to by the Latin phrase *Imago Dei*), the following meanings have been suggested:

- Humankind's nature. Because humans are created in the image of God, they have a moral and spiritual nature. Having a God-given freedom provides both dignity and responsibility.

- Humankind's position. Being made in the image of God implies personhood and attributes to human beings a unique relationship with God. As persons, humans are related to God in a manner different from anything else in the created order.

- Humankind's function. Since human beings are uniquely related to God by creation, the Old Testament states that their primary function is to worship and serve the Creator in every aspect of life. Furthermore, as God's vice-regents, they are given ecological responsibility over nature.

- The universality of the image. Genesis 1:27 tells us that both male and female are created in God's image. In the creation account, Adam and Eve represent all humanity. Indeed, the word "Adam" is not a proper name in Hebrew, but merely a word meaning "humankind." Likewise, the word "Eve" is the Hebrew word for "life" or "living." The *Imago Dei* is not the sole possession of one tribe or race or nation. Its potential applies to every human being without exception.

According to this understanding, while we humans are *in* nature, we stand *above* nature, for we have the freedom to acknowledge the claims of the Creator upon us and, within that relationship, to exercise dominion over the earth. Because they stand in a personal relation with God, humans are the crowning glory of God's creation (Ps. 8:5–8).

How then does Jesus fit into this perspective? Who is Jesus Christ, and why is he so important for the Christian faith? The Christian doctrine known as christology sets out to explore why the church believes that Jesus of Nazareth, a first-century Galilean peasant, holds the key to the nature of God and of human destiny. Christology is not simply about Jesus, though even as human he represents the ideal universal person, the embodiment of the highest and best in us all. Christology is also about Christ, in whom "all things hold together" (Col. 1:17). Such understanding has very much to do with us today. If christology is to be relevant today, it must relate to the central issues of our day, providing vision, focus, and coherence not only to religious concerns but also to political, economic, social, scientific, and aesthetic concerns as well. If we are interested in christology, it should be because of the vital issues of our day, not despite them. If, as psychiatrist Carl Jung, puts it, the Christ-figure corresponds to the archetype of the self, the God-image in us all, then this universality of the Christ figure, representing the ultimate dimensions of human existence, alone makes christology relevant today. In this sense, the discussion about Jesus addresses the relationship between the self and God, the mystery that lies at the center of reality. At this initial point in the discussion, the mystery of the Christ is not a matter of faith but rather one of recognition, not "Can you believe this individual to be the Son of God?" (that question comes later), but "Can you see the fullness of your humanity in him?"

The first Christians had a stunning array of titles, names, and expressions for Jesus, ranging from Rabbi, Messiah, and High Priest to Lord, Son of God, Word of God, Wisdom of God, and Spirit of God. Over the next three centuries these titles would be fleshed out to incorporate a Nicene understanding: Jesus Christ was of the same substance as God the Father; he was equal with God in status, authority, and power; he was the one through whom God created all things in heaven and on earth; there never was a time when he did not exist. These were all quite exalted things to say about an apocalyptic itinerant preacher from rural Galilee crucified as a would-be messiah, a failed claimant to the vacant Jewish throne of Judea.

By 381, this understanding of Jesus, recited in the Nicene Creed, served as a benchmark of orthodoxy for all succeeding mainstream Christian churches, whether Catholic, Orthodox, or Protestant. The classic Christian position, summarized in the "doctrine of the two natures," perfectly divine and perfectly human, was definitively stated by the Council of Chalcedon in 451. Generally stated, this position affirms the centrality of the two natures of Jesus Christ for the church, wisely noting that so long as we recognize that Jesus Christ is both truly divine and truly human, the precise manner in which this is articulated or explored is not of fundamental importance. Chalcedon defined the starting point for classical christology to be the recognition that in the face of Christ we find the face of God.

As stunning as these claims remain, what is even more surprising is the rapidness of the development of the early church's christology. According to biblical scholar Martin Hengel, more happened in the first decade or two after the death of Jesus than in the entire later centuries-long development of dogma. The historian of early Christianity, Bart Ehrman, concurs: "It must have been no more than twenty years after Jesus died, possibly even fewer, that the Christ poem in Philippians [2:6–11] was composed, in which Jesus was said to have been a preexistent being 'in the form of God' who became human and then because of his obedient death was exalted to divine status and made equal with God, the Lord to whom all people on earth would bow in worship and confess loyalty."[11]

During subsequent centuries, Christian thinkers devoted a great deal of study to the topic of christology, speculating about the two natures of Christ while closely connecting their study to doctrines of the incarnation, the atonement, and the Trinity. Over time, two main pictures developed: of a Christ who was God in disguise and of Jesus the perfect man. Sadly, both pictures, offered as objects of devotion and belief, distanced Jesus from ordinary people and led to his irrelevance for increasing numbers of people.

Dietrich Bonhoeffer spoke for many when he wrote from a Nazi prison in the 1940s: "What really bothers me incessantly is the question . . . who Christ really is for us today." For Jesus Christ to be "the same yesterday and today and forever" (Heb. 13:8), he has to be a contemporary of every generation and therefore different for every generation: he must be *their* Christ, *our* Christ.

The critical question is, "How does the 'Christ for us today' relate to the Christ for other ages—whether of the first century or the sixteenth or the twentieth?" One mistake of the liberal tradition is to wish too fervently that the biblical writers might say exactly what needs to be said today. It is the same error in reverse of the traditionalists who wish too fervently that the biblical message might be the exact word we ought to pronounce now. Our exploration of the meaning of Jesus Christ—then and now—presupposes a reality there to explore. According to a Quaker observation, "we do not 'seek' the Atlantic, we explore it." The same applies to Christ. Christians begin with a given, gracious reality. They cannot assume this dogmatically or narrowly, nor can they presuppose it of others. When Paul and other

---

11. Ehrman, *How Jesus Became God*, 370.

early Christians state, often uncritically, "to me, living is Christ" (Phil. 1:21), or confess, "Jesus is Lord" (1 Cor. 12:3), what did these mean to first-century Christians, and what do they mean to us today? The center, thankfully, is given in scripture, but the periphery is teasingly and liberatingly open.

In the words of J. M. Creed: "Christian theology need not claim that the Christian religion contains within itself all truth, or even all truth that is of religious value, but if it loses the conviction that in Jesus Christ it has found the deepest truth of God, it has lost itself."[12]

JESUS AS THE ARCHETYPE OF THE SELF

Religion (*re-ligio* meaning re-binding) is not doing its job if it only reminds us of our distance, our unworthiness, our sinfulness, and our inadequacy before God's greatness. Whenever religion increases the gap, it becomes antireligion instead. Such gap creating between God and creation is actually diabolical (*dia balein*, Greek for "to throw apart"). What we need, of course, are adequate symbols (*sym bolon*, "throwing together"), and that, precisely, is what the New Testament provides: an entirely symbolic way of understanding Reality.

Let us be clear; in his human mind, Jesus was limited. It seems likely, as modern biblical scholarship indicates, that Jesus did not fully know his True Self as the "Son of God" until after the Resurrection. Before his transformation, Jesus lived by faith and was like us in every respect except sin (Heb. 4:15). This means he never accepted the "lie of separation," which is the core meaning of sin. He could affirm, without hesitation, "The Father and I are one" (John 10:30). That affirmation, and other equally remarkable affirmations attributed to Jesus, such as "before Abraham was, I am" (John 8:58), are not so much declarations of uniqueness as indications that in Jesus we have the ultimate model and trustworthy leader for all humanity.

When we examine other well-known biblical passages in this light, they come alive in new ways. For instance, when Jesus says, "I am the vine, you are the branches" (John 15:5), there really isn't a division between vine and branches, even though we can tell the difference between them. And when Jesus says, "I am in my Father, and you in me, and I in you" (John 14:20), there is no implied separation of the Self and God. The same holds true in Acts, when Paul defines God as that in which "we live and move and have our being" (Acts 17:28).

Thus, when I use the word Resurrection in this segment, it is for its symbolic value. Despite its uniqueness in Jesus, Resurrection is not about

---

12. Creed, Divinity of Jesus Christ, 113.

psychological optimism, religious miracle, theological proof that Christianity is the true religion, or even an affirmation that there is life after death. Rather, I am referring to something more constant and universal than any of these, something intrinsic to almost everything in life, even things we fear or dislike.

When the eminent Swiss psychiatrist Carl Jung spoke of Jesus as "the Archetype of the Self," he meant that what happens in the life of Jesus happens always and everywhere.[13] Discovering in the Jesus story a map of the unconscious human journey, he feared that Western civilization could lose this pattern, and that the results would be disastrous. Jesus is our "Savior," then, because he is the one who charts and guides us on the necessary path. The contours of that path can be summed up in the twin concepts of death and resurrection, for they serve as the template for full and authentic human life, what Jesus called "abundant life" (John 10:10).

As resurrected Lord, the risen Christ is not being rewarded for a job well done as much as he is modeling the full, completed journey and goal of life. The New Testament depicts Jesus as the "pioneer and perfecter" of the entire human journey, as Hebrews 12:2 poetically states, the guarantee (Heb. 7:22) and pledge (Eph. 1:14) that life is stronger than death, that love is everlasting. Furthermore, this guarantee has been implanted in every heart by God's Holy Spirit.

THE THIRD INCARNATION OF GOD

Longing for God and longing for one's True Self are the same longing. Religion has only one job description: making one out of two. For Christians, that is the "Christ Mystery," the belief that God overcame the gap from God's side, doing "the heavy lifting," initiating the longing. What God is saying in the incarnation of Jesus is, "I am not totally Other. I have planted some of me in all things." Christians would say that it is God who is doing the longing in us and through us, by means of the divine indwelling we call the Holy Spirit. The core meaning of the Christian doctrine of the Holy Spirit is simply this, that God implanted a natural affinity and allurement between Godself and all God's creatures. Otherwise, the limited and the limitless would be incapable of union. Apart from God's Spirit, the finite and infinite could never be reconciled.

What we call Resurrection is one of the greatest and most compelling symbols available to human beings, for it discloses the universal pattern of the undoing of death. The three Abrahamic religions saw God as the one

---

13. Jung, AION, 5.70, 115–16, 124; 12.283.

"who gives life to the dead and calls into existence the things that do not exist" (Rom. 4:17). For Christians, this pattern of incarnation, death, and resurrection revealed in "the Christ" was true long before Jesus of Nazareth, from the very birth and death of the stars to the entire circle of life on this planet.

When we speak of Jesus, we also have in mind the eternal or Cosmic Christ. Christ is simply another word for "the body of God," another name for "God-as-materialized" (what scientists call the "Big Bang," which apparently happened about 13.8 billion years ago). This Cosmic Christ is God as revealed through every aspect of creation, as the New Testament makes clear (John 1:1–10; 1 Cor. 8:6; Col. 1:15–20; Eph. 1:3–14; Heb. 1:1–3; 1 John 1:1–3).

When ordinary people become Christians, that is, "little Christ's," they embody or enact in their lives the "third incarnation" of God, or the "second coming" of Christ.[14] Let me explain what I mean. The first incarnation is the moment described in Genesis 1 as "the first day," when God became the Universal Christ, joining in unity with the physical universe and becoming the light inside of everything. This is described in Genesis 1:3–4 by the statement, "Then God said, 'Let there be light'; and there was light . . . and God separated the light from the darkness." This teaching is affirmed in the prologue of John's Gospel, by the relationship between God and Christ (the Word/Logos): "In the beginning was the Word, and the Word was with God, and the Word was God . . . in him was life, and the life was the light of all people. The light shines in the darkness, and the darkness did not overcome it" (John 1:1, 4–5). The first incarnation—what we are calling the Cosmic Christ—is the divine presence pervading creation since the beginning. From this perspective, wherever the material and the spiritual coincide, we have the Christ.

The second incarnation of God and the "first coming" of Christ represent what Christians believe about the historical incarnation we call Jesus. Let us be clear: Christ is not Jesus' last name. The word Christ is a title, meaning Anointed One. When Christians speak of Jesus Christ, they include the entire sweep of the meaning of the Christ, which includes all the divine activity since the beginning of time (see Rom. 1:20). Of this activity, Jesus is the visible map, the one who brings this eternal message home personally.

The third incarnation of God (the "second coming of Christ") occurs whenever true discipleship occurs, when Jesus Christ is born in us. For

---

14. The concept of three incarnations, exemplified in what Richard Rohr calls an incarnational worldview, is articulated in his book The Universal Christ, 12–21.

Christians, evidence for the third incarnation appears in the Eucharist: "Eat it and know who you are," Augustine said. As any nutritionist knows, we are what we eat and drink. Christians are part of the Christ Mystery. No longer alienated from God, others, or the universe—at least in principle—Christians embody cosmic belonging, oneness with Christ, the name we give to everything purposeful and harmonious in the universe. Paul affirmed this truth when he declared, "It is no longer I who live, but it is Christ who lives in me" (Gal. 2:20).

Exhorting believers to adopt the mind of Jesus (Phil. 2:5), Paul also confirms that Christians incarnate Christ, since they possess "the mind of Christ" (1 Cor. 2:16). When individuals become Jesus people—incarnations of Christ—they exchange one mindset for another, their "monkey mind" (the obsessive, noisy chattering we observe during silent meditation) for the mind of Christ. This is likely what Paul meant when he called believers God's "new creation" (2 Cor. 5:17): "If anyone is in Christ, there is a new creation: everything old has passed away; see, everything has become new." For Paul, when the minds of believers are transformed into the mind of Christ, their bodies become temples, dwelling places of God's Spirit (1 Cor. 3:16–17; see Rom. 12:1–2).

As we travel inward, into the interior depth of soul, we discover that each believer is a chip off the old block, a miniature word of the Word of God, a mini-incarnation of divine love. This entails allowing God's grace to heal, hold, and empower us. It means entering the unknowns of our lives, and learning to trust the darkness, for the transformative power of divine love is already there.

QUESTIONS FOR REFLECTION

1. After reading this chapter, what did you learn about Jesus Christ?
2. Explain the relation between Christ's humanity and divinity and how those two aspects factor into your understanding of Jesus' life and ministry.

PART IV
Grace Revealed

Chapter 9

Living Graciously

> **Promenade.** Once we are ready to set aside dualistic frames of reference, we need further clarifications to live holistically with nature, others, and ourselves. In this respect, process theologians often appeal to some form of the mind-body analogy as a model for the God-world relation. This position can be expressed by saying, as does Charles Hartshorne, that God is essentially "the soul of the universe," related to the universe somewhat like the human soul is related to its body. Feminist theologian Sallie McFague, applying this approach to ecological issues, introduces models of God as mother, lover, and friend of the world, writing extensively on care for the earth as if it were God's "body."

ALBERT EINSTEIN WAS ONCE asked, "What is the most important question you can ask in life?" He answered, "Is the universe a friendly place or not?" In the first century CE, when Jesus lived and when the New Testament was being recorded, the most important question in the Mediterranean world was, "Are the angels friend or foe?" Since angels were understood to be the driving force behind the elements of the universe, it is clear that the people of that era wanted to know if the universe was a friendly place or not.

The early Christians had a definite response to Einstein's pressing question: The universe is a beneficent place, for it is created by a loving God, maintained by the Son, and renewed by the Spirit. I agree. This world teams with life, thanks to nature and its abundance. The rain falls on every creature, and the sun warms us all. There is a pattern and order to nature that when acknowledged proves to be both generous and hopeful. Humans, following nature, have adopted patterns and rituals that create boundaries and therefore order and meaning to their lives, expressed in families and neighborhoods, societies and nations, and in global citizenship. We have settled into jobs and careers and have devised disciplines, ideologies, religions, arts, technologies, and recreational activities to express our hopes and creative imagination as well as to meet our social, physical, and emotional needs. Life is so good, in fact, that humans have devised ways to enhance and prolong it.

THE PRIMACY OF GRACE

In 2016 I published *Living Graciously on Planet Earth*, a book on ethics. The starting point for that study was the premise that we live in a sacred and hence in a benevolent universe. This perspective challenges us to think about the purpose of life, which, as I suggested, is to find happiness for ourselves and to promote the happiness of all living beings.

Morality is often connected with spirituality, and rightly so. Every living world religion acknowledges a natural law, but such law is not the result of observation or of mere trial and error. Before there was a universe, there was a benevolent Spirit, graciously loving the emerging cosmos, instilling promise and bringing forth beauty. Ancient Jews and Christians viewed the natural world with awe, affirming it to be God's handiwork.

Because we humans are the product of divine promise, we are happiest when we bring beauty from ourselves and from others, and when we acknowledge and care for cosmic sacredness in its infinite manifestations. We do so best when we live virtuously, energized by faith, hope, and love, virtues so eternal and enduring that theologians have grouped them under the category of "theological" virtues.

The moral life is not to be lived dutifully or legalistically, but rather graciously, for without grace, all efforts at the moral life collapse. This I learned from scripture, my parents, and from scholars such as Karen Armstrong, Marcus Borg, C. S. Lewis, and Huston Smith, master teachers and pioneers in the field of morality and spirituality.

Humans are happiest when they live virtuously. This is the premise of all of the world's living religions. According to a long-standing tradition in Christianity, there are seven virtues. Four are called "natural" or "cardinal" (the word "cardinal" comes from a Latin word meaning "the hinge on the door"), signifying that they go back to the origins of human civilization and as such are recognized by all cultures as "pivotal" to moral behavior. These four—prudence, temperance, justice, and fortitude—represent how human beings can and should behave toward themselves and others. According to Thomas Aquinas, the great medieval theologian, these four virtues God expects us to attain, out of our own human resources. In that respect they represent "natural" human ability at its best.

In 1 Corinthians 13:13, the apostle Paul presents three additional qualities, so eternal and enduring that theologians have grouped them under the category of "theological" or "supernatural" virtues: faith, hope, and love. These virtues, transcending ordinary human activity such as devotion, optimism, and kindness, are considered divine gifts for they are viewed as originating with God and as attainable only with divine assistance. Historically, Christian authorities believed these virtues were not natural to human beings in their fallen state, but were conferred at baptism.

Before there was hope, there was faith; before faith, love; before love . . . grace! Faith, hope, and love, as habits of choice and action, cannot simply be learned through practice, as other human virtues are. Either we have them as gifts of God's grace, or our efforts at the moral life will be limited to the instrumental goodness that a disciplined cultivation of the cardinal virtues makes possible. The primacy of grace, then, is the foundation upon which all morality is based and perhaps life's most transformative concept. The starting point for all virtue is this: we live in a gracious universe, created by Love and perpetuated by Spirit. And this grace is available—already embraces—all creatures, indeed, all life.

Living Graciously examines the natural virtues individually, viewing their promissory role as social, moral, and spiritual building blocks, and the theological (supernatural) virtues in particular as symbolic of a deeper metaphysical ontology.

LEVELS OF REALITY

In his 1976 book, *Forgotten Truth*, the renowned scholar of comparative religions, Huston Smith, delves into the Perennial Tradition, the common, fundamental experience of humankind as found in the core teachings of the world's religions, identifying therein a cosmology based on the idea of an ontological gradation of reality.

According to Smith, perennial wisdom is perhaps best distinguished by its recognition of the many-layered nature of both reality and the self. Smith narrows these layers to four: reality is composed of the terrestrial, intermediate, celestial, and infinite levels, while the self is composed of the body, mind, soul, and spirit.

These tiers correlate in such a way that higher levels of reality correspond to deeper levels of the self:

- The terrestrial tier (also called the material, physical, sensible, corporeal, and phenomenal) corresponds to the body.
- The intermediate tier (also called the subtle, psychic, or astral) corresponds to the mind.
- The celestial tier (this realm views God as personal; here one speaks of God's attributes and personality) corresponds to the soul.
- The Infinite tier (this realm views God as transpersonal; this level is best spoken of through analogy, in negative terms, or through paradox) corresponds to the Spirit.

Smith's cosmological image shows the earth, symbolic of the terrestrial sphere, enveloped by the intermediate sphere, which in turn is enclosed by the celestial, the three concentric spheres together superimposed on a background that represents the Infinite. "Considered in itself, each sphere appears as a complete and homogeneous whole, while from the perspective of the area that encloses and permeates it, it is but a content. Thus the terrestrial world knows not the intermediate world, or the latter the celestial, though each world is known and dominated by the one that exceeds and enfolds it."[1] With each higher level, different laws apply, together with a different way of experiencing reality. The highest and deepest tiers, Infinite and Spirit, are, according to Smith, without limitation; while the Infinite is unbounded externally, the human Spirit is unbounded internally. These two levels, therefore, are in fact the same.

As one moves down the tiers of reality and out the tiers of selfhood, one encounters increasing levels of differentiation and/or materialization. In the primordial tradition, the possibility exists that one of the higher metaphysical levels can "break through" into one of the lower levels, in so doing overriding the laws of that lower level. While religion explores all four levels holistically, the laws of science are limited in their application primarily to the physical (terrestrial) level.

Whereas Smith places the body in the innermost circle, as the most accessible aspect, with the other levels expanding concentrically outward to the spirit, humanity's most expansive element, I think of the body as the outermost level, the container for the inner levels of selfhood. I begin with

---

1. Smith, Forgotten Truth, 61.

the body and emphasize its role for two reasons: (a) to counter longstanding religious misrepresentations of the body as the place and cause of sin, and (b) to highlight the body's vital role in spiritual health. One of the great tragedies of religious history occurred when the physical body was falsely accused for the sins of humanity. The idea that our most basic bodily functions, including our sensual pleasure and sexual passion, are unclean and unholy is not only a regrettable belief system, it is also profoundly ignorant. In her book *The Seeker's Guide*, Elizabeth Lesser affirms that "deep spirituality is not an out-of-body experience; it's an in-body experience."[2]

Body and mind are not separate; neither are body and emotions or body and soul. Humans are not spiritual beings trapped in a carnal existence. The self is like a diamond, each part a facet of the same essence. When we view our bodies as base and vulgar and our souls and spirits as pure and distinct, we affirm dualism, the bane of spirituality. If we recognize our bodies to be "materialized spirit," and therefore spiritually based, we are on our way to wholeness and truth. Care of the body, therefore, is the first and most important principle of religion. If we are to make spiritual progress, we must learn to love and care for our bodies. The physical is the doorway to the spiritual. This is the starting premise of all healthy spirituality.

Moving inward from body we come to mind, the seat of consciousness, conceived as distinct from the brain, which is part of the body. The mind is not our thoughts, but rather a container for life's continual creative impulses. According to Smith, there is no convincing materialistic explanation of mind, for mind cannot be measured quantitatively. Furthermore, mind conforms to laws that differ in kind from those that matter exemplifies.

The third level of selfhood is the soul (called by ancients *psyche*, *anima*, *atman*, *nephesh*, or *nafs*), the final locus of our individuality, its source and yet superior. The soul is closer to our essence than is the mind, with which we usually identify. While the soul is finite, it is the only possible bridge to Spirit, the fourth level of selfhood. If soul is the element in humans that relates to God, Spirit is the element that is identical with God, not with God's personal mode but with God's mode that is infinite. Mystics and theologians speak of identity at this level because here the subject-object dichotomy is transcended." While Spirit is infinite, humans remain finite because they are not Spirit only. Our specifically human overlay—body, mind, and soul—is said to veil the Spirit within us.

The key point in Smith's model is the realization that as far as selfhood is concerned, one cannot maintain harmony, equilibrium, and flow by jumping across levels. Each level builds consecutively and concentrically on

---

2. Lesser, Seeker's Guide, 242.

the preceding. In other words, the bridge to consciousness is the body. To understand the mind, one must be fully grounded in one's physicality. The link to soul is mind, and the link to Spirit is soul. Each level must be explored deeply and authentically before it can serve as conduit to the next. To acquire meaning and understanding, one cannot jump from body to soul or from mind to Spirit. For Smith, the final link, the door that leads from soul to spirit, is love: "For Spirit to permeate the self's entirety, the components of the self must be aligned: body in temperance, mind in understanding, and soul in love."[3]

GLOBAL CRISIS

It is no secret that our world is in a state of crisis. The prognosis is bleak and the conditions may be irreversible. The tip of the iceberg, evident to almost everyone nowadays, is the environmental fate of our entire planet. During the second half of the twentieth century we learned that deterioration in the quality of the air we breathe, the water we drink, and the soil in which we grow our crops seriously threatens our continued life and well-being on this earth.

In addition to environmental degradation and anticipated ecological factors such as unpredictable weather patterns, increasing number and severity of storms, and sea-level rise, we can add pandemics and the outbreak of new diseases, species extinction, malnutrition and widespread famine, terrorism, violence and crime, the breakdown of the family, increased addictive behavior, unemployment, corporate scandals, an increasing income gap between rich and poor, religious fanaticism and sectarian wars, and the list goes on and on.

The current crisis involves many factors: ecological, political, economic, sociological, and ethical. At its core, however, the problem is spiritual. The crisis of spirit, dubbed "the impoverishment of soul" by Matthew Fox, one of today's leading spiritual teachers, is particularly evident in our Western civilization today. It is characterized by imbalance, or more accurately, by dissociation between the spiritual and physical realms of life.

The current generation outpaces all others in history in terms of wealth, health, education, and convenience—yet it doesn't seem to be happier or more content than preceding generations. Perhaps, in our passion for acquiring things, we have actually lost something profound—something so valuable that we would never knowingly sell it or trade it away. Some may

---

3. Ibid., 92.

refer to values, standards, or patriotism, but what it comes down to is the loss of the sacred.

Rather than being rooted in a spiritual worldview and in principles espoused by the traditions of the world's great religions, particularly in their mystical approaches to reality, modern humans see the world through the lenses of crass materialism, scientism, and positivism. In his thoughtful volume, *Man and Nature: the Spiritual Crisis in Modern Man* (1997), Islamic scholar Seyyed Nasr takes the reader through history and explores the causes of the desacralization of nature in the West and the resultant ecological crisis we face today. He demonstrates how the West, by divorcing science from spirit, has wrecked havoc on our planet. He also argues that the Christian faith helped accelerate this process when it removed elements of its metaphysical doctrines that kept nature as a part of the divine.

Whether the current crisis is curable is debatable, but it will clearly require massive cultural reorientation. More importantly, it will require a transformation of the human spirit and a commitment of will. Only a relationship of genuine harmony with nature and a love of nature's God can transform humans from consumers to caretakers. When historians look back at the start of the twenty-first century, it is hoped that they might remember it most for two commitments: as a time when the peoples of the world made a profound commitment to one another and made an equal commitment to nature.

GLOBAL CITIZENSHIP: A PROFOUND COMMITMENT TO NATURE

The central defining characteristic of spirituality is an individual's sense of connection to a much greater whole. At its heart, spirituality involves an emotional experience of awe and reverence. Such experience is highly desired, fervently sought, endlessly disagreed upon, and thoroughly fascinating.

The world we live in today is the world we know through scientific observation, a much different world from the classical world where Western civilization first emerged. At that time, there was greater continuity between religion, culture, and nature. Today, however, we are experiencing a discontinuity unequaled in its order of magnitude. That is why there is suspicion and misrepresentation among the religions of the present time and why we are experiencing new fundamentalisms: Islamic, Jewish, Christian, Buddhist, Hindu, and Shinto.

Fundamentalism is a defensive tactic. It is one reason why few of the religions of the world are dealing with the ecology issue on a widespread scale. They simply do not feel equipped to deal with this new challenge. By not accepting a responsibility for the fate of the earth, there is a failure of religious responsibility to the divine, as well as to the human. We seem not to realize that as the outer world becomes damaged, our sense of the divine is degraded correspondingly.

Why did our ancestors have such a wonderful idea of God? Because they lived in an awesome world. They wondered at the magnificence of whatever it was that brought the world into being. This led to a sense of adoration. This adoration, this gratitude, we call religion. But now, as the outer world is diminished, our inner world is drying up.

Religion involves the sense of God, of the human, of creation, and of revelation. All of these aspects belong together, and they cannot be treated separately. We would have no sense of the divine without creation. Speculatively, we could talk about God as being prior to or outside creation or independent of creation, but in actual fact there is no such being as God without creation.

Pagans are seen as idolatrous because they worship the forces of nature and depict the divine in natural images and forms. But the divine always appears in some embodiment; no one ever worshiped matter as matter. Whatever is worshiped is seen as a mode of divine presence. Prior to the advent of monotheism, the divine was experienced by peoples generally as an all-pervasive presence of mysterious power in the universe. Biblical people drew together this all-pervasive presence in a transcendent, divine, personal creator related by covenant to a special people. People in the West, who inherited this outlook, gained a great deal, including a historical perspective, a sense of personal identity, and a sense of community. But they gradually lost the outer world, and when the outer world is lost, much of the inner world is lost as well.

Christianity allows for both the immanence and transcendence of God. The two polarities, however, must be maintained in tension. Excessive emphasis on the immanence of God can limit the divine to the range of purely natural phenomena. Excessive emphasis on the transcendence of God, however, can lead to apathy toward nature or even to misuse of its resources, thereby contributing to the destruction of the planet.

Of course, we have to recognize that immanence—this divine presence in creation—is understood differently in our present historical context than by our primal ancestors. Primal peoples related to nature immediately and intuitively; they simply observed and admired the natural world about them. Time was eternal—it moved in ever-renewing, seasonal cycles of change—and the universe existed as it always was and always would be. Humans could not really interfere with that or change it.

In the biblical world, however, a new sense of history came into being, an awareness that the universe emerged into being at a definite moment. Modern science, though it perceives the universe through a different set of intellectual lenses, with the aid of microscopic and telescopic instruments, reinforces the biblical perspective. Gradually, the Western world has come to understand that the universe is not simply a given, and that it did indeed have a beginning in time. And time, we have discovered, is irreversible. Our modern scientific view of the universe thus coincides with the biblical realm rather than with the non-biblical world.

There is something very important about the origin of the universe as we now know it. The beginning of the universe, we now understand, involved articulated energy constellations bound together in an inseparable unity. The various parts of the universe, while outwardly differentiated, were once inwardly bonded together in a comprehensive intimacy of each particle with every other particle.

Ecotheologian Thomas Berry indicates that at the beginning of the universe there were two forces: an expansive force, which resulted in a diversification process, and an attractive or gravitational force, which pulled things together in profound intimacy. While this attraction that everything has for everything else is vital, nobody knows its nature. Isaac Newton (1642–1727), who noted the laws of gravitation, said he did not know what gravitation was, and to this day no one can tell us what gravitation is. But we do know that these antithetical forces, the attractive force and the explosive force, together constitute what is called the curvature of the universe. According to Berry, "Everything that exists comes into existence within this context, the curvature of space. If this rate of emergence had been a trillionth of a fraction faster or a trillionth of a fraction slower, the universe would have either exploded or collapsed . . . If the attraction overcame the expansion, it would collapse. But if the expansion overcame the attraction, then it would explode."[4] Gravitation, built into this process, binds everything together so closely that nothing can ever be separated from anything else. Alienation, therefore, of one human from another or of humans from nature, is only a perception, for it is a cosmological impossibility.

As Berry points out, the other thing that is so important to this process is the relationship of origin: everything in the universe is derived from the same source. Science indicates that, and so does theology. If that is so, then everything in the universe is cousin to everything else. There is literally one

4. Cited in Dunn and Lonergan, Befriending the Earth.

family in the universe, one bonding. Community is not something we humans invented. And if the planet is a single community of existence, then all living beings are interconnected and all things are vital. In a universe where everything is related by origin, nothing is unimportant, nothing is marginal.

The current crisis of humanity is, in essence, a crisis of a lack of relationship. Humans are out of touch with themselves—with one another, with nature, with their past, with their future—but also with the Creator, the God of the universe. As this crisis grows, so does the yearning for relatedness. And that is the good news. Crisis precedes transformation and actually fuels or serves as a catalyst for transformation.

In the journey of life upon which we have all embarked, the most important task is to cultivate a sense of trust. Nothing will serve us better than a profound and ever deepening trust in the Creator, the sovereign power that keeps the vast panorama of universal existence moving along. Yes, the world is in poor shape, and many of its problems grow worse with each passing day. We must do what we can, but we must not fall into despair. If we focus on the big picture, we will realize that the universe is in a continual state of change. And we must remember that our planet is only a small part of the whole, that our crises are but fleeting instants in the eternity of time. There is perfection to the order and flow of this grand universe that is not absent from our tiny earth or our present time.

RECAPTURING THE SACRAMENTAL SENSE OF REALITY

John F. Haught, professor of theology at Georgetown University, argues that when it is wholesome, religion maintains four components: sacramental, mystical, silent, and active. Each of these dimensions suggests a distinct "way" of being religious, he argues, "but religion is most healthy and alive when it blends all four ways harmoniously. And it begins to dissolve into something other than 'religion' whenever any of the four aspects is isolated from contact with its three partners. In the actual world of religious life, such sundering of one aspect from the others is not unusual. But when this splintering occurs, religion rapidly decays into magic, escapism or obsession with esoteric teachings, or into cynicism, iconoclasm or vacuous activism."[5] When, on the other hand, religion concretely preserves the four components in a balanced way, it will function in an ecologically supportive way.

---

5. Haught, Promise of Nature, 73–75.

What fascinates me most about these aspects is the sacramental dimension. Religion is sacramental in the sense that it can speak of unspeakable mystery only through the use of symbols, or what theology calls sacraments. A sacrament, in its broadest sense, includes any object, person or event through which religious consciousness is awakened to the presence of sacred mystery. Historically, most of religion's sacraments have been closely related to nature. For example, the luminosity of sunshine, dawn, and dusk; the experience of wind or breath; the purifying power of clean water; the fertility of soil and life—all of these natural phenomena, and many more, have been used by religions to symbolize the way in which ultimate mystery affects us.

Since nature provides many of the fundamental sacraments of human religion, it is easy to see how the conservation of nature is indispensable for the survival of religion. If we lose the environment, we lose God as well. And it is equally true that when religion loses touch with its sacramental origins, it begins to grow indifferent to the natural world. A sacramental vision, Haught reminds us, makes nature, at least in a fragmentary way, transparent to divinity. In this sense it concedes to nature an inherent value without allowing it to become a substitute for God. According to this Christian perspective, nature is worth saving not because it is sacred, but because it is sacramental.

Of course, religion can exaggerate its sacramental side. It does so when it loses its association with mysticism, its essential polarity, as well as silence and action, another set of opposites that exists in a sort of tension with sacramentalism. When mysticism is lost, the sacrament becomes an end in itself, losing its symbolic value. But mysticism alone, if it diminishes the value of nature by looking exclusively beyond the natural order, can decay into sheer escapism. Occasionally it has even gone to the extreme of hating the earth and everything natural. Mysticism and sacramentalism are necessary, as are silence and action, but they need to be delicately balanced. Mysticism dissociated from a vigorous sacramentalism promotes the doctrine of "cosmic homelessness," whereas sacramentalism without the mystical aspect of religion collapses into idolatry or pure naturalism (the view that nature is all there is).

In his book *The Luminous Dusk*, Dale Allison explores the loss of wonder in Western society and its negative impact on our relationship to the cosmos. Arguing that early Christians favored the desert to the city, finding it natural to practice Christianity in solitude and silence, he laments that modern people forsook the wilderness and filled the cities. And the closer humans came to themselves, the more uncertain and cynical they became.

He mentions a poll of scientists taken some years ago, whose object was to gauge their belief in God. Although few acknowledged belief in God, of those that did, there was a significantly higher percentage of cosmologists than biologists, and a significantly higher percentage of biologists than psychologists. The results led Allison to conclude that "the closer one's profession took one toward human beings, the less belief [in God] there was."[6]

QUESTIONS FOR REFLECTION

1. After reading this chapter, how would you answer Einstein's question? Is the universe a friendly place or not?
2. After reading this chapter, what did you learn about grace?
3. After reading this chapter, what did you learn about the role of the body and the natural realm in vital spirituality?

---

6. Allison Jr., Luminous Dusk, 13.

Chapter 10

The New Creation

Promenade. Modern Christians spend a great deal of time trying to connect the dots, attempting intellectually to penetrate the core of reality to see what is good, beautiful, true, lasting, and transcendent. While most early Christians sought the same things, they did not approach life and faith analytically, as we do today. Rather, they applied what they believed mystically, spiritually, and intuitively. As a result, they lived kindly, in harmony with nature and others. Although they did not use the word "nondual," the idea was consistently assumed, implied, and even taught for at least sixteen hundred years. Since the Enlightenment, modern believers have approached reality in a more detached and scientific way, looking to facts, evidence, and objective truth for hope and truth, favoring doctrine over direct experience. In trying to defend its ground in the face of rationalism and scientism, modern religion tried to become "rational" and lost its alternative consciousness. Losing access to the higher levels of consciousness—the transrational, transpersonal, and transcendent—many Christians settled for finality and conformity, content to rest in shallow waters rather than plumbing the depths. Tragically, many lost the inner experience that underlies the outer belief system. That is the heart of religion's problem today, taking the symbols too literally, and now the emerging generation is throwing them out as useless. Without searching, nothing will be found, but how one searches will determine what one finds or even expects to find.

CORPORATE PERSONALITY

In 2018 I published *The New Creation*, a book on church history, raising questions about the church's nature, its role in society, and whether the church has lived up to its nature and destiny as God's new creation. When Christians hear the phrase "the new creation," they tend to think of Isaiah's prophecies or of Revelation's vision of "a new heaven and a new earth" (Isa. 65:17; Rev. 21:1). Others think of unbelievers converted to Christianity or of believers transformed by the Holy Spirit.

The Bible portrays Israel as God's people, not simply a collection of persons but a divine company ("a priestly kingdom and a holy nation"; Exod. 19:6; 1 Pet. 2:9). Out of families, clans, and tribes God formed a nation, with a corporate personality: When one person suffered, everyone suffered; when one person was blessed, the people enjoyed the benefits; when one person sinned, the whole nation participated in the judgment; when one person received a promise, he or she did so on behalf of the nation.

Americans today live in a pluralistic society, with diverse cultures, religions, and societal values, and we are taught to be tolerant. Ancient societies were quite the opposite; they were homogeneous, with little tolerance or diversity, and with no such thing as freedom of religion. The concept of corporate personality provided Israel with stability, solidarity, and unity during the period of its ascendency. These qualities enabled Israelites to maintain social and religious cohesion in a sea of paganism. Their laws, rituals, and values provided them with a distinctive way of life, which has preserved them to this day.

The first Christians acknowledged individual transformation, but they would have viewed it corporately rather than in isolation. When God gave individuals a vision or called individuals to service, it was for the larger good. When Jesus spoke of the good shepherd leaving the fold for the sake of one lost sheep, he had the flock in mind. When Paul spoke of believers, he had the church, the "body of Christ," in mind. Though individuals are deeply beloved of God, they are members of a larger entity. Likewise, when Jesus tells his followers that they will do the works he does and even "greater works than these" (John 14:12), he had in mind not the deeds of individual disciples but the corporate endeavors of his followers.

Their origin as a "little flock," ongoing and expanding throughout history, would proliferate to a global religion of staggering size and pervasive presence whose faith, resulting in deeds of kindness and compassion, would literally "move" social and economic mountains (see Mark 11:23). Despite these accomplishments, Jesus reminds his disciples that they are to abide in him, the true vine, for individually and apart from him, they can do nothing

(John 15:1–8). Only by following his example, propelled by his vision and empowered by his Spirit, would they fulfill their God-given destiny.

The letter to the Ephesians, written by a devoted admirer of Paul during the last two decades of the first century, is influenced by a dominant concern, namely, the unity of the church under the headship of Christ. The church at this time had become predominantly Gentile and was in danger of losing its sense of continuity with Israel. The author of Ephesians, desiring to underscore the larger history and tradition that defined Christianity, as well as the mystical unity of believers in Christ, portrays that oneness in three predominant images: the church is (1) the body of Christ (1:22–23), (2) the building or temple of God (2:20–22), and (3) the bride of Christ (5:23–32). The church's solidarity, Paul makes clear in Galatians 3:28, has social implications, namely, challenging racial, social, and sexual barriers. Because Christ is one, church members are united. Because Christ is one, church members are equal. Because Christ is one, church members are free to serve one another.

WHY STUDY CHURCH HISTORY?

As loss of memory in an individual is a psychiatric defect calling for medical treatment, so too any community that has no social memory is suffering from illness. While historians have the crucial task of helping each generation find its bearings, the recording of history tells the story of the human family.

Christianity is essentially a historical religion. It cannot be understood simply through a set of dogmas, a moral code, or a view of the universe. For through the stories of Israel, Jesus, and the developing church, Christianity acknowledges the revelation of God in action. As an institution, the church has an identity and a mission, and as an organism, it necessarily develops from infancy to maturity, undergoing the growing pains of adolescence, young adulthood, and midlife as well as periodic transformation due to changing cultural needs and challenges.

It is important to remember that when anyone—politician, social activist, or church reformer—calls for a radical new start, a complete break with the past, he or she is shooting at the moon, for no clean break with the past is possible. Every generation, just as every individual, is the result of the subtle yet dominant influences of the past. The philosopher Bertrand Russell claimed that one of the great faults of the twentieth century was that it limited itself to a "parochialism in time," viewing the old as antiquated and irrelevant and only the new as pertinent. Lord Acton made the same point:

"history must be our deliverer not only from the undue influence of other times, but from the undue influence of our own."

History, then, has to do with the study of the "otherness" of the past. It involves trying to allow that "otherness" to speak to us. If we are to be liberated from the tyranny of the present, we must try to see life with the eyes of centuries other than our own. In that way we embrace the past in the present. We must allow individuals of the past to pose their own questions rather than imposing upon them our own fascinations, hopes, and neuroses. Only in this way will the study of the past open up to us a larger present.

Another benefit from the study of church history is that study of the past can be useful in shaping proper attitudes toward scripture. While Christians value the Bible, they do not always agree on its message. Studying the history of Christianity provides perspective on the interpretation of scripture, for it acquaints us with vast differences in how the Bible has been used and understood. Because its members and leaders are human, the church is not perfect, as its history makes abundantly clear. For that reason, the study of church history should increase our humility about who we are and what we believe. In addition, historical study helps us distinguish between biblical chaff and wheat, preserving our deepest commitment only to those aspects of Christian faith that deserve such commitment, while enabling us to act with even greater toleration in a cultural climate becoming increasingly diverse.

While many Christians value the study of church history, some disparage it as unnecessary and irrelevant to their spiritual wellbeing. Unlike traditional Roman Catholic or Eastern Orthodox Christians, who value tradition, evangelical Christians typically go directly to scripture for guidance or inspiration, neglecting the value of tradition for faith and practice. They often appeal to Martin Luther and other Protestant Reformers, who argued for the primacy of scripture above all other authorities.

When Protestant thinkers such as Martin Luther coined the phrase *sola scriptura*, establishing the Bible as the source and sole authority of their faith, they were protesting the role of tradition—particularly the medieval accretions that defined Latin Christianity—as equally binding. Their methodology, encapsulated in the phrase *ad fontes* (back to the sources), defined their strategy. They believed the scriptures, practically and clearly interpreted, to be adequate and sufficient for faith and practice. In addition, they argued, the church stood in need of purification from excessive reliance upon secular medieval institutions and practices such as state, culture, philosophy, and reason. Rejecting the synthesis mentality of the thousand-year-old Holy Roman Empire, which valued equally scripture and tradition, the Protestant Reformers attempted to return to an undiluted biblical way of thinking, without realizing that the scriptures upon which they were relying also included a synthesis mentality, as yet undetected. Unfortunately, the Reformers' search for purity resulted in the further fragmentation of Christendom, first into four sectarian bodies (Lutheran, Reformed, Anglican, and Anabaptist), and eventually into hundreds of denominations and thousands of sects.

While Protestants and non-denominational Christians remain influenced by biblical ideals, some reject the suspicion and anxiety produced by schisms of the past. As Christians of all denominations, cultures, and races are discovering, unity is better than discord, and cooperation more beneficial than isolation. Learning from history, modern Christians are setting aside ecclesiastical and sociological differences, affirming the trajectories that provide forward momentum to the faith.

A fragmented world awaits this unified church, its members working together for the healing of the nations. This cannot take place unless believers join hands, informed by their varied traditions and beliefs and empowered by the larger Christian narrative. What transpired during the canonical process—one Bible representing multiple voices and perspectives—needs to occur yet again, one church representing many voices, cultures, and traditions. Such unity in mission and service does not occur automatically, but only through an informed appreciation of a mutual heritage, a common scripture, and a shared story. Twenty-first-century Christians can no longer ignore church history. Aside from keeping Christians provincial and divided, such ignorance prevents them from fulfilling their destiny as the body of Christ.

THE CHURCH: FOUR DEFINITIONS

In my days as a seminarian and then as a young professor, I heard people speak of the church as central not only to the New Testament but also to the Old Testament. This idea perplexed me, for it appeared ignorant. After all, the birth of the church is recorded in the book of Acts. Could the church preexist its own birth? Over time, I became less literal in my understanding of biblical concepts, and I now find the idea of the church in the Old Testament attractive and even accurate, particularly if by "church" we mean something mystical and invisible rather than institutional. The Christian church did come into existence on the Christian Pentecost, but the prototype goes back to "Father Abraham," the founding member of God's church.

The New Creation defines the church as "the people of God," a reality traceable to God's covenant with Abraham. It is this concept I address in that study, related but not equivalent to Israel or to the institutional church.

Paul speaks of this church as God's "remnant people" (Rom. 9:27–29; 11:5), an entity known to God but not discernible organizationally. Using Pauline language, the New Testament church is a "wild olive shoot" grafted into the olive tree (true Israel), and the "branch" of Gentile Christians is supported by the roots that reach deeply into God's choice of Israel and God's faithful dealings with this people (Rom. 11:17–24). *The New Creation* assumes that from the beginning God had in mind what we term the church, a people chosen from every race and nation to enact the divine will and plan, and that this church is present in every generation.

The New Creation distinguishes between four uses of the term "church," maintaining consistency in the meaning and use of the term when possible. The general practice is to capitalize the term when it refers to a specific ecclesiastical organization, such as the Greek Orthodox Church, the Roman Catholic Church, or the Lutheran Church. However, when speaking of Christianity or the Christian church in general, we do not capitalize the term. If we are speaking of a local church or group of churches in a region such as Jerusalem, Alexandria, Constantinople, or Rome, lower-case usage is appropriate, but when by the Roman Church we mean Roman Catholicism, or the papacy, upper-case usage is appropriate.

This text introduces another subtlety, the possibility of a mystical body of believers, whether in the pre-Christian period or throughout the Christian era, embedded in particular ecclesiastical organizations yet not confined or defined by such membership. This notion of God's people as an invisible church is biblical and yet was generally unknown throughout church history until it became widely acknowledged in the Reformation and post-Reformation periods. For this understanding of "church" we may use the term "*kirk*," based on the Greek adjective *kuriakē*, "belonging to the Lord." This term, found in several northern European languages, is often associated with the Scottish Church.

Though the tension between these perspectives of the church runs throughout Christian history, the New Testament writers did not distinguish between them. After all, the ecclesiastical structure was in its infancy, and the biblical writers assumed that "card-carrying" Christians, while worshipping in a local congregation, also belonged to the larger "body of Christ." Like an iceberg, the church was strategically visible yet largely invisible.

When we speak of the church, then, we envision four overlapping entities:

1. Christianity in general, in which case the term "church" is not capitalized.

2. A visible ecclesiastical organization such as the Catholic, the Anglican, or the Lutheran Church, in which case the term "church" is capitalized.
3. A local congregation of believers, in which case the term "church" is not capitalized.
4. The invisible church (*kirk*) throughout the ages, an entity on earth sometimes called "the church militant" (as contrasted with "the church triumphant," a reference to departed brethren). While the term "militant" suggests antagonism between the church and the world, used ecclesiastically the word refers to the church on earth working to overcome defective dimensions of human existence.

THE NEW CREATION: AN OVERVIEW

While scholars date the birth of the church to the celebration of Pentecost on or about the year 30 of the Common Era, *The New Creation* takes a more nuanced approach. The church—God's people—has not one but rather two biblical foundations:

- The Great Command (Gen. 12:1–3), when God said GO!, and
- The Great Commission (Matt. 28:18–20), when God said GROW!

The story of the church begins with Abraham in the second millennium BCE, long before Jesus or the birth of Christianity, and it proceeds through three epochs:

1. Formation (c. 1850–4 BCE)
2. Transformation (4 BCE–1500 CE), and
3. Reformation (1500–present).

To understand the biblical concept of community one must begin with Abraham. God started with one family, declaring a promise so wondrous as to engender laughter, creating something in Sarah's womb when she was unable to conceive: "Is anything too wonderful for the Lord?" (Gen. 18:14). From Isaac came Jacob, and from him the twelve tribes of Israel. They took his name, his personality, his style of life, and the covenant he had with God. They would call themselves "*bene* Israel," sons of Israel. The doctrine of election was not arbitrary. Rather it reminded them that they were beloved, God's new creation. They were not one nation *out of* many, but one nation *for* many. In such unity there is resolve, resilience, and strength.

The first Christians lived in a Greek world, dominated by alien values and beliefs. As Jews, they drew on Hebraic customs and beliefs, themselves shaped by alien cultural influences: Sumerian, Amorite, Egyptian, Hittite, Phoenician, Aramean, Assyrian, Babylonian, and Greek. Over time, these and other ancient neighbors in the Eastern Mediterranean world had supplied beliefs and practices that resulted in views of God grouped variously under the rubric called ethical monotheism. Like their forebears, the first Christians tried to reconcile diverse visions of deity, and the results, far from uniform, elicited unstable answers to unending questions.

Affirming the action of God throughout the entirety of human history, *The New Creation* envisions primeval, pagan, and patriarchal origins as preparatory to the Israelite period (first millennium BCE), and the latter as preparatory to the apostolic period (first century CE). An apt metaphor is the hourglass, the sands of time flowing from the upper globe through a narrow opening to the lower globe, or, as biblically conceived, from creation, through Christ, to consummation.

The New Creation examines the church as God's mechanism to inspire and enable select individuals (such as patriarchs, prophets, apostles, priests, martyrs, monks, and laypeople), groups (such as the Israelite nation and later the Christian church), and reforming movements throughout history, to be the salt and light of the world. Their purpose is to live consistently, powerfully, lovingly, and faithfully, thereby challenging families, neighbors, clans, nations, and people around the globe to actualize their God-given potential. It is my contention that this movement did not appear as an afterthought, but that it was initiated and shaped by God from the beginning of recorded history.

The New Creation provides a concise survey of the Christian church, God's instrument for the providential care of the earth and its human family. It divides church history into nine units, each discussed as a phase in the church's organic growth and development. In addition to the narrative, each chapter identifies significant events and turning points for an epoch of church history.

THE EPHEMERAL NATURE OF CHRISTIAN UNITY

Christians have always sought unity. Yet they seem more divided today—certainly more diverse in practice and belief—than ever before. At its inception, the Christian movement was characterized by great diversity of beliefs and practices, some Jewish, some pagan, and others uniquely Christian. During the second and third centuries of the Common Era, Christianity was threatened by conflict within (orthodoxy versus heterodoxy) and without (conflict with other elements of society, such as pagan philosophers and imperial persecution by the Roman state), but by the fourth century, Christianity was searching for agreement and unity. As the early church expanded into the prevailing Greek and Roman cultural worlds and simultaneously eastward and southward into Persian, Asian, and African cultural worlds, powerful organizational forces emerged that established uniformity, providing ethical and theological boundaries to the movement. Unity was necessarily fragile, and when achieved, it was at great cost, initially by imperial persecution and eventually through coercion and by inquisition.

Unity demanded a universal version of the church and over time there developed a term of great resonance for Christianity, the word "catholic," from an ordinary Greek adjective for "general," "whole," or "universal." Bishop Ignatius of Antioch provides the first known use of the term in his letter written to the Christians of Smyrna, in the early second century. Since he did not bother to explain what he meant by the "catholic church," he evidently expected his readers to be familiar with the expression. This was a momentous development, for Christians have never abandoned their hope for unity, despite their general inability to sustain it at any stage in their history.

During the second century, the church stood at a crossroads. Could it draw clear lines between true worship of Jesus Christ and the era's multitude of Greek, Roman, and Middle Eastern philosophies and mystery religions that also featured revelations from a high God and appeals for dedicated moral life on earth? The answer is affirmative, but the journey was long and arduous before Christian orthodoxy prevailed.

An umbrella of protection was needed, broad enough to accommodate the masses, yet specific enough to deal with deviant belief and behavior. Many Gentiles, formerly pagan, began joining the church. Most were illiterate, in a state of spiritual infancy, and not yet ready for the freedom Paul had spoken about in Galatians (see 3:23–26; 5:1). Like all adolescents, they needed guidance and protection. By the year 112, Ignatius, leader of the Christian church in Antioch of Syria, urged fellow believers to "follow the bishop as Jesus Christ followed the Father." On his way to martyrdom in Rome, he wrote letters to the churches of Asia Minor and to Rome. In each letter, he calls for submission by the members to the bishop and the elders and requests respect for the deacons. In his letter to Polycarp, bishop of Smyrna, Ignatius declares, "Let nothing be done without your approval." His injunction revealed the emergence of a system of church organization constructed around locally powerful bishops.

By 150 CE, a fairly well-defined rule of governance by bishops was firmly in place, and catholic orthodoxy—meaning a universal rule of faith binding upon all Christians—was taking shape. By the time of Ignatius there circulated among the expanding Christian congregations two collections of Christian documents, one consisting of the four gospel accounts of the life of Jesus as attributed to Matthew, Mark, Luke, and John, and the other containing copies of the letters credited to the apostle Paul. Soon Christians would add to these the Acts of the Apostles and other sacred writings, set alongside the Hebrew Bible to provide written guidance for the church. In roughly the same period that witnessed the evolution of an episcopal system of church organization and a scriptural record of Christ and the early church, there also appear short, concise summaries of what it meant to be an orthodox Christian. These creeds (from the Latin *credo*, "I believe"), proved immensely useful both as a way of marking out the boundaries of Christian faith and as an introduction for inquirers or the children of believers. Some creeds were baptismal, formulated as a way to teach catechumens (converts undergoing instruction).

Together with the episcopate and the canon of scripture, the early creeds became the anchors that stabilized the church in its early subapostolic history. The importance of creed, canon, and episcopacy for the development of orthodox Christianity cannot be overestimated, but behind each word lies a historical process complex as it was important.

Much changed in 312, when Constantine defeated his rival Maxentius at the battle of Milvian Bridge. During what became a crushing victory for Constantine, Constantine had a dream in which he saw a cross in the heavens and the words, "In this sign conquer." A year earlier the Emperor Galerius, on his deathbed from a disease he believed was punishment from God, had decreed pardon to all Christians and toleration for their faith. In 313, Constantine's Edict of Milan guaranteed that their freedom would continue. Within a century, Christianity would become the official state religion. At the time of Constantine, perhaps one in twenty—some estimate one in ten—were Christians. A century later, most people in the Mediterranean world were at least nominally Christian.

Throughout the first four centuries of the church's existence, a running debate occurred between people who called themselves Christians. This debate focused on beliefs (doctrines), but it also impacted morality. The debate culminated in the great church councils that began in the fourth century, where the "official" position emerged as orthodox and the rejected views were declared heterodox (heretical). Doctrinal debates centered on the areas of hristology (the deity of Christ, his two natures, the incarnation), the Trinity, and soteriology (the redemptive work of Christ, as well as the relation between faith, grace, and good works). Other areas of debate included the nature of revelation and inspiration (the orthodox position culminated in the selection of the twenty-seven books that make up the New Testament), anthropology (how humans are unique, how they relate to God, and the influence of sin on their nature), and eschatology (views regarding the end of the world, the resurrection of the dead, and the afterlife).

During the Reformation of the sixteenth century, Protestant thinkers began questioning doctrines and practices established during the medieval period, including ecclesiastical hierarchicalism, the authority of the pope, the estrangement between laity and clergy, sacramentalism, monasticism, the veneration of relics and saints, the emphasis on good works as meritorious for salvation, and the sale of indulgences. In so doing, most Protestants were not rejecting church authority, but rather subordinating it to biblical constraints. While retaining the ancient creeds and the theological formulations of the great ecumenical councils of the fourth and fifth centuries, mainline Protestants rejected those doctrines, practices, and ceremonies for which no clear warrant existed in the Bible, or which seemed to contradict its letter and intent.

The spirit of reform erupted with surprising intensity in the sixteenth century, giving birth to Protestantism and challenging papal leadership of Western Christendom. As mentioned above, four major traditions marked early Protestantism: Lutheran, Anabaptist, Reformed, and Anglican Christianity. Shortly thereafter, Roman Catholic Christianity regrouped and, led by the Jesuits, recovered its moral zeal. Bloody struggles between Catholics and Protestants followed, and Europe was ravaged by war before it became obvious that Western Christendom was permanently divided.

Everything the Protestant Reformation represented was rejected at the Council of Trent, Catholicism's Counter Reformation. The council met in three main sessions: 1545–1547, 1551–1552, and 1562–1563. Throughout the sessions the Italians were strongly represented, while other areas, notably France, were underrepresented. During the second series of sessions, a number of Protestants were present, but their voice was negligible. From start to finish the council reflected Rome's militant stance.

The Reformers emphasized that justification is imputed to the believer by faith alone. The council held that justification is both external to the believer as well as internal, infused into the believer through the sacraments. The Reformers stressed salvation by grace alone; the council emphasized grace and human cooperation with God. The Protestants taught the religious authority of scripture alone; the council insisted on the popes and bishops as the essential interpreters of the Bible.

Thus, the Council of Trent guaranteed that modern Roman Catholicism would be governed by divine and human collaboration. The pope remained, as did the seven sacraments, the sacrifice of the Mass, and belief in saints and in practices such as confessions and indulgences. The one thing that did not endure, however, was the unity of the church. The Protestant Reformation and the Catholic Counter Reformation shattered the religious unity of Western Christendom.

Since the sixteenth century, much has happened, including the birth of the ecumenical movement and the Second Vatican Council, an attempt to bring Catholicism "up to date." Upon the election of Pope Francis in 2013, most Catholics view the future with hope, for in electing the first pope from the Americas and the first Jesuit, the Church was signaling its willingness to chart a new course. Choosing his papal name in honor of Francis of Assisi, Francis is noted for his humility, his concern for the poor, and his commitment to interfaith dialogue.

Like their Protestant "separated brethren," Catholics find their journey through the twentieth and into the twenty-first centuries a perilous and often uncertain pilgrimage. The distance between Protestants, Catholics, and Orthodox Christians has narrowed, as has the distance between Christians and non-Christians in general. The ecumenical dream, based on Christ's prayer for unity, is more alive today than ever.

Will the church as we know it survive? The answer remains uncertain, but what is certain is that if the church as we know it will survive, it must involve both head and heart. Despite its vital past, the greatest days of the church may still lie in the future. In that emerging church, worship will be lively, authentic, high tech, and free. The leadership will include women equally with men and will be racially representative. It will be ecumenical and non-sectarian. In other words, church worship and the Christian life will be hopeful, dynamic, and spontaneous, for that is the essence of newness, the church's resplendent quality.

QUESTIONS FOR REFLECTION

1. After reading this chapter, what have you learned about the church's nature and role in society?
2. In your estimation, has the church lived up to its nature and destiny as God's new creation?
3. After reading this chapter, what have you learned about the benefits of studying church history? Explain your answer.
4. After reading this chapter, are you optimistic about the future of the church? Explain your answer.

PART V
Power Revealed

Chapter 11

In the Potter's Workshop

Promenade. Most of us live with a steady stream of consciousness, with a continual flow of ideas, images, and feelings, clinging to these ideas and feelings as if they were us. They are us, but not our True Self. To ascertain our True Self, we must discover "the face we had before we were born," who we are behind our thoughts and feelings. This is the first goal of contemplation. As Einstein said, "No problem can be solved from the same level of consciousness that created it." For this reason, a contemplative stance toward life provides an entirely new way of knowing reality, providing the power to help us move beyond mere ideology and dualistic thinking. Mature religion will always lead to some form of prayer, meditation, or contemplation to balance our calculating mind. Such a way of seeing gives us the capacity to be comfortable with paradox and mystery. "Presence," for the contemplative practitioner, is the word for this encounter, this way of knowing. Most of us call it awareness, as opposed to judgment or thinking. Whatever we call it, this nondualistic way of seeing the moment refuses to be pulled into the emotional and mental tugs of war essential to dualistic life. A vulnerable approach, lacking all sense of control, sitting in silent meditation, is necessary to experience joy and truth simultaneously in this world.

UNLESS ONE IS AN atheist or an avowed skeptic, the highest human aspiration is to experience God in this life, to encounter the divine in some objective and direct way. For such encounters would affirm our uniqueness as human beings, confirm our relatedness to our Ground of Being, and sustain our sense that we live in a purposeful universe. This topic—experiencing the Divine Presence in everyday life—is the subject of my 2019 book, *In the Potter's Workshop*.

"Can God be known directly and personally by humans?" Apart from a handful of mystics, who throughout history have claimed oneness with the divine, the question seems misguided, for the Christian tradition, by enlarge, directs us to a lesser yet equally valuable goal, namely, to experience the presence of God rather than the person of God. Such a goal—indirect rather than direct intimacy with the divine—is not only commendable but actually attainable by the majority of Christians, and it is this goal that I addressed *In the Potter's Workshop*. There, we are led by a seventeenth-century monk named Brother Lawrence, an unlearned Carmelite brother who authored a series of Conversations and Letters published as *The Practice of the Presence of God*. This brief Christian classic contains the reflections of an individual who sought to make the love of God the end of all his thoughts and actions, no matter how trivial. Seeking God in all things, he desired God alone and nothing else, not even God's gifts or blessings. For Brother Lawrence there is no higher goal, nothing equally commendable. Can this be our goal as well?

The closing words of Richard Rohr's influential book, *Falling Upward*, are perhaps his most important: "God, like nature, abhors all vacuums, and rushes to fill them." Viewed from a spiritual perspective, the goal of life is to live directly in the presence of God, experiencing God's magnificent love and will in all things, an emptying process described by the framers of the Westminster Shorter Catechism as the "chief end of man," namely, "to glorify God and enjoy God forever." If our task on earth is to glorify God, the benefit of such a way of life is the consequent enjoyment of God, an attitude and way of life available to believers here and now and not simply in the afterlife.

In his book, a persuasive discussion of the spiritual stages of the first and second halves of life, Rohr addresses his readers directly: "Nothing can inhibit your 'second journey' except your own lack of courage, patience, and imagination. Your second journey is yours to walk or to avoid." Pain and self-emptying, he adds, are part of the deal, but only "for the sake of a Great Outpouring."[1]

What Rohr calls the second journey or the second half of life I call "practicing the presence of God." Such a way of life involves a coalescing of one's will, attitudes, and priorities around one goal: "To glorify God and

---

1. Rohr, *Falling Upward*, 160.

enjoy God forever." If there is a world of spiritual reality, how do we get in touch with it?

THE WESTERN CHRISTIAN SPIRITUAL TRADITION

Religious practice is common the world over, a natural way for human beings to remain open to the wider world of spiritual experience. Nevertheless, to cultivate our experience of God, we need not look to other traditions or search for exotic non-Christian ways to experience the holy. For that we need only become acquainted with the richness of the Western Christian spiritual tradition.

The spirituality of the West arises out of the Western worldview, with its distinct perspective. How one views spiritual reality, particularly its core or center, influences religious practices and outcomes. For example, worship of the warlike Norse god Wotan can produce Hitler and Nazism, whereas worship of a loving Christ can produce Francis of Assisi and Mother Teresa. Furthermore, how one envisions the goal of the faith journey will shape that person's experience of God. In this respect, the psychotic who denies the reality of the physical world and dwells almost exclusively in the inner or psychoid dimension of life is not far worse than the consistent materialist, who by denying the existence of the spiritual world dwells exclusively in the physical realm. The mature adult who chooses to live in both realms simultaneously is far healthier for doing so.

However, if the goal of the religious adult is simply experience, bliss, or a flight away from physical reality with its challenges and responsibilities, the results may lead not only to pride and egomania, but to psychoses as well. In *Care of the Soul*, psychotherapist Thomas Moore indicates that a spiritual life of some kind is necessary for psychological health, but he cautions that excessive or ungrounded spirituality can be dangerous, leading to compulsive and even violent behavior.[2] It is far better for religious seekers to embrace a historical religion, one in which religious practices have been tested and refined over time, than to experiment solo or by joining some new sect that pretends to have a new revelation of final truth. There is, however, an equally great and grave danger when people blindly accept the practices, methods, and beliefs of any established religion, for religious practices and beliefs that are not tested by individual experience or subjected to criticism and change can degenerate into bigotry and brainwashing. A wise therapist once noted that brainwashing occurs whenever someone is made to feel guilty for doubt.

2. Moore, Care of the Soul, xii–xiii.

The spirituality of the West arises out of the Christian worldview, which affirms both the physical and spiritual realms as real, valuable, and interrelated. As sense experience and sense images connect us with a real physical world, so inner images can connect us with a real spiritual, metaphysical, realm. We need to develop sensitivity, awareness, and a capacity for critical thinking in order to deal with each realm. If we accept sense experience uncritically, we can fall into all sorts of delusion, such as the flatness of the earth, the rising and setting of the sun, and the earth as the center of the universe. Likewise, if we take images from dreams and visions or religious symbols and teachings as ultimate and final representations of reality, we can fall into similar absurdity.

Western spirituality regularly views the motivating and creative core of the universe as Divine Love. This is true of institutional and mystical Christianity. However, there is a vast difference between being absorbed into the cosmic One (such unity is the goal of much of Christian apophatic prayer[3] and of many Eastern mystical traditions) and encountering Divine Love, which is the goal of Christian kataphatic prayer.[4] Unfortunately, some writers on spirituality such as Jacob Boehme, Meister Eckhart, Thomas Traherne, and Matthew Fox, and poets and "nature mystics" such as Byron, Wordsworth, Blake, Emerson, Thoreau, Whitman, and Annie Dillard, attempt to rescue mysticism and direct spiritual experience by describing spirituality as an ecstatic experience of the physical world. By so doing, they stop short of the experience we seek, namely, intimacy with the personal God of the Christian tradition.

East and West offer similar disciplines for the beginning of the spiritual quest. Both emphasize detachment, quiet, stilling the emotions, withdrawal, receptivity, listening, and ceasing ego activity and striving. The reason is clear: if we are to find the spiritual realm and its central meaning in God, we need to detach ourselves from *exclusive* preoccupation with the physical realm.

At this point, the spiritual understanding of the West diverges from that of the East. The Eastern way plunges into the depths of detachment

---

3. The term "apophatic" refers to ways of knowing God that are direct and not mediated. Apophatics reflect an intuitive form of spirituality, which views God as ineffable and indescribable. Apophatics are comfortable with ambiguity and, when speaking of God, they prefer terms such as Mystery or Spirit. They prefer to worship God in silence or by striving for justice and peace in the world.

4. The term "kataphatic" refers to ways of knowing God that are indirect and mediated. Kataphatics reflect a sensate form of spirituality, which prefers concrete images of God. Kataphatics are often divided into two groups: those who prefer to worship verbally and sacramentally and those who prefer to worship spontaneously and wholeheartedly, with the senses and the emotions.

and imagelessness, seeking extinction of the subject-object duality and individual consciousness. For the Western spirituality we are describing, once detachment has been achieved, the individual is redirected back to attachment, in this case to human love, compassion, and all the positive activity associated with beauty, goodness, and healthy vitality that accompany attachment to the Divine Lover. Here one relies on a host of images and symbols, natural and supernatural, that enable individuals to achieve greater wholeness and integration of their complex inner selves. Such integration, according to Western masters of spirituality, leads the individual into a relationship with the Divine Lover, which results in the transformation of the individual into the likeness of that to which he or she relates and beholds.

SPIRITUAL AND PSYCHOLOGICAL APPROACHES

In this scientific age, Christians need to resist the tendency to reduce spirituality to psychological terms. While there are similarities of interest and areas of overlap between spiritual and psychological realms, they represent fundamentally different disciplines. Psychological methods and attitudes are far more objective and tangible than their spiritual counterparts. To formulate too strict a separation, however, to divorce mind from spirit, is artificial and obstructive. We are human beings, with body, mind, and spirit all reflecting aspects of our unified being or soul. To consider the spirit (the dynamic force of being) without addressing the mind is unhelpful, like caring for the mind while ignoring physical health. Thus, some kind of balanced attitude is required.

The most obvious difference between psychotherapy and spiritual formation is that the former focuses more on mental and emotional dimensions such as thoughts, feelings, and moods, while the latter focuses more precisely on spiritual issues such as prayer, religious experiences, and the sense of relationship to God. While some kind of balanced attitude is needed, we must beware the danger of collapsing mind, emotions, and relationships under the general rubric of spirituality. Likewise, spirituality must avoid focusing attention excessively on extrasensory psychic experiences or on dream analysis. In such cases the means have surpassed the goal.

For people on the spiritual journey, the goal is not spiritual experience in itself. Exciting and dramatic experiences can actually distract us from our goal of constancy toward God. Gerald May makes this distinction in *Care of Mind, Care of Spirit*, his study on the psychiatric dimension of spiritual direction: "Although spiritual journeys often begin in the context of experience, and although experiences constitute major vehicles of insight, growth, support, and service along the way, the goal of the journey can never legitimately be experience itself. The goal is beyond experience, and has to do with our actually becoming who God means us to be and doing what God means us to do. Experiences can sometimes be a helpful means towards this end, and they can sometimes get in the way. But they are never the end in themselves."[5] Our task is not to trust experience but to trust God.

For those pursuing spiritual goals, it is a good rule of thumb to ask questions such as, "What does it mean to focus on God?" or "What things are preventing the working of the Holy Spirit in my life?" All human experiences can be said to be spiritual in the larger sense, but spirituality focuses most clearly on those areas that reveal the presence or leading of God in one's life.

Thus, primary attention should be given to personal prayer life; to practices such as meditation and contemplation and other ways to simplify and slow things down; to awareness of God's presence, absence, or callings; to experiences of fundamental meaning; to personal longing for God; and to the multiplicity of factors that seem to help or hinder fullness of living in God's presence.

In general, psychotherapy encourages effective living, and its values often reflect prevailing values in the surrounding culture. For example, psychotherapeutic approaches focus on helping patients achieve autonomous mastery over self and circumstance, whereas spirituality seeks liberation from attachments and self-surrender to the discerned power and will of God. In stricter forms of psychiatry, the physician assumes the role of healer while the patient remains a compliant object whose deficiencies are corrected. In more humanistic psychotherapies, therapist and client form a healing team together.

In spiritual formation, however, the true healer, nurturer, sustainer, and liberator is God, and the disciple is a hopeful channel of grace. In their spiritual pursuit, seekers must reject two extremes, the temptation to play God (that is, substituting personal mastery for surrender to divine will), and the risk of apathy, whereby seekers avoid their own graced potential for action by refraining from doing anything at all. If examined closely, both extremes reflect excessive willfulness, the former by aggrandizing personal power, and the latter by restricting it. The one denies the transcendence of God; the other denies God's immanence and human responsiveness to God.

The question is deceptively simple to ask yet exquisitely difficult to answer, "Am I truly seeking to do God's will, or mine?"

---

5. May, Care of Mind, 38.

WHY I AM NOT AN ATHEIST

Years ago J. B. Phillips, translator of the celebrated *New Testament in Modern English* (1958), wrote a small volume titled *Your God is Too Small*. If, in describing my understanding of God in this book, I am found to be heterodox in my view, I trust it will be because my God is too big rather than too small. If my views are not in the mainstream of current Christian orthodoxy, it is because they belong to that tradition of Christian orthodoxy described as apophatic, rather than in the prevalent Western theological tradition characterized as kataphatic.

My understanding of God builds on a mystical yet deeply intellectual tradition in Christianity, represented biblically in the Wisdom literature of the Old Testament (primarily in Job and Ecclesiastes), but also in the prophets and in the spirituality of Jesus and the apostle Paul. It is also found represented in Christian thinkers of all ages.

In a letter to one he was guiding, Abbé Huvelin, one of the most accomplished spiritual directors of all times, spoke from personal experience when he wrote: "In faith we have just enough light to follow the right way, but on either side there is an abyss." The abyss of agnosticism, manifested in cosmic rootlessness, can cause unbelievable pain and suffering, as we learn from the writings of atheistic existentialists such as Sartre and Camus. Feeling alone in a meaningless world, however, often results in more than existentialist despair. It has emotional and physical consequences as well.

In his autobiography, *Memories, Dreams, Reflections* (1963), and in his earlier works, such as *Modern Man in Search of a Soul* (1933), Swiss psychiatrist Carl Jung tells how he was jolted from the rational, materialistic agnosticism of his medical training. A colleague of Freud, he broke with Freud after discovering there was a nonphysical dimension or reality, observable to anyone who would take the trouble to experience it. It was, he said, as experienceable as were the two moons of Jupiter to those in Galileo's time who were willing to look through his telescope. Jung believed that one of his most important therapeutic tasks was to free people trapped in the constricting materialistic outlook of modernity and open them up to a more adequate view of reality. He viewed the person caught up in materialism as more sick than amoral or immoral.

One of Jung's important contributions to modern psychology and theology was his recognition that the inability to believe in anything, or the belief in a meaningless world, could be classified as disease or sickness and could cause as much damage as childhood trauma, acute tension, or a dose of poison. Believing that one has no meaningful place in the universe is not only a disease or sickness, but it can result in actual emotional and physical illness. Numerous devastating emotions may result from the sense of living in a hostile or indifferent universe, ranging from fear, anger, and stress to loneliness and depression. Studies show that 60 percent of those under continuous stress actually suffer some serious physical illness within twelve to eighteen months.

Much of the drug dependency of our time is surely related to the psychic sense of meaninglessness in the universe, coupled with the fear that no one loves and accepts us we are. From this perspective, life seems unfair, particularly if it ends with extinction at death. When there is no friendliness in the universe, there is little reason to expect it from other human beings, and less reason to reach out to others. Our separation from social meaning can lead to isolation, loneliness, and depression, which makes us susceptible to contamination by the fear, anger, depression, stress, and hopelessness of others. Psychic infection usually strikes below the conscious level and is difficult to deal with consciously. Rebuilding seems hopeless, and people tend to give up on life, inwardly and outwardly. How can human beings overcome inner anxiety and rage without a sense of purpose and the hope of some meaning in this world and beyond?

One of the functions of the church is to provide a decompression chamber into which we can step out of the negativity and hopelessness so rampant in our society. However, when the church fails to offer an environment of love, meaning, and concern, both human and transhuman, and when it becomes caught up in its own survival, reflecting the fears and suspicions of its weakest members, has it not lost its way? If salt has lost its savor, of what value is it?

THE INADEQUACY OF DISBELIEF

If we remain within the framework of a meaningless materialistic world, how do we control the effects of destructive emotions such as fear, anger, stress, loneliness, and depression? Without therapy and medication, we simply can't. And even these solutions tend to be temporary, for they don't really target the problem. They merely result in dependency. Without divine assistance, there is simply no way out of the materialistic maze, although it should be noted that right- and left-brain studies show that women are more balanced and less one-sided than men, and often not as defeated in finding meaning as men. However, as we learn from psychiatrists and therapists such as Jung, the cause of much mental and physical sickness is rooted in agnosticism and unbelief. Many of Jung's patients were brilliant scientists who suddenly found that life had lost meaning. This realization left them unable to cope with life and led Jung to the conclusion that among all his patients in the second half of life, that is, over thirty-five, every one of their problems was in some way related to finding a religious outlook on life.

Many years ago William James noted that the inability of people to believe and be converted to religious faith was often intellectual in origin. Afraid to trust their instincts, they became tied to pessimistic and materialistic beliefs, which led them to view faith as something weak and shameful. Intellectually speaking, people should question blind faith and total disbelief, but they should also remain open to valid and helpful alternatives.

Reason, particularly when used as an extension of subjective assumptions or fears, or when based on the views of someone else's authority, can be unreliable and untrustworthy, as modern philosophy teaches. Few people nowadays are convinced of the existence of God by purely rational arguments or "proofs." Skepticism can be a good thing, even of reason, for by relying on reason alone people can prove nearly anything they wish to prove, particularly if their starting point is erroneous. For example, many today accept the assumptions of postmodernism, the Zeitgeist of our day, affirming in conscious and unconscious ways that no final truth exists and that reality is ultimately ambiguous, open-ended, and contradictory. Succumbing to logical reductionism, they disavow objectivity altogether, affirming that what some call truth is nothing but opinion. Thus, they conclude that there is no objective truth, but only "truths," which are essentially subjective preferences and opinions. The loss of absolutes results in relativity and uncertainty.

During medieval times, as evidenced by the contributions of Thomas Aquinas, Christian theology and faith became tied to one or more system or rational thought. This approach, deductive in nature, was formulated by Aristotle, and during the medieval period it became the basis of scholastic theology. Euclidian geometry and basic logic, with its use of syllogisms, illustrate this method, for here one starts with axioms and proceeds to absolute and certain conclusions. But what happens when the axioms are subjective or faulty? Immanuel Kant, the late eighteenth-century German philosopher (1724–1804), saw the logical fallacies in deductive thought and pointed them out with relentless clarity. He understood that logic could not unlock the secrets of either the subjective intellect or the objective physical world. According to Kant, human knowledge results from the interaction of two realities, the phenomenal (physical reality) and the noumenal (non-physical reality). Caught up in a materialistic worldview, Kant believed that only phenomenal experience could be described, and that its understanding could be probed exclusively by reason.

Questioning all authorities and traditions of the past, Kant and his fellow Enlightenment thinkers substituted a virtually unbounded faith in human reason. Kant's "Copernican Revolution," as it has been called, was to reverse the process by which knowledge occurred. Rather than believing that one's mind is influenced by the objects and events it experiences through the senses, Kant maintained that objects and events we know through experience must conform to the operation of the mind. The phenomenal world (the external and natural realms), since it exists apart from our experience of it, is thereby unknowable to the human mind, as is the noumenal world (the spiritual and supernatural realms), meaning that knowledge of God, the soul, and the afterlife are unattainable to human beings. Since the finite mind cannot experience or know infinite things, the best it can do is to postulate or infer their existence. By assuming a sharp dualism between phenomenal and noumenal reality, Kant radically redefined what could be known. Thinkers before him, such as Plato and the church fathers, had assumed that both realms could be known, but Kant limited knowledge only to the phenomenal realm, and even that knowledge to be severely restricted.

Despite Kant's pietistic upbringing, he became known as the father of theological liberalism, a view that denies divine revelation altogether. Kant's dualism between noumenal and phenomenal reality led to modern skepticism, which limits knowledge to what can be apprehended only by means of the senses, and denies that spiritual reality can be known at all. The effect of Kant on liberal Christian theology has been enormous. His philosophical approach plunged generations of seekers after knowledge into an "abyss of subjectivism."[6]

The uncertainty left by Kant stimulated the idealistic philosopher Hegel to develop his own dialectic. Through his method one starts with any thesis (such as Kant's), and allows it to turn to its antithesis. Hegel's antithesis of Kant became the view that all reality was spiritual in nature, meaning that everything manifested absolute mind. Hegel's views became the rage of the middle nineteenth century, a landslide reaction to the agnosticism of Kant and to the even more pervasive agnosticism of the naturalistic and materialistic perspective that swept through Europe at that time. Karl Marx later adopted Hegel's thesis to develop his theory of dialectical materialism, which affirms that only matter exists, a view that became the basis of communist thought. For all idealistic ideologies, intelligence is the supreme value. In Hegel's case, an abstract force guides history, not a divine intelligence.

---

6. MacKenzie, "Kant's Copernican Revolution," I:289.

Hegel's intellectual idealism was in harmony with another method of finding certainty about reality and its ultimate nature, the method of René Descartes (1596–1650), who analyzed the nature of experience through the lens of methodical doubt. Descartes began the history of modernity with his *Cogito ergo sum* ("I think therefore I am"), thereby precipitating what L. L. Whyte described as one of the most colossal blunders of modern thought, making knowledge dependent upon logic and the thinking self. Descartes's efforts resulted in a new starting point for human knowledge, self and logic, rather than God and faith. This shift in priority produced uncertainty about what to believe or not to believe. While Descartes was not a skeptic, his view led to a world in which skepticism flourished. Thus, modernist humans found implausible the idea that there could be supernatural intrusion into human life, and that this could undergird a theology of experience.

On the whole, if one's view of the universe (whether held consciously or unconsciously) is that of deterministic materialism, it is almost impossible for that person to take seriously the religious life or worldview of Christianity. Of course, some Christians opt for blind faith, throwing away their rationality entirely, as is done in most fundamentalist sects, but this extreme is not reflective of mature Christianity. It is possible to present the Christian message in a way that does not violate intelligence, and that is our intention. Traditional Christians often find their religious convictions stretched during times of sickness, uncertainty, or personal crisis. Rather than threaten or reduce our faith, such events can actually strengthen faith and expand awareness of the divine.

During the twentieth century, science became increasingly dissatisfied with rational materialism as a comprehensive answer to the nature of things, thereby transforming and challenging many cherished scientific beliefs. Freud and Jung offered new hypotheses about the nature of reality that had much in common with the classical views of Plato and the church fathers. Jung, in particular, opened the eyes of many to an understanding of the world that had been lost to most Westerners for several hundred years.

During the twentieth century, Jerome Frank and Roger Walsh showed the importance of faith and the value of spiritual discipline for the health of the mind, emotions, and body. Likewise, Andrew Greeley gave evidence of the correlation between emotional maturity and mystical experience. In addition, Loren Eiseley and Pierre Teilhard de Chardin demonstrated that natural selection does not account for all the data of biological development. Parapsychology, too, has come of age, providing evidence of nonsensory data. In 1969, after years of rejection, the Parapsychological Association was accepted into the prestigious American Association for the Advancement of Science. This acceptance is an indication that the scientific community has come to believe that human beings are not limited to the five senses. Mystics, as Richard Rohr reminds us, "often intuit and live what scientists later prove to be true."[7]

Aldous Huxley, the English novelist and philosopher, perhaps best known for his dystopian novel *Brave New World* (1932), moved to California in the late 1930s. In 1970, after experimenting with the mind-expanding drug mescaline, he reflected upon his experience in a short book, *Doors of Perception*. He concluded that human beings are open to a vast array of experiences, many of which are forgotten, overlooked, or go unnoticed because the function of the brain and nervous system is to protect us from being overwhelmed and confused by this large mass of knowledge, much of it useless and irrelevant. This leaves only a small and special selection that may have practical value, including the practices of spirituality, conscious and unconscious, described at length by William James in *The Varieties of Religious Experience* and by Morton Kelsey in *Companions on the Inner Way*. Human insight, imagination, and intuition supply convincing evidence of the pervasive and comprehensive spiritual nature of the universe, including seemingly unlimited opportunities for experiencing the sacred.

As Huxley suggests, many human beings rest content with the meager trickle of experience that remains after the total possibilities of experience have been funneled through the "reducing valve" of our brain, sense organs, and nervous system. The problem is compounded when we try to express this reduced awareness of the universe through language. Language and writing provide access to other people's experience, but they can also limit our view of reality by confirming the idea that this reduced awareness is the only experience available. Furthermore, humans frequently get in the habit of confusing concepts for data and words for actual things.

Over time, different cultures have developed many words for things that are important to them and few words for what they consider unimportant or "nonexistent" aspects of reality. Eskimos, for example, have a great many words to describe different kinds of snow. Greeks have five words for "love" and twelve different words to describe encounter with nonphysical dimensions of reality. Hindus have over twenty words that describe various aspects of spiritual experience, but few words to deal with different aspects of the physical universe. By contrast, the English language has only one vague and much abused word to describe human encounter with the spiritual realm, the term "mysticism." Something is surely wrong with our religious imagination, if not with our spirituality. In the language of Western culture, the supernatural realm has surely suffered from reduced awareness.

---

7. Rohr, *Falling Upward*, 157.

If this reductionist trend in the Western religious sensibility continues, we will become a nation of spiritual orphans.

Thankfully, modern thinking is making room for spirituality, disclosing ways by which we can open up our capacities of knowing and coming into contact with contrasting realms of experience available to us. Those who would use reason to argue God out of experience no longer have precedence over than those who use reason to argue God into reality.

Having examined the limitations of various modern forms of disbelief, is there an alternative? I believe there is, and that it has been in the West all along. The alternative is found in the writings and beliefs of Plato; the Hebrew prophets; Jesus; early Christian thinkers such as Origen, Athanasius, and Augustine; medieval monastics and mystics such as Bernard of Clairvaux, Francis of Assisi, Julian of Norwich, Catherine of Siena, Catherine of Genoa, and Bonaventure; the Spanish mystics Teresa of Ávila and John of the Cross; reformers such as Martin Luther, John Calvin, and Ignatius Loyola; revivalists such as Jonathan Edwards, John Wesley, and George Whitfield; and more recently William James, Carl Jung, and philosophers of science such as Heisenberg and T. S. Kuhn. To find it, however, we must use our imagination and insight, thereby breaking with the materialistic presuppositions of the last thousand years of Western thought. This way will confirm that what we experience spiritually is real, however partial and imperfect our understanding and comprehension.

Our knowledge of reality and our experience of its underlying spiritual essence can grow if we observe and adopt the methodology developed by the physical sciences. This approach, essential to science, is called the inductive method (despite combining induction with deduction). This method follows a four-step process, beginning with the painstaking process of observation and comparison of the data on the subject under consideration, in our case, the subject of spiritual experience. This initial step is followed by a second, whereby one arrives at a hypothesis regarding how and why the data are relevant. Significantly, this process is guided less by reason than by intuition and imagination. Paul Feyerabend, a respected philosopher of science, suggests that if society wishes to produce creative scientists, the development of their imagination is of greater importance than the development of their purely logical and rational capacities. Once a hypothesis is framed, we use our best powers of rational analysis and deduction to sketch out the implications of our theory. If some of the data of experience do not agree with the theory that has been formulated, and these continue to appear, then a new hypothesis is required, and the whole process begins anew. A new hypothesis is imagined, which is then subjected to further testing, and so the process of understanding continues.

Human beings have the capacity to see beyond the appearance of things and grasp their essence. Plato spoke of a mathematical intuition by which humans perceive the structure of reality. It was through this kind of insight that Isaac Newton constructed his monumental vision of the order with the cosmos. Kurt Gödel spoke of the insight through which mathematicians perceive the truths of their discipline and compared this to how Plato believed humans encounter eternal forms and essence (called Ideas or Ideals). Such "seeing through" ordinary reality, if carried far enough, can bring religious observers to a religious understanding of reality, though with obvious limitations.

Young children live comfortably between two worlds. It takes years of training in our materialistic culture to persuade them that only the physical world is real. Children tend not to distinguish between outer and inner reality; their imagination is for them as real as hard physical reality. There are few better descriptions of this aspect of childhood than Frances Wickes's *The Inner World of Childhood*. The poet William Blake was beaten because he insisted he saw spirits in the streams and trees, and although he learned to distinguish the external from the internal, he never gave up his inner vision. Hallucination occurs when we attribute to the outer world what has come to us only through the inner one. A sound ego helps us from being overwhelmed by the contents of the unconscious psyche.

Fantasy literature, such as the popular novels of J. R. R. Tolkien or the children's stories of C. S. Lewis, has long ushered adults and children alike across the boundaries of the purely physical realm, fostering real encounters with other dimensions. Likewise, religious ritual uses poetry, incense, stained glass windows, architecture, music, sculpture, painting, dance, and storytelling to expand human horizons and provide a taste of the divine. Greek and Russian Orthodox Christians have long used icons as windows into heaven. Great music, drama, and literature have long transported believers beyond the limits of a purely materialistic world.

Artistic inspiration is one of the most important natural ways by which we receive glimpses of the spiritual world and its importance. With few exceptions, nearly every religion uses artistic expressions to mediate their experience of the divine source of life. In fact, most religious rituals have their root in dramatic reenactment, reliving sacred events so that devotees can participate in them. The Christian Eucharist allows believers to step by divine play into the drama of redemption. Like all great drama, religious rituals enable human beings to step into another world, introducing us to a deeper dimension of life.

Related to imagination is our capacity for intuition, the perception of meanings and realities other than those perceived through the five senses.

Jung, in his important distinction between psychological types, suggested that we have two quite different ways of taking in data, one through the senses, which he called sensation, and another that he called intuition. Nearly all human beings have intuitions—hunches or vague flashes of understanding. All humans share this capacity. Those who develop this capacity most highly could call their ability insight. The Myers-Briggs Type Indicator, developed in conjunction with Jungian psychological typology, is a device that helps analysts determine how much their clients prefer to use their capacity for intuition. Through intuition, human beings sometimes learn about physical and nonphysical realities within or beyond their psyches.

THE FACE WE HAD BEFORE WE WERE BORN

Modern Western society presents a rosy picture: the journey ahead is upward and onward. You can be successful, and you can do it by yourself. Jesus, however, presents us with a different model, that of death and resurrection—a pattern of renewal, of daily dying to self. The True Self is who you are from the beginning, in the heart of God, the "face we had before we were born," as the Zen masters say. In this light, Carl Jung offered a momentous insight: "Life is a luminous pause between two great mysteries, which themselves are one."

Sometimes the end is the beginning, and the beginning points toward the end. Agreeing with Jung, we can affirm that the One Great Mystery is revealed at the beginning and forever beckons us toward its full realization. Many of us cannot let go of this implanted promise. Some call this homing device their soul, some call it the indwelling Holy Spirit, and others think of it as nostalgia or dreamtime. Whatever we call it, we cannot ignore it. It calls us both backward and forward, to our foundation and our future at the same time. The soul lives in such eternally deep time.

Speaking of this mystery, Richard Rohr notes that we are called forward by "a kind of deep homesickness," an inherent dissatisfaction that comes from our original and radical union with God.[8] Like loneliness, sadness, and depression, sickness, loss, and deprivation can serve as beacons to light our way home. One of the reasons the Wizard of Oz has such lasting appeal is because Dorothy is guided forward to Oz and back to Kansas by her constant love and desire for home. Restlessness and dissatisfaction in life can serve as pointers to our destiny in God. The moment that we find ourselves in the presence of God is the moment we also find ourselves inside God.

8. Material in this segment is adapted from Rohr, *Falling Upward*, 65–96.

The end was planted in us at the beginning, and it gnaws at us until we get there freely and consciously. Suffering, tragedy, and all episodes of loss in our lives are potentially sacramental. As Carl Jung put it, "when you stumble and fall, there you find pure gold." God hides, and is found, precisely in the depths of everything, especially so in the deep fathoming of our pain, suffering, weakness, and failure. This "something real" is what all the world religions point to when they speak of heaven, nirvana, bliss, or enlightenment. Their only mistake is to push it off into the next world. "If heaven comes later, it is because it is first of all now."[9]

How does God operate? We really don't know. However, so many have encountered God in their weakness that we realize God's strength is God's ability to be patient, to refrain from overt use of power. From our perspective, then, we can say that God is a god of weakness, acting as much by persuasion as by direct action.

In tragedy and sickness, we are no longer in charge. That is good news, because all attempts to engineer or plan our own enlightenment are doomed to failure, since they are ego driven. The ego's job is to protect the status quo, so failure and humiliation force us to look beyond our comfort zones. Thus, we must stumble and fall. We must get out of the driver's seat for a while or we will never learn how to give up control to our soul's True Guide.

In the spiritual world, we do not really find something unless we first lose it, choose it, long for it, and personally find it again—only now on a new level. In Luke 15 we find three parables about losing something—a sheep, a coin, a son—searching for them anew, and finding them once again. This new appreciation is followed by the kind of sincere celebration that comes with any new realization.

If you desire to grow spiritually, eventually some idea, event, or relationship will enter your life that you are not equipped to handle, using your present skill set. Richard Rohr calls such a situation a "stumbling stone," an event that causes you to leave your comfort zone in life.[10] Often such an experience involves physical or mental suffering. In this case, suffering will not solve any problem mechanically so much as it discloses the chronic problem in our lives, the refusal of our ego to let go. In such cases, suffering has a mentoring role, that of opening up new spaces within us for learning and loving. Francis of Assisi noted that when he kissed the leper, "what had been nauseating to me became sweetness and life." He marked that moment

---

9. Rohr, Falling Upward, 95.
10. Ibid., 68.

as his conversion, as the defining moment in his life, when he tasted his own insufficiency and began drawing from a different source.[11]

Catholic theologian Friedrich von Hügel, valued more highly in his day as a spiritual director than as a theologian, found practical outlets for his significant intellectual skills. At the age of eighteen, sickened with typhus fever and left practically deaf, he embarked on a theological career. While he spent most of his life as a Catholic layman dedicated to theological and philosophical writing, at the age of forty he met the Abbé Huvelin, a distinguished spiritual director serving in a Parisian parish. Through his influence, von Hügel experienced a profound spiritual transformation that led him from his intellectual pursuits into the field of spiritual counseling, and it was as a guide and counselor that he made his greatest contribution. Von Hügel's final words, written to his niece, fittingly summarize life: "Remember, no joy without suffering, no patience without trial, no humility without humiliation, no life without death."[12]

What von Hügel learned at eighteen from his own spiritual director, Father Raymond Hocking, when he decided on a career in theology, he applied as a spiritual counselor: "You want to grow in virtue, to serve God, to love Christ? Well, you will grow in and attain these things if you will make them a slow and sure, but utterly real, mountain-step plod and ascent, willing to have to camp for weeks in spiritual desolation, darkness, and emptiness at different stages in your march and growth. All demand for constant light, all attempt at eliminating or minimizing the cross and trial, is so much soft folly and puerile trifling."[13]

These words reflect what Jesus taught his followers about the cost of discipleship: "If any want to become my followers, let them deny themselves and take up their cross and follow me. For those who want to save their life will lose it, and those who lose their life for my sake and for the sake of the gospel, will save it" (Mark 8:34–35). A more realistic description of the Christian spiritual journey has not been recorded. However, the story does not end here, for Jesus also teaches his followers that wherever they go, he will accompany them (Matt. 28:20). Those who are yoked to Jesus experience exhilaration and joy daily, even in times of trial, for Christ's burden is light (Matt. 11:30).

---

11. Ibid., 69–70.
12. Steere, Spiritual Counsel and Letters of von Hügel, 34.
13. Ibid., 4.

QUESTIONS FOR REFLECTION

1. After reading this chapter, what did you learn about the difference between Eastern and Western spirituality?
2. After reading this chapter, what did you learn about the difference between spiritual and psychological approaches to health and vitality?
3. After reading this chapter, what did you learn about atheism and unbelief?
4. After reading this chapter, what did you learn about experiencing God?

Chapter 12

Walking on Water

Promenade. When we think metaphysically, even using analogies and metaphors, most of us think dualistically, using paired opposites such as good and evil, light and darkness, male and female, and yin and yang to depict reality. However, this way of seeing places limits on our understanding. The essential religious experience is that you are being "known through" more than knowing anything in particular yourself. Yet despite this difference, it will seem like true knowing. This is what we call nondualistic thinking, third-eye-seeing, or true prayer. Such seeing takes away our anxiety about figuring things out, or needing to be right in our beliefs, ideologies, or perspectives. "At this point, God becomes more a verb than a noun, more a process than a conclusion, more an experience than a dogma, more a personal relationship than an idea."[1] To live in such a way is to possess an unexplainable hope, because your life will seem more expansive than your own. In fact, it is not your own life, and yet, paradoxically, you are closer to your True Self than ever before. The False Self is energized by problems, challenges, and self-created goals. The True Self is energized by a different fuel: union, contentment, and particularly, deep resonance (meaning) of any kind. Once you know that life and death are not separate but part of a whole, you will begin to view reality in a holistic way, and that will change everything. This is the initial birth of nondual consciousness.

---

1. Rohr, Naked Now, 23.

ARISTOTLE SAID DEMOCRACY WOULD only work in a culture committed to virtue; Jesus said we must know the truth, for only truth can set us free (John 8:32); the book of Proverbs maintains that where there is no vision, there is no common restraint (29:18). In the past, society was guided by common principles, inspired truth. Today there is no communal myth to guide us, no common vision to inspire us, no transcendent images to shape us. It is a sad and dismal world if I alone am its center. If we have to start at zero, our lives are too short to discover wisdom on our own, too brief to learn how to love, too arrogant to identify our place and role, and too myopic to define our proper significance and value.

Given our divisive attitudes and perspectives, a single cultural myth or national story may no longer be possible. Many today are unable to offer one another basic respect, engage in civic dialogue, or honor the human struggle. Modern humans have become adept at dissecting, critiquing, disagreeing, shaming. Despite its ubiquity, however, faultfinding is not an art form. It does not represent the kind of deep passion or positive faith that can stand up to war, vengeance, or injustice. To survive, we must learn to walk on water.

"How did Jesus do it?" people always ask after reading the Gospel story of Jesus walking on the sea. Reading this story literally, solely as an account of a miracle, leads them to miss its metaphorical message, that walking on water is not something only Jesus could do, but also something all people of faith can and should do. Perhaps this is what Jesus had in mind when he declared in John's Gospel, "Very truly, I tell you, the one who believes (trusts)[2] in me will also do the works that I do and, in fact, will do greater works than these" (John 14:12).

Human beings need to find that rare ability to live happily in a broken world and still work for its reform. It is a way of living that I believe only spirituality can achieve. Mere ideology is not sufficient for the task. Conservative ideologues, in my opinion, often have no practical goal beyond preserving the status quo, and liberal ideologues no useful objective beyond maintaining personal and social freedom. While this is a generalization,

---

2. Prior to the seventeenth century, "to believe" meant, "to give one's heart to someone or something"; the concept indicated loyalty, commitment, and trust. In the centuries following the Enlightenment, the terms "belief" and "believe" came to be associated with ideas in one's mind rather than with the disposition of one's heart. By the nineteenth century, when knowledge consisted chiefly of empirical facts, belief became the opposite of knowledge. From that point, a person's belief in God was reduced to his or her belief system, that is, to unprovable statements of faith that person judged to be true. The greatest downside to this conflation is that when faith is reduced to belief in creeds and doctrines, many thoughtful people decide they no longer have faith, thereby experiencing a great loss.

what ideologues often lack is a spiritual center, a reference point beyond the individual "I" or corporate "We." Lacking a God who gives source, pattern, and external goal, they create gods in their own image, becoming their own god. Contrast that to the prophets of old, all claiming an authority beyond their own, a Center outside of themselves.

What does it mean to be human? we ask. What makes a person unique? Does biology have priority? Are personality and spirituality equally significant factors? What about race, gender, and social class? To what extent are we shaped by our upbringing or education, by our friends and loved ones? What roles do our jobs and accomplishments play in our self image and identity?

When our Western forebears thought of personhood, they searched the realm of art and drama for guidance, settling on the term "person" as definitive. The word "person" comes from the Latin word for "mask" or for the actor's role in a drama. The Judeo-Christian tradition built on this idea, viewing human personhood as an organic participation in the one personhood that is God. In other words, the human self has no meaning or substance apart from the Selfhood of God. God's personhood, however, is not a mask, but the face behind all masks. We humans are the masks of God, and we play out God's image in myriad ways.

The problem we face in a secular society is that we do not know we are the masks of God. Hence, we are compelled to create our own significance, our own masks and personhood. This makes us—like atoms—inherently unstable. When we do not see our lives as a participation in Another, we are forced to manufacture our own private significance. Needing a word for this phenomenon, modern psychology chose the Latin word for "I," or "ego." This is the atomized self, the small self, the false self, which does not really "exist" at all. In such a state of insecurity, it overly defends and overly defines itself. This imperial ego becomes the basis for all illusion and evil. It is Adam and Eve trying to survive outside of the Garden, something they cannot do.[3]

Many people, I find, have a God who is too small, a God they fear, hate, or ignore. Naturally, we cannot admit that to ourselves. However, if we are afraid of God, or experience God as cold and absent, as someone who toys with us or sabotages our plans, we have only one alternative: Lose the false images that no longer serve us, the images of God that are insufficient and the images of ourselves that are likewise inadequate. God is transcendent, even of the name "God." God is beyond names and forms. The medieval Christian mystic, Meister Eckhart, said it best when he declared that the

---

3. Rohr, What Mystics Know, 24–25.

ultimate and highest leave-taking is leaving God for God, leaving our notion of God for an experience that transcends all notions.

Faith is first a verb before it becomes a noun, a way of trusting and living before it becomes a way of believing. Unfortunately, most of us reverse that equation. We start with belief, and then we try to act accordingly. That approach only lasts so long before it collapses from failure, inertia, or exertion. To discover the truth, we must become the truth. First, we must act, and then we will understand. That is the mysterious wisdom of faith. Called the "primacy of action," it is the wisdom we learn only when we are on the way. This is a lesson nobody can teach us; we must go down this road ourselves. This is the place of the soul, the place of wisdom, toward which we must move. In the end, truth is an encounter much more than a concept that can be argued. We are realigned with truth when the real person meets the real God, which is exactly the stuff of spirituality, theology, and conversion.

There are two necessary paths enabling us to move toward wisdom: a radical journey inward and a radical journey outward. For too long we have confined people to a sort of secure middle position, a safe midpoint between these two great teachers. Failure and falling short are the best teachers; success has practically nothing to teach on the spiritual path. Through education or by temperament, most of us fall into one of two camps, mysticism (the focus is inward) or activism (the focus is outward). Unfortunately, these two types seldom come together, and thus they both miss half the truth.

The great temptation of Western Christians has been to imprison the gospel in their heads. Up there, one can be right or wrong, a position correct or false, but in any case, everything must remain firmly under one's control. On the other hand, action never allows the illusion of control, at least not for long. For this reason alone, it seems obvious that we must begin primarily with action.

In 2019 I wrote my twentieth book, *Walking on Water*. That book describes a path, based on unfailing vision and enduring truth. Exploring ideas common to the Perennial Tradition and the Judeo-Christian heritage, *Walking on Water* helps us become wise at the deepest level, living harmoniously with ourselves, others, the earth, and the Creator. The following ideas summarize that book:

1. The goodness of God fills all the gaps of the universe, without discrimination or preference. The space between everything is space at all but God's Spirit.

2. Death is not just physical dying, but hitting bottom, going the distance beyond when the ego is in control, fully beyond what we are now. Grace is found at the depths and in the death of everything. After

these smaller deaths, the only "deadly sin" is to swim on the surface of things, where we never see, find, or desire God and love. This includes even the surface of religion, which might be the worst danger of all.

3. When we go into the full depths and death, even the depths of our own sin, we come out the other side—and the word for that is resurrection. None of us crosses over by our own effort or merits, purity or perfection. We are all carried across by unearned grace. The tomb is always finally empty. There are no exceptions to death, and there are no exceptions to grace or resurrection.

PERENNIAL WISDOM AND ULTIMATE REALITY

Given the quandary we face, socially and environmentally, exacerbated by our complicity with racism and our propensity for exploiting natural resources, America needs help. Ironically, if solutions exist, they must come not from exclusively American expertise—from uniquely modern, scientific, or Christian values—but from the Perennial Tradition, from peoples, beliefs, and customs North Americans have traditionally overlooked, discarded, or displaced in their strident surge onward.

When I speak of the Perennial Tradition, sometimes called Perennial Philosophy or simply "the wisdom tradition," I am referring to the view that the world's major religions share common teachings, and that these truths transcend culture, time, and place. Jews, Christians, or members of any specific religion, should not feel they were the first to know God's eternal patterns and presence. After all, those patterns are perfectly plain, because God has made it plain. "Ever since the creation of the world [God's] eternal power and divine nature, invisible though they are, have been understood and seen through the things [God] has made" (Rom. 1:19–20). How else could it be? How could any God worthy of the name squeeze Being itself into any specific timeframe, culture, or vocabulary? That is what we mean by the Perennial Tradition.

People who value perennial wisdom share core existential questions with other human beings, only they do not confine their search for answers to any one religion. What I call "core existential questions," what philosophers call "ultimate questions," can be reduced to four: (1) "Is there an ultimate reality?" (2) "Can I relate to that reality?" (3) "How does that relationship affect the way I live?" and (4) "What can I hope for?" Because these questions never go away, they form the heart of almost every spiritual quest.

It is the main business of religion to answer life's existential questions. A useful place to start is the Perennial Tradition, by which I mean not the distinct perspectives of other religious traditions—for the goal of spiritual transformation is a deeper understanding of one's own faith tradition, not conversion to some alternative religious tradition—but rather the congruence of values and beliefs (absolutes) across cultures, those unchanging beliefs that unite human traditions that seek wisdom in ancient texts and modes of life. According to perennial wisdom, every religious tradition, when one explores its mystical side, articulates common answers to humanity's existential questions, answers that emerge repeatedly throughout human history and across human culture.

Perennial wisdom, found in most human cultures, religions, and civilizations, begins not with time, space, matter, or even with ontology (speculation about divine essence or Being), but with a common singularity we call Unity, or better yet, Mystery. As Lao Tzu, the sixth-century BCE author of the *Tao Te Ching*, says in his opening poem, "The Tao that can be named is not the eternal Tao. The name that can be named is not the eternal name . . . Darkness within darkness. The gate to all mystery."

The Perennial Tradition says that there is a capacity for divine reality inside all humans, but we initially cannot see what we are looking for because what we are looking for is doing the looking. God, the name most of us give to Ultimate Reality, is never an object to be found or possessed as we find other objects, but the One who shares our deepest subjectivity by virtue of being only Subject, never object.

Dualistic people use knowledge, even religious knowledge, for the purposes of ego enhancement, shaming, and the control of others and themselves, for it works very well in that way. Nondual people use knowledge for the transformation of persons and structures, but especially to experience transformation, seeing reality with a new eye and heart.

This realization helps to explain the great paradox we all must face—and embrace—that God is both perfectly hidden and perfectly revealed in all things. God has written the pattern in things as they are, and yet we never see the full pattern without divine assistance. Thus, faith (trust in the divine) is always necessary to see what is "natural."

In the context of comparative religion, it is wrong to claim that all Gods are the same, or that all Gods are variations of a specific context. If you want to study Allah, study Islam. If you want to learn about Krishna, Vishnu, Shiva, and the rest of the Gods of India, study the many schools of Hinduism. In the study of world religions, each deity must be allowed to speak in its own way, or at least to reflect the values of its priests, prophets, sages, and gurus.

The Perennial Tradition, however, does not seek such distinctions. Rather, it sifts through the scriptures and teachings of many cultures looking for those teachings that transcend the limits of specific cultures and point to the Reality that cannot be named, defined, or figured out.

Is the Perennial Tradition, the perspective that all the world's religions share a single truth or origin, consonant with Christianity? For many, this perspective is false, misleading, and heretical. For others, however, it is not only compatible with Christianity, but it represents an essential and oft overlooked aspect of Christianity, perhaps its deepest insight and teaching.

A person's view of God is vital because it serves as a lens through which people view reality, influencing their perspective of life, the cosmos, others, and of themselves. As one's view of self provides a microcosm of reality, so one's view of God serves as a macrocosm of that reality. If one's view of God is positive—such as lover or friend—then the universe seems benevolent, others are valued, and the self is considered good. However, if one's view of God is negative—such as angry antagonist or vindictive judge—then the universe seems harsh, others are devalued, and the self is considered evil or sinful.

THE TWO SELVES

The ultimate adventure, the grandest game, the greatest challenge, is the spiritual transformation of the self. As I discuss in *Walking on Water*, the role of authentic spirituality is letting go of the False Self, one's incomplete self trying to pass for one's True Self. Our True Self, our inherent soul, is that part of us that sees reality accurately, truthfully. It is divine breath passing through us, dwelling with us. Our False Self is the egoic self that is limited and constantly changing. It masquerades as true and permanent but in reality is passing, tentative, and fearful of change. It is that part of us that will eventually die. The role of true spirituality, of mature religion, is to help speed up this process of dying to the False Self.

Not surprisingly, we cannot accomplish—or even understand—what we have not been told to look for or to expect. This staggering change of perspective—that our ego is not our True Self—is what Jesus came to convey to humanity. It led Thomas Merton, the Trappist monk who first suggested use of the term False Self, to his radical rediscovery of the meaning of Jesus' teaching that his followers must lose their False Self in order to discover their True Self (see Mark 8:35).

This realization—what some people call "mindfulness" and mystics call "being present"—is the heart of religious transformation (meaning, "to change forms"). For Christians, the model and exemplar of such transformation is Jesus, who came to tell us—and show us—that our human form is also divine, that what is human also shares in the divine nature, a divinely implanted reality that can be experienced here and now, in our present mortal state. Initially, that possibility might sound far-fetched, but I assure you, that concept is both true and truly Christian.

The Greek word *theosis*, often used by Eastern Christians and perhaps best translated as "divinization" or "deification," speaks of this reality. Bishop Irenaeus taught the concept in the second century when he wrote that "God had become what we are, that He might bring us to be even what He is Himself."[4] Likewise, Bishop Athanasius of Alexandria at the end of the fourth century declared: "Jesus Christ was made human so that he might make us gods."[5] The clearest biblical antecedents for this teaching are 2 Peter 1:3–4, "His divine power has given us everything needed for life and godliness . . . so that through them you may escape the corruption that is in the world . . . and may *become participants in the divine nature*," and 2 Corinthians 5:16–17, "From now on, therefore, we regard no one from a human point of view. . . . So if anyone is in Christ, there is a new creation: everything old has passed away; see, everything has become new!" Elsewhere Paul uses words like "adopted" (Gal. 4:5) and "joint heirs with Christ" (Rom. 8:17) to make the same point.

Unfortunately, many people today, including religious and non-religious conservatives and other traditionalists, have become and remain quite rigid in their thinking, living, and believing because they have been taught that happiness, success, and stability require adherence to the religious status quo, and with it unquestioned obedience to the guardians of tradition. Such people are often moral and productive—even model citizens—but they simply never learned much about wisdom, paradox, or mystery, and their centrality to the faith traditions they espouse. When so many religious practitioners, including most professional clergy, attend worship and observe rituals faithfully without experiencing spiritual transformation at any deep level, religion becomes a duty that actually prevents transformation from taking place. This has been going on for centuries, and in all faith traditions.

In Jesus' day, most of his contemporaries, particularly social, religious, and political leaders, simply could not see what he saw (Matt. 13:13–17). This was not due to Jesus' unique identity or access to truth, for he keeps saying, in effect, "You should all know better. You do not know your own wonderful Jewish tradition." The same could be said of conventional

---

4. Against Heresies 4, 38.
5. De Incarnatione 54, 3.

Muslims, Buddhists, Hindus, or Christians today, "You do not know your own wonderful religious heritage."

Like any true reformer or prophet, Jesus evaluates his tradition from within, by its own criteria and its own documents. This is what I hope to do here for Christianity or any religion. Too often, religion offers doctrinal conclusions, additional competing truth claims in the increasingly growing marketplace of religious claims, but seldom does it give people a vision or process whereby they can legitimate those truth claims for themselves by inner experience and actual practice. As German Jesuit theologian Karl Rahner often remarked, "Devout Christians of the future will either be 'mystics' or else cease being anything at all."[6]

DEATH AND THE FALSE SELF

Mature religion talks about the death of any notion of a separate, False Self, while recognizing that only a deep security in a larger love will give you the courage to do that. The True Self can let go because it is secure at its core. Our False Self, however, does not let go easily.

As Jesus and other great spiritual teachers made clear, there is a self that must be found and another that must be renounced. This teaching is found in each Gospel (see Matt. 10:39; 16:25; Mark 8:35; Luke 9:24), but is central to John's Gospel, where it is coupled with "dying to the self": "unless a grain of wheat falls into the earth and dies, it remains just a single grain; but if it dies, it bears much fruit" (John 12:24). Hence, "those who love their life lose it [that is, their False Self], and those who hate their life [their False Self] in this world will keep it [their True Self] for eternal life" (John 12:25; see also 1 Cor. 15:36–37, 42).

In one way or another, almost all religions say that you must die before you die—and then you will know what dying means, and what it does not mean. What it does mean, of course, is the relinquishment of selfish, possessive living, of egoic existence. The ego self is the self before death; some form of death—psychological, spiritual, relational, or physical—is the only way we will loosen our ties to our small and separate False Self. Only then does it return in a new shape, which we call the soul, the True Self, or the Risen Christ.

There are four major splits from reality that we have all made in varying degrees to create our False Self:

---

6. Cited in Rohr, Naked Now, 38.

- We split from our shadow self[7] and pretend to be our idealized self.
- We split our mind from our body and soul, and live in our minds.
- We split life from death and try to live without any "death."
- We split ourselves from other selves and try to live apart, superior, and separate.[8]

Each of these illusions must be overcome, either in this world or at the moment of physical death. Spirituality, pure and simple, is overcoming these splits from Reality. Anything less than the death of the False Self is inadequate religion. The False Self must die for the True Self to live, or, as Jesus put it, "If I do not go, the Advocate [the Holy Spirit] will not come to you" (John 16:7). Theologically speaking, what this verse is telling us is that Jesus (a good person) still had to die for the Christ (the universal presence) to arise. This is the pattern of transformation, where the letting go of the original indispensable self results in the arrival of a better reality.

Your True Self sees truthfully and will live forever. Your False Self is constantly changing and will eventually die. Your False Self is your necessary warm-up, the ego part of you that establishes your separate identity, especially in the first half of life. It is your incomplete self trying to pass for your whole self. The role of true spirituality, of mature religion, is to help speed up this process of dying to the False Self. Whatever one calls it, true spirituality is the form of living embodied by Jesus and taught by the Buddha. Such calm, egoless approach to life is invariably characteristic of people at the highest levels of doing and loving in all cultures and religions. These are the ones we call sages or holy ones.

Without what Jesus called "the sign of Jonah" (see Matt. 12:39–40)—the pattern of new life only through death—Christianity remains a largely impotent ideology, another way to "win" instead of the "way of the cross" characterized by Jonah, Jeremiah, Job, John the Baptist, and Jesus. Viewed this way, Jesus become the teacher of the path rather than the cosmic problem-solver. The Jonah-Job-Jesus pattern has been hard for Westerners to recognize and accept, but it is taught by what we call Eastern religions. The sign of Jonah is at the heart of the matter.

---

7. The shadow self, something everyone possesses, represents the least developed part of one's personality. The shadow uses relatively childish and primitive forms of judgment and perception, often as an escape from the conscious personality and in defiance of conscious standards. One's shadow includes "good" qualities as well as "bad" or "shameful" qualities that one denies. As one makes room for one's polarities, one becomes healthier and more open to transforming grace.

8. Rohr, Diamond, 29.

Psychologically, the large fish (whale?) represents "the power of life locked in the unconscious. Metaphorically, water is the unconscious, and this creature in the water is the life or energy of the unconscious, which has overwhelmed the conscious personality and must be disempowered, overcome, and controlled. . . . In the story of Jonah, the hero is swallowed and taken into the abyss to be later resurrected—a variant of the death-and-resurrection theme."[9]

The egoic self is real, precious, unique, but temporary, for your False Self is what changes, passes, and ends when you die. There is no escape from death when the "you" is the egoic self. It is a manifestation of the True Self, but it tends to forget this and imagines itself to be apart from God rather than a part of God. However, such thinking is in error. There is no "you" separate from God, just as there is no wave separate from the ocean. When you die—psychologically and spiritually but also physically—you are still what you were and are: holy, sacred, and immortal.

If all you have at the end of your life is your False Self, there will not be much to eternalize. However, there is no death when the "you" is the divine Self, for the True Self lives forever. When you are connected to the Whole, you no longer need to defend or protect the isolated part. You are now connected to something Real, eternal. When you are able to move beyond your False Self—at the right time and in the right way—it will feel like freedom and liberation, as if you had lost nothing.

It is no surprise that we humans would deny death's certain coming, fight it, and seek to avoid the demise of the only self we have known. This process of transformation is something we both deeply desire and desperately fear. It is the phenomenon Rudolph Otto termed the *mysterium tremendum*, an experience both alluring and frightful at the same time. Originally described in the language of symbol and myth, this experience has been acted out in ritual and other kinds of human activity long before it became a topic of philosophical and theological discussion. It is the union that will liberate us, yet we resist and flee.

The path of dying and rising is exactly what in-depth spiritual teaching must address. It is the letting go of all you think you are, moving into a world without any experienced context, and becoming the person you always were at depth and yet did not know on the surface. The surrender of our False Self in the final days and hours in any conscious dying have been called "enlightenment at gunpoint" by Kathleen Dowling Singh, a woman who spent her life in hospice work.

---

9. Campbell, Power of Myth, 146.

We put off enlightenment by decades if we are not present at deaths—and births. Remember, salvation is not so much a matter of *if* as *when* you get it, and maybe how much we can handle.[10] It makes us wonder why we have turned the spiritual journey into a forced march or into a game of *Survivor*, instead of a joyous proclamation of this necessary but good process of surrender into love. The reason seems obvious; it is because the False Self prefers win-lose over win-win, even, strangely enough, when it ends up defining itself as a loser. The ego will always choose trumped-up competition over calm cooperation. Such a mindset—more "hell" than "heaven"—seems almost the American way.

Once you know you are sharing in "the force field of resurrection," you can always live within it, drawing from its power.[11] Nevertheless, the price of such momentous realization is that you must first go into the tomb with Jesus, "so that, just as Christ was raised from the dead by the glory of the Father, so we too might walk in newness of life" (Rom. 6:4).

As the mystics and sages teach, the path of dying and rising is one continuous movement. It begins with learning to love one's life, and then with allowing oneself to die into it—and never to die away from it. Once death is joyfully incorporated into life, you are already in heaven, and there is no possibility or fear of hell. This is the Way, modeled by Jesus and enacted by his followers. "The Gospel is not a fire insurance policy for the next world, but a life assurance policy for this world."[12]

LEARNING HOW TO SEE

As all mystics know and teach, spirituality is about seeing rightly, for "how one sees is what one sees." As Jesus says in Matthew 6:22, "The eye is the lamp of the body. So, if your eye is healthy, your whole body will be full of light." Moses could never have seen burning bushes as divine, could never have persevered with so much unknowing, unless he had moved to a higher level of seeing. William Blake, the seminal mystic poet who worked to bring about change both in the social order and in common ways of thinking, taught that "All we need to do is cleanse the doors of perception, and we shall see things as they are—infinite."

While Western religions have been preoccupied with telling people *what* to know and believe, mystics approach things differently, teaching people *how* to see. That, according to Luke's Gospel, is what took place when

---

10. Rohr, Diamond, 141.
11. Ibid., 144.
12. Rohr, Eager to Love, xxii.

the resurrected Jesus joined two ordinary travelers on their way home in Emmaus. He invites them to "open up" by telling their story of heartbreak. In the process, he explains to them his own life narrative. Through this act of intimacy and disclosure, they learn to see; their eyes are opened "and they recognized him" (Luke 24:31). Later that day, Jesus also appears to his sequestered disciples, transforming their vision from despondency to resurrection reality (Luke 24:36–49).

In the Gospels, Jesus praises God for hiding divine wisdom "from the wise and the intelligent" and for having revealed it "to infants" (Matt. 11:25). What is it that the learned and the clever often miss, and why is it that only infants and children see it? The learned and self-sufficient ones often see themselves as "having arrived," and by such arrogance, they remain outsiders to divine mystery. Their resistance and cleverness block its possibilities and hinder its reciprocity. Because of their vulnerability and dependence, children are avid learners, open to growth and newness. That is why children have a head start. When vulnerable exchange happens, there is always an augmentation of being on both sides. We are improved people afterward, bigger and better selves.

During the medieval period, two influential Christian philosophers at the monastery of St Victor in Paris—Hugh of St. Victor and Richard of St. Victor—wrote that humanity was given three different sets of eyes. The first was the eye of sensation, the second the eye of reason, and the third the eye of understanding. The third eye—the mystical gaze—builds on the first two, yet goes further. It represents the full goal of all seeing and knowing.

The first two ways of seeing, when separated from the third, result in dualistic thinking, an "us versus them" way of seeing, the foundation of much violence and discontent in the world. The third way of seeing—typifying the seer, the poet, the saint, and the authentic mystic—grasps the whole picture. Today's world has many eccentrics, fanatics, rebels, and self-promotors. What the world needs is more mystics who see with all three sets of eyes. Such people are both humble and compassionate, for knowing that they do not know, they experience the unknowable.

Some call such knowing conversion, some call it enlightenment, some transformation, and some holiness. This way of knowing is Paul's "third heaven," where he "heard things that are not to be told, that no mortal is permitted to repeat" (2 Cor. 12:2–4). Far too often, organized religion has a stake in keeping members in the first or second heaven, for this keeps them coming back, and keeps clergy in business. This is not always intentional, but rather an extension of the principle that you can lead others only as far as you yourself have gone. Lacking the contemplative gaze, such leaders remain functionaries and technicians, their parishioners without the resources to guide them into Mystery. Theological training without spiritual experience is protectionist, not progressive.

What I call the contemplative gaze is not a technique for acquiring benefit, for getting ahead, or even a requirement for entry into heaven; nor is it a pious exercise that somehow pleases God. It is much more like practicing heaven now.

Paradoxically, if we misuse spiritual awareness, or keep it to ourselves, it "hides," and we cannot go deeper. This is why many remain at the level of mere "religion," and it is surely what Jesus means when he says, "For to those who have, more will be given, and they will have an abundance; but for those who have nothing, even what they have will be taken away" (Matt. 13:12). How does the "secret" of God's kingdom, of God's reality and nature, become "unhidden"? It is disclosed when people stop hiding—from God, themselves, and others. The emergence of our True Self discloses the secret of God's kingdom, the mystery of reality.

All who witness this mystery, who experience its reality, "become children of God" (John 1:12), and, as Paul puts it, if children, then also "heirs of God and joint heirs with Christ" (Rom. 8:15–17; see also Gal. 4:7). While the Judeo-Christian tradition tells us we are already children of God, made in "God's image and likeness" (Gen. 1:26–27), most of us have no clue what this means, and far fewer live out of its resources.

Twenty-five hundred years ago the Indian sage Siddhartha Gautama—the historical Buddha—experienced enlightenment. After years of training in the austerities of his native Hinduism, he was no closer to Truth than before he began. Then something changed. He took responsibility for his own awakening. He ceased to walk the path his teachers followed and simply sat down. He sat beneath a large fig tree in Bodh Gaya, India, and observed what he could of the world within and without. Then the veil lifted, and he realized what he was unable to see previously. Transformed, he knew what he was—he was awake.

OVERCOMING DUALISM

How does one overcome dualism? How does one awaken to nondualistic awareness? If you have read this far, you deserve to know. The answer, of course, has been there all along.

Chapter 3 introduced two competing models for truth, the circle and the ellipse. While the circular model is one-dimensional and exclusionary, viewing everything by its relation to the center, the elliptical model is holistic and inclusive. A circle has a single center, whereas an ellipse contains two circles, and hence two centers or foci, with areas of overlap between them. The symbol of a circle leads to dualistic seeing, the ellipse to nondualistic seeing.

To arrive at nondualism, two approaches are available, one unitary and the other ternary. Let me illustrate. To understand the unitary approach to reality, a good place to begin is the principle taught by the Perennial Tradition (the timeless truths of the world's religions) that there is only one ultimate Reality. This Reality, called by many names, is the source and substance of all existence. Every human being is a manifestation of this Reality, as is every object in nature.

One way to understand this interrelationship is to examine the body's relationship to its natural surroundings. While accepting the uniqueness of one's individual body, it seems obvious that the body cannot function effectively in isolation. While we can agree, for example, that the lungs are part of the human body, what would happen if they were removed from the body? Of course, one would die, for their function—taking in oxygen and eliminating carbon dioxide—is essential to one's survival. And where is oxygen produced? Not by the body, certainly, but rather by trees and plants and the ocean. If we humans cannot survive without trees, plants, and the ocean, why not recognize them as part of our body? If we do that, why stop there? Trees, plants, and oceans don't exist in isolation either; they need the earth and sun to live and produce oxygen, so why not see them as part of our body as well? Perhaps they should be understood as part of our bodies no less than lungs, heart, and brain.

The sun doesn't exist in isolation either. It is in relation to the earth because of our solar system, and our solar system is the way it is because our galaxy is the way it is, and so on. If this is true, the entire universe is one's body. That's the position of perennial wisdom: if all this is you, and all is God, then you are God. In Sanskrit, this is summed up in the phrase, *tat tvam asi*; in English, You are That! You and I are the entirety of being and becoming. Each of us is an expression of the universe as the universe is an expression of God.[13]

Another way to understand the unitary approach to reality is through the doctrine of incarnation. Jesus came to reveal the dualism of the spiritual and the secular as untrue and incomplete. In his incarnation—by his existence—Jesus modeled for us that these two seemingly different realities are and always have been one. Incarnation is always hidden beneath the surface of things. To experience this unity is to be "in Christ."

---

13. Shapiro, Perennial Wisdom, 59–60.

A second way to counter the binary nature of the human brain is through ternary perspectives. When we think metaphysically, even using analogies and metaphors, most of us think dualistically, using paired opposites such as good and evil, light and darkness, male and female, and yin and yang to depict reality. However, this way of seeing places limits on our understanding. To expand our horizons, Christian scholar Cynthia Bourgeault suggests that we replace binary systems with ternary perspectives, adding a third "mediating" or "reconciling" principle to the mix. For instance, instead of focusing on man and woman, emphasizing man, woman, and child, and instead of envisioning black or white, seeing black, white, and gray. This principle is evident in the Christian Trinity, with the incarnated Christ as its culminating expression. According to this perspective, the third force is not a product of the first two, as in the classic Hegelian synthesis, but is independent and coequal with the others. According to Bourgeault, the interweaving of the three produces a fourth force or realm of possibility. In contrast to binary systems, which seek completion in stability, through the balance of opposites, ternary perspectives create a synthesis at a completely new level, seeking completion in newness. In *The Holy Trinity and the Law of Three*, Bourgeault advises that we not limit this metaphysical principle to one triad (Father, Son, and Holy Spirit), but rather that we envision the Holy Trinity as one of many triads, each revealing different facets of the divine wholeness.

Dualism balks at any notion of Trinity, because it cannot possess it. Trinitarianism, one form of nondualistic thinking, is helpful, for it says that God is more a verb than a noun. God is three "relations," more than three persons, which boggles our minds. To understand the Trinity, that is a good place to start, with mystery and newness rather than with certainty and rationality.

Christianity teaches that God the Father is formless, God the Son is form, and God the Holy Spirit is the energy between those two. The three do not cancel each other, nor do they replace one another. Rather, they do exactly the opposite: they are relationship, and known in relationship, not only in the human realm, but also in the realms of biology, cosmology, and physics. The world of science—from molecular biology to astrophysics—now affirms this trinitarian truth, although from different angles. These disciplines see all things as interdependent, reality as a force field of constantly changing forms.

Viewed perennially, ternary perspectives defeat the dualistic mind and invite human beings into nondual, holistic consciousness. They replace the argumentative, limiting, binary principle of two with the dynamic, mediating principle of three. It takes us into the wonderfully transformative realm of "not one, but not two either." When we add a third, overlapping element to the elliptical model, unity is more readily apparent.

More than a way of thinking, nondualism is a way of living. Such living teaches us how to experience all experiences, whether good, bad, or ugly, and how to let them transform us. The dualist mind gives us sanity and safety, and that is good enough for survival. But to address our social and religious problems in creative and final ways, we need something bigger, better, and more profound. We need a new mind, "the mind of Christ" (1 Cor. 2:16). Non-polarity thinking is "the mind of Christ."

LIFELONG LEARNING

Personal transformation—openness to change; the desire to be all that we are; to defeat negative habits, attitudes, and beliefs; to overcome fear, anxiety, and distress—underlies the concept of lifelong learning, so widespread in academia today.

What does it mean to be a learner, particularly a lifelong learner? What does it mean to truly grow and evolve over a lifetime? Defined pedagogically, learning often involves the acquisition of requisite information about such disciplines as math, science, language, literature, and communication. Socially, learning cultivates emotional intelligence, the ability to live happily and harmoniously with others and oneself. Philosophically, learning introduces a mode of thinking about "fact," "theory," and "truth," that discerns their commonalities as well as their distinctions.

Defined scientifically, learning requires openness. Scientific facts, for example, are never final; hence, they are labelled "theories." The same should hold true for other disciplines, including philosophy and religion, yet in these areas, particularly religion, bias and arrogance often masquerade as revelation. When science and philosophy speak with finality, they are falling short of their own standards. When it is true to its own principles, science does not seek to impose its findings on nature, but instead humbly interrogates nature and takes seriously what it finds. Such science constantly prods, challenges, and seeks contradictions or persistent errors, proposing alternative explanations, encouraging heresy. Science gives its highest rewards to those who convincingly disprove established beliefs.

Whenever possible, religion should follow suit. In religion there should be something comparable to scientific humility. Such a perspective, attitude, and approach to life, learning, and truth is what we call spirituality.

Humans love labels; in the field of political science, as in economics and religion, we create spectrums of perspective, of thinking and living, and then we place people in categories along that spectrum, using terms such as conservative, moderate, progressive, and liberal to type people and their views. Of course, others may be extremists, but most of us seem to place ourselves conveniently and consistently in the moderate mean, never at the fanatical poles. There is a place for specificity, but when we use such terms stereotypically, we lose the greater perspective of the fluidity and dynamism of life. The Romantic poet William Wordsworth put it best in his poem *The Tables Turned*: "We murder when we dissect." When we define categories rigidly, placing others into static perspectival straightjackets, we embark on a path that leads ultimately to conflict and futility.

Take, for example, the supposed conflict between science and religion, "supposed conflict" because opposition between the two requires a "winner take all" mindset. Using the notion of "a hierarchy of explanation," namely, that most phenomena can be explained from numerous levels that make sense at their own level, we can affirm an approach that in religion, as in science and all of life, various explanations can coexist without contradicting or competing with one another.

Ultimately, it doesn't matter what you call yourself, what your worldview is, or where you place yourself on the ideological spectrum. There is only one reality that works. This reality, which we call spirituality, represents adulthood, citizenship, maturity, health, and wellbeing; it is organic, dynamic, growing, and ever changing. This is what Jesus meant by the kingdom, by eternal life, and why John's Gospel depicts Jesus as the only way to God (John 14:6).

Lifelong learning is attitudinal, for it espouses that one can and should be open to new ideas, decisions, skills, or behaviors.

NONDUALITY AND TRANSCENDENCE

Nondualism is not monism. Monism reduces all things to the same thing, erasing all diversity and difference. Nondualism celebrates difference and affirms diversity. It simply refuses to see this diversity as anything other than the greater unity of a singular Reality. As contemplatives have always known and modern-day ecology and quantum physics is only now discovering, all things in nature are both metaphysically distinct and one at the same time. Nondualistic thinking or "third-eye" seeing is not a technique for acquiring things, a pious exercise that makes God happy, or a requirement for entry into heaven. It is more like practicing heaven now. Such experience is invariably the same—relinquishing particularity, one's sense of separate self, to an egoless awareness that leaves one with an unshakeable sense that all is God.

In *The Eye of Spirit*, Ken Wilber offers a stunning perspective on nonduality and its power of transcendence. When we look at any beautiful object, whether natural or artistic, we suspend all other activity. Enraptured, all we want to do is contemplate the object. We don't want to eat it, own it, run from it, or alter it; we only want to observe, and we never want it to end.

In that contemplative awareness, our own egocentric grasping comes momentarily to rest. We relax into our basic awareness, resting with the world as it is, not as we wish it to be. We are not agitating to change things, but we contemplate the object as it is. Great art has this power to grab your attention and suspend it. Think of the most beautiful person you have ever seen. Think of the moment you first looked into his or her eyes, and for a fleeting second you were paralyzed: you couldn't take your eyes off that vision. You stared, frozen in time, caught in that beauty. Now imagine that identical beauty radiating from every object in the universe, every rock, plant, animal, cloud, stream—even the disappointments and broken dreams—radiating that beauty. You are quietly frozen by the gentle beauty of everything that surrounds you. You are released from grasping, even released from time, when you contemplate the unending beauty of the artistry of the universe, and its Spirit.

That all-pervading beauty is not an exercise in creative imagination. It is the actual structure of the universe. If you remain in this "eye of the Spirit," as Wilber calls it, every object displays radiant beauty.[14]

QUESTIONS FOR REFLECTION

1. After reading this chapter, what did you learn about Perennial Wisdom?

2. After reading this chapter, what did you learn about Ultimate Reality?

3. After reading this chapter, what did you learn about the False and the True Self?

4. After reading this chapter, what did you learn about nonduality?

---

14. Wilber, Eye of Spirit, 44.

Epilogue

MOST AMERICANS ARE FAMILIAR with the short story of "Rip Van Winkle," Washington Irving's classic tale of a man who falls asleep for twenty years, sleeping through the American Revolution. When Rip awakes, the cultural setting has changed entirely, and Rip undergoes what can be understood as a crisis of identity. Confronted with his grown-up son and with a grandson as well, Rip experiences an existential collapse. Social and political life has changed so surrealistically that Rip cannot adjust. On one level, the story is about change, and about some people's inability to adjust or grow into adulthood. I see in Rip's story an account of the transition from first-half-of-life living and thinking to second-half-of-life possibilities. For some people, like Rip, the transition is alien and unwelcome. For others, it is a welcome and exhilarating change.

As a child I was an achiever, fully embracing first-half-of-life tasks. Given a job, I did it to the best of my ability, quickly and efficiently. I was task oriented, and the sky was the limit. No task was insurmountable. Tasks required commitment and discipline, which I had in spades. These are essential virtues for the first half of life. However, first-half-of-life virtues can only take you partway home.

Evidence suggests that there is another great undertaking to human life. The first task is to build a strong "container" or identity; the second is to find the contents that the container is meant to hold.[1] The first task—surviving successfully—is obvious, one we take for granted as the purpose of life. We all want to complete successfully the task that life first hands us: establishing an identity, a home, a career, relationships, friends, community, and security, all foundational for getting started in life. Many cultures throughout history, most empires in antiquity, and the majority of individuals in the

---

1. Rohr, Falling Upward, xiii.

modern period have focused on first-half-of-life tasks, primarily because it is all they have time for, but also for lack of vision.

Most of us are never told that we can set out from the known and the familiar to take on a further journey. Our institutions, including our churches, are almost entirely configured to encourage, support, reward, and validate the tasks of the first half of life. Shocking and disappointing as it may be, we struggle more to survive than to thrive, focusing on "getting through" or on getting ahead rather than on finding out what is at the top or was already at the bottom. As wilderness guide Bill Plotkin puts it, many of us learn to do our "survival dance," but we never get to our actual "sacred dance."

According to Plotkin, the stage of adolescence—beyond which most adults never move—holds the key to both individual development and human evolution. In this stage individuals develop their distinctive ego-based consciousness, which represents both their greatest liability as well as their greatest potential. If they are to become fully human and move to the stages of genuine adulthood, people in the adolescent stage must let go of the familiar and comfortable while submitting to a journey of descent into "the mysteries of nature and the human soul." Individuals who remain within the constraints of a largely adolescent world regress into "pathological adolescence," characterized by materialism, sexism, competitive violence, racism, egoism, and self-destructive patterns. Patho-adolescent societies are perpetuated by leaders and celebrities described as self-serving politicians, moralizing religious leaders, drug-induced entertainment icons, and greedy captains of industry. If society is going to develop soulcentrically, it must be overseen by wise elders, not by adolescent politicians and corporate officers. We must also leave behind first-half-of-life spirituality, venturing into the wilderness of challenge, growth, and transformation.

WALKING THE WIRE

On the evening of June 15, 2012, 33-year-old daredevil Nik Wallenda went for a 25-minute walk, becoming the first person to walk on a tightrope 1,800 feet across Niagara Falls (Horseshoe Falls), starting on the American side. A crowd of 4.000 people watched on the American side and 125,000 on the Canadian side, in addition to millions of TV viewers. Along the way, Nik prayed aloud. When customs agents asked him for his passport, which he presented, he was asked the purpose of his trip. Nik's response was classic: "I want to inspire people around the world."

This feat was the fulfillment of a lifelong dream as well as an opportunity to honor his great grandfather, the legendary Karl Wallenda, who died after falling from a tightrope in Puerto Rico in 1978, the year before Nik was born. When Nik Wallenda walked the high wire across the Niagara Falls, he was building on a family tradition that dates back centuries. Nik represents the seventh generation of the Flying Wallendas, a traveling family circus troupe that traces its history back to 1780s Europe. "People say I'm insane," he remarks, "but they don't understand this is something I've done since I was two. It's just in my blood."

I would like to relate this illustration to our general human condition, building on the well-known account of the first humans found in Genesis 2 and 3, known ironically as the "Fall of Man." These chapters are one of the best known, yet most baffling portions of scripture. What are they about? Theologians and commentators differ widely on their interpretation. Are they about sexuality and the loss of innocence? About gaining a conscience? About moral knowledge, evil, or original sin?

Rather than focusing on the details of the account, as if it were an allegory, I would like to suggest that we examine one aspect of the story—the two trees in the Garden—and consider them as two types of existence possible for humans in a universe provided by God.

The first type of existence, symbolized by the Tree of Life, represents

a. plateaued existence in a garden of bliss; a gilded-cage existence, somewhat like the pleasure-palace into which the young Siddartha (later to become the Buddha) was placed by his father so that he might control the destiny of his son and keep him on the path to becoming a powerful ruler rather than a compassionate healer;

b. a universe of aggressive Providence, where God is everywhere present and everywhere active.

Under the dynamics of a Tree of Life existence, the needs of humanity and the vicissitudes of nature are handled by a hands-on God, who like a helicopter parent hovers over humans as though they were infants in a comfortable home. All is lush and relatively problem-free. Human growth and dignity are sacrificed on the altar of bliss. All is taken care of.

By contrast, the second type of existence, symbolized by the Tree of Knowledge, represents an opposite set of dynamics, including:

a. a life of challenge, freedom of choice, and responsibility

b. the reality of temptation

c. an aggressive pursuit of knowledge

d. pain and joy in great extremes
e. a life of independence and risk
f. mortality by virtue of natural and moral evil
g. a higher potential for moral good and for moral evil
h. diminished Divine Providence, and
i. the possibility of a lifestyle based on faith.

According to this scenario, human individualism, creativity, and capacities for good and for growth will have a greater arena for expression but so also human cruelty and natural calamity. By seeking to manage their environment and to nurture it, rather than to have it handed to them on a silver platter, humans living in the Tree of Knowledge type of existence come closer to a true image of God than they do in the Tree of Life scenario.

Biblical support for this understanding comes from the syntax of Genesis 2:9, where the phrase commonly translated as "and the tree of the knowledge of good and evil" literally reads: "and the Tree of Knowledge, good and evil," or it could very well be translated: "and the Tree of Knowledge; consequently good and evil."

So we have two ways of life; two complete sets of dynamics: the dynamics of the Tree of Life and the dynamics of the Tree of Knowledge. And these sets are mutually exclusive. One may not simultaneously operate under both sets of dynamics at the same time. One cannot possess full freedom and full knowledge. Nor can humans have the "best" elements of each set simultaneously. For example, according to the dynamics of the Tree of Knowledge, we cannot know ourselves fully or know God directly. Such universal truths are elements of the Tree of Life paradigm.

According to this understanding of Genesis, it was actually humans who determined the expulsion from the Garden of Bliss, seeking the destiny of the Tree of Knowledge with all that the choice implies. Therefore, by choice and of necessity, humans no longer live in the Garden of Bliss, but rather East of Eden, where mortality and uncertainty but also faith and freedom dwell.

We have been taught that Adam and Eve sinned in partaking of the Tree of Knowledge and I would like to question that understanding. My interpretation is that while Adam and Eve acted contrary to divine caution, the category of classic "sin" here is not applicable. Rather Adam and Eve, the symbolic parents of humanity, exercised their divinely granted measure of freedom to decline the warning of the Divine, thereby choosing the path of dynamics known by the title "Tree of Knowledge." This high-risk approach to life, which humans embraced, may not have been favored by God, but it was definitely permitted. And the essential choice of that path, if one follows the story literally, was made by Eve, the mother of mankind. The one who bears the child and suffers the pain in childbirth chose to set her children along the more arduous, but hopefully more rewarding path of the Tree of Knowledge.

This approach raises the question of evil, suggesting that with the creation of potential for good—which is required for humans to reach their spiritual capacity—potential for evil indirectly came into existence as a consequence. Perhaps this is what Augustine meant when he noted that "Evil has its source in the good," and what Thomas Aquinas had in mind when he stated "There is no possible source of evil except good." These views represent consistent and classical monotheism, refreshing in the light of the rampant dualism that characterizes the mindset of many contemporary Christians, Muslims, and other so-called monotheists.

One last principle needs to be mentioned about the two trees in the Garden, namely that the two sets of dynamics they represent are in inverse proportion. The more one increases the influence and magnitude of elements inherent in one set, the more one decreases the influence and magnitude of the dynamics inherent in the other set. Those who embrace the security and certainty of the Tree of Life paradigm, including a full and aggressive Divine Providence, decrease the elements of the Tree of Knowledge paradigm—including the elements of challenge, freedom, and responsibility. Those who embrace the Tree of Knowledge way of life choose freedom and responsibility but also risk and uncertainty. The expansion of one set implies the contraction of the other.

In the concluding book of the Bible, the author of the book of Revelation illustrates this point when, in describing the new Paradise, the Heavenly Jerusalem, in chapter 22, there is no mention of the Tree of Knowledge but only of the Tree of Life. Only at the end, in this final paradigm, is there no night, no mortality, no illness, and no evil, but only the set of dynamics implicit in the Tree of Life option.

Those of us who live here and now, according to the dynamics of what we have called The Tree of Knowledge—and that would be all of us—must exchange that final certainty, security, and bliss ("walking by sight") for uncertainty and insecurity ("walking by faith"). On at least the level of faith, I encourage you to join the Flying Wallendas, to become tightrope walkers.

When Nik Wallenda walked the tightrope across the Horseshoe Falls on June 15, 2012, all the dynamics of the Tree of Knowledge type of existence came into play. He was taking a huge risk; the conditions were treacherous, and there were no guarantees of success. But three factors were in his favor:

1. Tradition: he was backed by the wisdom and experience of generations of ancestors;
2. Safety harness: he was tethered to the wire, supported by a security system that he could count on if the unpredictable winds and the misty conditions proved to be overwhelming;
3. Balancing pole: he carried a balance beam attached by a brace to his neck to keep him grounded, focused, and stable.

Without these three, he would have been unable to cross the wire to the other side.

So it is in our lives: as we walk the tightrope of our earthly existence, we find we must leave the security and safety of the Garden of our infancy and walk the tightrope of life, heading across the gorge to the other side. And we will make it safely to our destination if by faith we keep moving, simply placing one foot in front of the other, focusing on the goal before us, and relying on three factors:

1. Our faith tradition, a two-thousand-year-old tradition of tightrope walking known as the Christian Church;
2. The person of Jesus, the pioneer of all our tightrope-walking efforts;
3. And the balance beam of scripture and worship, which keep us grounded and balanced in life.

And as we do, let us rely on the primary promise of that scripture, made by Jesus, the pioneer of walking by faith, when he assured his disciples: "I am with you always, wherever you go, and I will never leave you nor forsake you."

RIDING THE TIDES

One of the great stories of human ingenuity comes from World War II, when the Italian forces were driven out of Eritrea, a country along the Red Sea. In an effort to make a major harbor unusable to the Allies, the Italians filled great barges with concrete, and then sank them across the entrance to the harbor. When the Allies took control of the region, they inherited a massive problem: finding a way to remove those barges in order to make use of the harbor.

The solution was ingenious. They sealed great empty gas tanks, the kind used by oil refineries to store fuel, and they floated them in the sea above the sunken barges. When the tide went out, they chained the floating tanks to the barges. When the tides came in, the tanks exerted their tremendous buoyancy to tug the barges free from the bay's sucking sand. Think of the power in that sequence of events. The barges were chained to the tanks, and the tanks were dependent upon the tides. The tides were pulled by the gravitational attraction of the moon, and the moon was moving in accord with the entire universe.

"There is a tide in the affairs of men, which, taken at the flood, leads on to fortune; omitted, all the voyage of their life is bound in shallows and in miseries" (*Julius Caesar*, Act 4, scene 3, 218–24). Shakespeare is saying that the tides not only have great power, but that they cannot be stopped or retrieved. Their lifting strength comes for a few hours and then is gone. And if we miss the flood, then we will be left "in shallows and in miseries." So there are moments in our lives when the tide is up, when opportunities for growth must be harnessed. If ideas are not cultivated as they surface, they may be gone forever. And so it is with the Spirit of God, who is described as a wind that blows where it will. There are times when the hot breath of the Spirit is all around us, when God's presence is palpable. At such times, great opportunities lie close at hand.

Examine the opportunities before you now—opportunities to be faithful, to repent, to obey, to bind up the brokenhearted, to serve. They might never rise again. Ride the tide while it is yours. The tide may mean living with ambiguity, uncertainty, and doubt; such living is a code word for faith. Take risks with your life and faith, for that is how you grow spiritually.

Appendix A

The Road of Life

AT FIRST, I SAW God as my observer, my judge, keeping track of the things I did wrong, so as to know whether I merited heaven or hell when I die. God was out there sort of like a president. I recognized God's picture when I saw it, but I really didn't know God.

Later on in life, when I met God, it seemed as though life were rather like a bike ride, but it was a tandem bike, a bicycle built for two, and I noticed that God was in the back helping me pedal.

I don't know just when it was that God suggested we change places, but my life has not been the same since. When I had control, I knew the way. It was rather boring, but predictable. It was the shortest distance between two points.

But when God took the lead, God knew delightful long cuts, up mountains, and through rocky places at breakneck speeds; it was all I could do to hang on! Even though it looked like madness, God said, "Pedal!"

I was worried and was anxious and asked, "Where are you taking me?" God laughed and didn't answer, and I started to learn to trust. I forgot my boring life and entered into the adventure. And when I'd say, "I'm scared," God would lean back and touch my hand.

God took me to people with gifts that I needed, gifts of healing, acceptance and joy. They gave me gifts to take on my journey, my Lord's and mine. And we were off again. God said, "Give the gifts away; they're extra baggage, too much weight." So I gave them away, to the people we met. And I found that in giving I received; and still our burden was light.

I did not trust God, at first, in control of my life. I thought God would wreck it; but God knows bike secrets, knows how to make it bend to take sharp corners, knows how to jump to clear high rocks, knows how to fly to shorten scary passages.

And I'm learning to shut up and pedal in the strangest places, and I'm beginning to enjoy the view and the cool breeze on my face with my delightful constant companion, God. And when I'm sure I just can't do anymore, God just smiles and says . . . "Pedal."

—author unknown

Appendix B

Chronological List of Publications by Dr. Vande Kappelle

2006 [republished in 2018] *Love Never Fails: The Story of Jacob and Bertha Vande Kappelle, Missionaries to Latin America*

2010 *The Invisible Mountain: A Journey of Faith*

2011 *Into Thin Places: One Man's Search for the Center*

2011 *Blue Notes: Profiles of Jazz Personalities*

2012 *Beyond Belief: Faith, Science, and the Value of Unknowing*

2013 *Iron Sharpens Iron: A Discussion Guide for Twenty-First-Century Seekers*

2013 *Hope Revealed: The Message of the Book of Revelation–Then and Now*

2014 *Truth Revealed: The Message of the Gospel of John–Then and Now*

2014 *Wisdom Revealed: The Message of Biblical Wisdom Literature–Then and Now*

2015 *Dark Splendor: Spiritual Fitness for the Second Half of Life*

2016 *Living Graciously on Planet Earth: Faith, Hope, and Love in Biblical, Social, and Cosmic Context*

2016 *Securing Life: The Enduring Message of the Bible*

2017 *Grace Revealed: The Message of Paul's Letter to the Romans–Then and Now*

2017	*The Scandal of Divine Love: A Study on Biblical Christology for Skeptics, Seekers, and Survivors*
2018	*Refined by Fire: Rethinking Essential Teachings of Scripture*
2018	*The New Creation: Church History made Accessible, Relevant, and Personal*
2019	*In the Potter's Workshop: Experiencing the Divine Presence in Everyday Life*
2019	*Addiction: How We Get Stuck and Unstuck in Compulsive Patterns and Behavior*
2019	*Power Revealed: The Message of Luke–Acts: Then and Now*
2020	*Walking on Water: Living into a New Way of Thinking*

Bibliography

Allen, Diogenes. *Christian Belief in a Postmodern World: The Full Wealth of Conviction.* Louisville, KY: Westminster John Knox, 1989.
Allison, Dale C., Jr. *The Luminous Dusk: Finding God in the Deep, Still Places.* Grand Rapids, MI: Eerdmans, 2006.
Anderson, Bernhard W. *Rediscovering the Bible.* New York: Association Press, 1951.
Armstrong, Karen. *The Case for God.* New York: Anchor, 2010.
———. *A Short History of Myth.* New York: Canongate, 2005.
Borg, Marcus. *The God We Never Knew.* San Francisco: HarperSanFrancisco, 1998.
———. *The Heart of Christianity: Rediscovering a Life of Faith.* San Francisco: HarperSanFrancisco, 2003.
———. *Meeting Jesus Again for the First Time.* San Francisco: HarperSanFrancisco, 1995.
———. *Reading the Bible Again for the First Time.* San Francisco: HarperSanFrancisco, 2002.
———, and N. T. Wright. *The Meaning of Jesus: Two Visions.* San Francisco: HarperSanFrancisco, 2000.
Bourgeault, Cynthia. *The Holy Trinity and the Law of Three.* Boston, Shambhala, 2013.
Brueggemann, Walter. *Genesis.* Interpretation: A Bible Commentary for Teaching and Preaching. Atlanta: John Knox, 1982.
Campbell, Joseph. *The Power of Myth: with Bill Moyers.* New York: Doubleday, 1988.
Countryman, L. William, *Biblical Authority or Biblical Tyranny? Scripture and the Christian Pilgrimage.* Valley Forge: PA: Trinity International, 1994.
Creed, John M. *The Divinity of Jesus Christ.* Fontana ed. London: Collins, 1964 [1938].
Dawkins, Richard. *The God Delusion.* New York: Houghton Mifflin, 2006.
Dobzhansky, Theodosius. "Nothing in Biology Makes Sense Except in the Light of Evolution," *The American Biology Teacher* 35 (1973) 125–29. Online: http://people.delphiforums.com/lordorman/light.htm.
Dunn, Stephen, and Anne Lonergan. *Befriending the Earth.* Mystic, CT: Twenty-Thrird Publications, 1991.
Ehrman, Bart. *How Jesus Became God.* New York: HarperOne, 2014.
Fowler, James. *Stages of Faith: The Psychology of Human Development and the Quest for Meaning.* San Francisco: HarperSanFrancisco, 1995.
Friedman, Richard Eliot. *Who Wrote the Bible?* New York:HarperSanFrancisco, 1997.
Griffin, David Ray. *Reenchantment without Supernaturalism: A Process Philosophy of Religion.* Ithaca, NY: Cornell University Press, 2001.

Hamilton, William. *The New Essence of Christianity*. New York: Association, 1966.
Haught, John. *Deeper Than Darwin: The Prospect for Religion in the Age of Evolution*. Boulder, CO: Westview, 2003.
———. *God After Darwin: A Theology of Evolution*. Boulder, CO: Westview, 2000.
———. *The Promise of Nature: Ecology and Cosmic Purpose*. Mahwah, NJ: Paulist, 1993.
———. *Responses to 101 Questions on God and Evolution*. Mahwah, NJ: Paulist, 2001.
Hendry, George S. *Theology of Nature*. Philadelphia: Westminster, 1980.
Jung, Carl G. *AION: Researches into the Phenomenology of the Self*. In *Collected Works*, 9:2. New York: Pantheon, 1953.
Kelsey, Morton T. *Companions on the Inner Way: The Art of Spiritual Guidance*. New York: Crossroad, 1983.
Knox, John. *The Humanity and Divinity of Christ*. Cambridge: Cambridge University Press. 1967.
Küng, Hans. *Does God Exist?* Translated by Edward Quinn. New York: Doubleday, 1980.
Lesser, Elizabeth. *The Seeker's Guide: Making Your Life a Spiritual Adventure*. New York: Villard, 2000.
MacKenzie, Charles. "Kant's Copernican Revolution." In *Building a Christian World View*, edited by W. Andrew Hoffecker, 1:278–93. Phillipsburg, NJ: Presbyterian and Reformed, 1988.
Mackintosh, H. R. *The Doctrine of the Person of Jesus Christ*. Edinburgh: T. & T. Clark, 1913.
May, Gerald G. *Care of Mind, Care of Spirit*. San Francisco; Harper& Row, 1982.
McGrath, Alister E. *Christian Theology: An Introduction*. 5th. ed. Malden, MA: Wiley-Blackwell, 2011.
Moore, Thomas. *Care of the Soul: A Guide for Cultivating Depth and Sacredness in Everyday Life*. New York: Harper Perennial, 1992.
Newberg, Andrew. *The Spiritual Brain: Science and Religious Experience*. Course Guidebook. Chantilly, VA: The Great Courses, 2012.
Packer, James I. *Knowing God*. Downers Grove, IL: InterVarsity, 1973.
Polkinghorne, John. *Quarks, Chaos and Christianity: Questions to Science and Religion*. New York: Crossroad, 1996.
Richardson, Alan. *Genesis I–XI*. Torch Commentary. London: SCM, 1953.
Rohr, Richard. *Eager to Love: The Alternative Way of Francis of Assisi*. Cincinnati, OH: Franciscan Media, 2014.
———. *Falling Upward: A Spirituality for the Two Halves of Life*. San Francisco: Jossey-Bass, 2011.
———. *Immortal Diamond: The Search for Our True Self*. San Francisco: Jossey-Bass, 2013.
———. *The Naked Now: Learning to See as the Mystics See*. New York: Crossroad, 2009.
———. *Quest for the Grail*. New York: Crossroad, 1994.
———. *The Universal Christ*. New York: Convergent, 2019.
———. *What the Mystics Know*. New York: Crossroad, 2015.
Schneider, Robert J. "Science and Faith: Perspectives on Christianity and Science." No pages. Online: http://community.berea.edu/scienceandfaith/default.asp.
Schulweis, Harold M. *For Those Who Can't Believe*. New York: HarperPerennial, 1995.
Schweitzer, Albert. *The Quest of the Historical Jesus*. New York: Macmillan, 1968.
Shapiro, Rami. *Perennial Wisdom for the Spiritually Independent*. Woodstock, VT: Skylight Independent, 2013.

Smith, Huston. *Forgotten Truth: The Common Vision of the World's Religions.* San Francisco: HarperSanFrancisco, 1976.
———. *Why Religion Matters.* San Francisco: HarperSanFrancisco, 2001.
———. *The World's Religions.* San Francisco: HarperSanFrancisco, 1991.
Spong, John Shelby. *Eternal Life: A New Vision.* New York: HarperOne, 2009.
Starr. Mirabai. *Wild Mercy: Living in the Fierce and Tender Wisdom of the Women Mystics.* Boulder, CO: Sounds True, 2019.
Steere, Douglas V. *Spiritual Counsel and Letters of Baron Friedrich von Hügel.* New York: Harper & Row, 1964.
Vande Kappelle, Robert P. *Beyond Belief.* Eugene, OR: Wipf & Stock, 2012.
———. *Dark Splendor.* Eugene, OR: Wipf & Stock, 2015.
———. *In the Potter's Workshop.* Eugene, OR: Wipf & Stock, 2019.
———. *Into Thin Places.* Eugene, OR: Resource Publications, 2010.
———. *The Invisible Mountain*, Eugene, OR: Resource Publications, 2010.
———. *Love Never Fails.* Mustang, OK: Tate, 2006 (republished by Wipf & Stock, 2018).
———. *The Scandal of Divine Love.* Eugene, OR: Wipf & Stock, 2017.
———. *Securing Life.* Eugene, OR: Wipf & Stock, 2016.
Walls, Andrew F. *The Missionary Movement in Christian History: Studies in the Transmission of Faith.* Maryknoll, NY: Orbis, 1996.
Walsch, Neale Donald. *Conversations with God: An Uncommon Dialogue.* 2 vols. Charlottesville, VA: Hampton Roads, 1997.
Whitehead, Alfred North. *Science and the Modern World.* New York: Free Press, 1967.
Wilber, Ken. *The Eye of Spirit: Integral Art and Literary Theory.* Boston: Shambhala, 1997.

Index

Abraham (patriarch), 28, 155, 157
accommodation, 81
Adams, John, 69
adventure, ix, 18–19, 23–24, 58, 67
  quest for, 61–63
afterlife, 31, 52, 85, 88, 91, 110, 115, 166, 174
agnostic(ism), 29, 30, 71, 72, 73, 85, 87–88, 171, 172, 174
Allison, Dale, 65
angels, 139
apophatic, 168n3, 171
Apostles' Creed, 101, 124
Aquinas, Thomas, 42, 79, 81, 90, 141, 173, 206
Aristotle (philosopher), 76, 81, 173, 184
Armstrong, Karen, 65, 74, 140
Athanasius of Alexandria, 177, 190
atheism, 30, 36, 66, 71, 72, 73, 92, 165
attachment, 47, 169
Augustine (bishop), 21, 42, 79, 81, 98, 135, 177, 206
awakening, 63

Bacon, Francis, 80
Baronius, Caesar (church historian), 79
Barth, Karl, 90
beauty, 201
belief(s), x, 6, 16, 23, 25–26, 30, 31, 37–39, 41, 42, 45, 50, 51, 73, 123, 150, 160, 167, 183, 186, 188
  See also disbelief, inadequacy of
believe, 40, 41, 42, 175, 184n2, 186
Berry, Thomas, 147
Bible, The. See scripture

binary perspective, 198
Blake, William, 168, 178, 194
Bloom, Allan, 17
Bodhidharma (Zen Buddhist philosopher), 47
body, physical, 70, 142–43, 144, 197
Bonaventure (theologian), 177
Bonhoeffer, Dietrich, 73, 74, 88, 131
Borg, Marcus, 30, 65, 96, 127, 140
Bourgeault, Cynthia, 198
Brother Lawrence, 166
Buber, Martin, 98
Buddha, 47, 63, 65, 192, 196, 204
Buddhism, 47, 48, 50, 73, 105, 145
  Zen, 47, 73, 179
Bultmann, Rudolph, 73, 74
Bunyan, John, 74
Burnett, Howard J., ix, 23, 58

Calvin, John, 79, 81, 111, 177
Campbell, Joseph, 61, 62
Catherine of Siena, 85, 177
Center, the, 61–63, 65
change, xii, 28, 33, 34, 37, 46–48, 49
Chautauqua Institution, 50, 74
Christ, the universal, 26, 65, 130, 134
  as first incarnation of God, 133–35
  second coming of, 134
christology, xiii, 120, 160
church, the, 26, 152–53, 155
  definition of, 155–57
  history of, 152–62
  notes of, 27
  unity of, 153, 155, 158–62
compassion, 21, 40, 57, 116, 195

Constantine (emperor), 25, 160
contemplation, 52, 57, 165, 170, 200, 201
conversion, 7, 11, 52, 63, 71, 98–99, 109, 126, 180–81, 185–86
corporate personality, 152–53
cosmology, 70, 78, 82
Countryman, William, 109
creation, doctrine of, 84, 97, 117
    covenant of, 27
    and design, 94, 95
    as promise, 93–96
    spirituality, xii, 99n13
    as unfinished, 93
creationism, 76
creed, 40, 41, 122, 160
Creed, J. M., 132
critical understanding, 29–30, 67, 72, 73
Crossan, John Dominic, 74
cycling, 9, 24, 58, 209–10

Darwin, Charles, 75, 76, 78, 84, 93, 94, 95
Dawkins, Richard, 69, 72, 74
Dead Sea Scrolls, 122
Descartes, René, 175
detachment, 47, 168–69
Dillard, Annie, 168
disbelief, inadequacy of, 172–79
discipleship, 27, 40, 115–16, 134, 181
Dobzhansky, Theodosius, 76
doubt, 33, 37, 42, 43, 73, 108, 208
dualism/dualistic, xi, 3, 23, 25, 45, 53, 66, 82, 85, 99, 119, 139, 143, 165, 174, 183, 188, 195
    overcoming, 196–99

Eastern Orthodoxy, 58, 130, 154, 156, 162, 178
Eckhart, Meister, 75, 168, 185
Ehrman, Bart, 131
Einstein, Albert, 76, 139, 165
Eiseley, Loren, 175
Eliot, T. S., 33
enlightenment, 47, 69, 180, 194, 195, 196
eschatology, x, 15, 16, 65, 161
evangelical, 16, 37, 76, 98, 99, 154
evangelism/evangelistic, 6, 7, 13, 36
evolution, biological, 75–76, 83–84, 88, 93–96

experience, authority of, 86–87

faith, x, xii, 3, 7, 12, 16, 17, 18, 21, 30, 31, 36, 37, 44, 67, 73, 95, 99, 171, 175, 184, 186, 188, 206, 207, 208
    definition of, 37–45
faith journey, ix, xi, xii, 21, 30, 33, 38, 61–62, 67, 72, 95, 99, 113, 166, 167, 179–81, 186
faithfulness, 43
False Self, 183, 185, 189–94
Feyerabend, Paul, 177
first half of life, 23, 32–33, 49, 50, 192, 202–3
Fox, Matthew, 99n13, 144, 168
Francis of Assisi, 162, 167, 177, 180
Frank, Jerome, 175
Freud, Sigmund, 65, 171, 175
Friedman, Richard, 106, 107
fundamentalism, x, 42, 48, 68, 69, 106, 108, 112, 146, 175

Galileo Galilei, 80, 81, 171
God, 11, 14, 70, 71, 115, 119, 124, 146, 170, 179–80, 183, 186, 188, 189, 193
    as creator, 93–96, 146–47, 148
    See also creation, doctrine of
    and evolution, 84, 93–96
    existence of, 66, 71, 72, 73
    images of, 8, 70, 83, 84, 89–98, 185–86
    incarnation of, 133–35
    as intelligent designer, 79, 93, 94
    as metaphor, 36
    as monarch, 96, 97–98
    as mother, 139
    and nature, 139
    as personal, 84, 93, 185
    as Persuasive Lover, 93
    quest for, 67, 70
    relationship with, 28–29, 30, 31, 38, 44–45, 67, 71–72, 97–98, 165–81
    and scripture, 106
    as Spirit, 96–98
    as Ultimate Reality, xiii, 95, 187, 188
    as unchangeable, 37
Goddard, John, 23

Gödel, Kurt, 22, 178
Gospels, 15, 25, 40, 109, 114, 117, 121, 122, 124, 127, 195
grace, 99, 115, 135, 140, 141, 161, 170, 186, 187
Greeley, Andrew, 175
Griffin, David Ray, 92
Grove City College, 15, 16

Hartshorne, Charles, 139
Haught, John, 77, 93, 94–96, 148, 149
heaven, xii, 16, 31, 33, 79, 85, 91, 99, 152, 178, 180, 194, 195, 196, 200
Hegel, Georg W. F., 29, 88, 174, 175, 198
Heisenberg, Werner, 22, 177
hell, xii, 16, 33, 85, 91, 99, 194
Hengel, Martin, 131
Heraclitus (Greek philosopher), 46
Herder, Johann G. von, 112
heroes, 17–19, 62, 63
heterodox(y), 25, 27–28, 111, 123, 159, 160, 171
Hindu(ism), 105, 145, 176, 188, 191, 196
Hodge, Charles, 79, 80, 81
holiness, 100, 129, 195
Holy Spirit, 19, 38, 79, 81, 96, 111, 112, 125, 133, 152, 170, 179, 192
Howard, David, 18, 19n3
Hügel, Friederich von, 181
Hugh of St. Victor, 195
Huvelin, Abbé, 171, 181
Huxley, Aldous, 176

Ignatius of Antioch, 159
image of God, 46, 97, 129, 205
imagination, 59, 110, 114, 176, 177, 178
incarnation, doctrine of, 197
inspiration, biblical, 16
intuition, 178–79
Irenaeus (theologian), 190
Irving, Washington, 202
Islam, 84, 188

Jacob (patriarch), 17, 157
James, William, 126, 173, 176, 177
Jefferson, Thomas, 69
Jerome (theologian), 40

Jesus Christ, xiii, 19, 63, 152, 177, 184, 190, 191, 192, 207
  as archetype of the self, 130, 133
  belief in, 40
  core message of, 52–53, 189–90
  and eternity, 52
  as exemplar, xiii, 189
  humanity of, xiii, 26, 123, 125, 130
  identity of, 9
  as Jewish, 126–27, 127
  as Lord, 122–28
  as preexistent, 125, 131
  as priest, 115
  as Revealer of the Father, xiii, 39
  role of, 27, 128–29
  as Savior, 79, 128
  as teacher, xiii, 119, 181, 184, 191
  and Ultimate Reality, 53
  views about. *See* christology
Jews/Jewish/Judaism, 28, 58, 68, 74, 84, 101, 140, 158
John, Gospel of, 9–10, 117, 132, 134, 152, 184, 191, 192, 200
John of the Cross, 177
John the Baptist, 126, 192
Jonah, sign of, 192–93
Julian of Norwich, 177
Jung, Carl, 23, 65, 66, 130, 133, 171, 172, 173, 175, 177, 179, 180

Kant, Immanuel, 173–74
kataphatic, 168n4, 171
Kelsey, Morton, 73, 176
Kepler, Johannes, 46
Kierkegaard, Søren, 28–29, 88–89
kingdom of God, 27, 40, 85, 100, 120, 196, 200
King's College, The, 12, 14, 48
Knox, John, 125
Kuhn, T. S., 22, 177
Küng, Hans, 84

Lao Tzu, 188
Latourette, Kenneth Scott, 14
Lesser, Elizabeth, 143
Lewis, C. S., 16, 60, 61, 122, 140, 178
Lindsay, T. M., 79

literal(ism), x, 15, 31, 32, 37, 53, 77, 79, 84, 101, 109, 110, 111, 117, 123, 155
Loftus, John W., 50
love, 3, 34, 84, 85, 93, 144, 168
Loyola, Ignatius, 177
Luther, Martin, 28, 111, 123, 154, 177

Maslow, Abraham, 63–64
Marx, Karl, 29, 174
Mary Magdalene, 47
May, Gerald, 169–70
McCluggage, Denise, 46
McFague, Sallie, 139
McGrath, Alistair, 100
McLaren, Brian, 74
meaning, quest for, 63–64
meditation, 63, 165, 170
Merton, Thomas, 189
metaphor, 36, 100, 183
   "Bible" as, 116–18
   circle and ellipse as, 45–46, 196–97
   "death" as, 179, 186–87, 191–94
   "God" as, 36
   "heart" as, 40, 45
   "resurrection" as, 132–33, 133–34, 179, 187, 193, 194
   "water" as, 184
Metzger, Bruce, 15
Mill, John Stuart, 91
Moore, Thomas, 167
morality, 28, 91, 99, 112, 140, 141
Moses, 28, 63, 81, 107, 108, 194
Muhammad, 63
Muslim, 58, 105, 191, 206
Mussorgsky, Modest, xi
Myers-Briggs Type Indicator, 179
mystery, 3, 36, 66, 149, 165, 179, 188, 190
mystics/mysticism, 25, 30, 36, 52–53, 84, 98, 143, 148, 149, 155, 166, 168, 171, 175, 186, 188, 191, 194, 194–96
myth(ology), 64, 65, 74, 184

Napoleon Bonaparte, 120
Nasr, Seyyed, 145
naturalism, 94, 149, 174

nature (natural realm), ix, 25, 44, 45, 47, 68, 70, 88, 93–96, 139, 140, 144–48, 149, 151, 172
   as extension of the human body, 197
   and God, 149
   as God's "body," 139
   origin of, 147–48
   as promise, 93–96
   sacramental sense of, 148–50
Newton, Isaac, 76, 93, 147, 178
Newton, John, 52
Nicene Creed, 130
nirvana, 47, 180
nonduality, xi, 21, 25, 57, 85, 105, 119, 151, 165, 183, 188, 198, 200

original sin, xii, 99, 204
Orr, James, 79
orthodox(y), 25, 27, 41–42, 123, 124, 160–61
   alternative, 25–27
Otto, Rudolph, 193
Outsider Test for Faith, 50, 51, 73

panentheism, xii, 92
pantheism, 92
Pascal, Blaise, 39
Paul (apostle), 18, 19, 26, 28, 44, 49–50, 51, 57, 72, 87–88, 131–32, 135, 141, 152, 153, 156, 159, 171, 190, 195, 196
Peacocke, Arthur, 83, 93
Perennial Tradition, 141, 186, 187–89, 197
person, personhood, 185
Phillips, J. B., 171
pietism, 112
Plato (philosopher), 174, 175, 177, 178
Plotkin, Bill, 203
pluralism, 31, 32, 66, 112
Polkinhorne, John, 39
polytheism, 92
Postcritical Paradigm, xii, 30, 31–32, 46
   Bible and, 116–18
postcritical understanding, xii, 30, 51, 72
postmodernism, 29, 64, 68, 89, 113, 124, 173
Precritical Paradigm, 30, 31, 32, 45, 122

precritical understanding, 29, 51, 72, 73
Presence, 52
Princeton Theological Seminary, 15, 16, 23, 48, 51, 52, 72, 73
Protestant Reformation, 41, 161, 162

Rahner, Karl, 191
reason, 86–87
religion, 32
    definition of, 67, 132
    inadequate, ix–x, 38, 52, 53, 69, 84, 85, 151, 195, 196
    mature, 33, 38, 52, 57, 66, 68, 69, 146, 148, 187–88, 191
    and ritual, 68, 178
    and science, 75–84, 199
    and spirituality, 67–70
Renan, Ernst, 120
Richard of St. Victor, 195
rites of passage, 63, 64
Robinson, John A. T., 73, 74
Rohr, Richard, 32, 119, 134n14, 166, 176, 179, 180
Roman Catholicism, 112, 130, 154, 156, 161–62
Russell, Bertrand, 153

sabbath, 108
sacred, sense of, 65, 66
salvation, 16, 65, 98–101, 161
    definition of, 99
Schumacher, E. F., 75
Schweitzer, Albert, 17, 121
science, 22, 31, 39, 67, 73, 147, 150, 177, 198, 199
    and design, 79, 94, 95
    hierarchical model of, 83
    limits of, 83
    and religion, 75–84, 200
    See also evolution, biological
scientism, 77, 78, 151
scripture, xiii, 16, 66, 68, 77, 98, 105–6, 188, 207
    authority of, 86, 107, 109, 161
    as canon, 160, 161
    as holy, 116
    inerrancy of, x, 37, 68, 71, 106, 112
    inspiration of, 106–13

    interpretation of, 79–80, 154
    multivalence/polyvalence of, 49, 113
    and Postcritical Paradigm, 116–18
    purpose of, 82
    and science, 78–84
    views on, 16, 105–18
second coming of Christ. *See* Christ, second coming of
second half of life, xii, 23, 32–34, 49, 50, 66, 166, 202
Sermon on the Mount, 43
shadow self, 192n7
Shakespeare, William, 208
sin, 97, 98, 100, 101, 132, 187
Singh, Kathleen Dowling, 193
Smith, Huston, 140, 141–44
soul, 21, 47, 65, 135, 139, 142, 143, 179, 189
spirituality, 22, 32, 36, 37, 50, 52, 53, 69, 145, 176–77, 186, 189, 192, 194, 199
    Eastern, 168–69
    and personality, 22
    postmodern, 68
    primal, 68
    and psychology, 169–70
    and religion, 68–70
    Western, 167–69. 186, 194
Spong, John Shelby, 74, 91
Starr, Mirabai, 23
Stinson, Daniel, 67
Stony Brook School, the, 11–12, 48
story/storytelling, 19, 66, 113–16
Strachan, Harry and Susan, 5

Teilhard de Chardin, Pierre, 76, 175
Ten Commandments, 43, 108
Teresa of Ávila, 177
ternary perspective, 197, 198
Tertullian (theologian), 80
theism, supernatural, 45, 71, 90, 91, 92
theological task, 67–68, 114, 125
theology, 89–98, 185–86
    and science, 93–96
    as story, 113–16
theosis, 190
thin places, 59–61
Tillich, Paul, 73, 74

Tolkien, J. R. R., 178
tradition, authority of, 86
transformation (personal), xiii, 7, 38, 52, 63, 126, 135, 148, 188, 189–90, 195, 199
Tree of Knowledge, 204, 205, 206
Tree of Life, 204, 205, 206
Trent, Council of, 161
Trinity, doctrine of, 128, 131, 198
True Self, 132, 133, 165, 179, 183, 189–96
trust, 39, 40, 42–43, 44, 148, 184
truth, xii, 36, 45, 48, 50, 57, 66, 86, 87–89, 184, 186
Two Books, God's, xiii, 78–84

ultimate questions, 67, 187
Ultimate Reality, 52, 85, 187, 197, 200
and beauty, 201
union (divine), 53

Vande Kappelle, Bertha and Jacob, 3–19, 58
Vatican Two, 162
virtue(s), 140–41

Wallenda, Nik, 203, 204, 206
Walsch, Neale Donald, 69
Walsh, Roger, 175
Warfield, Benjamin B., 79
Washington & Jefferson College, ix, 16, 50, 58, 72
water. *See* metaphor, "water" as
Wells, H. G., 120
Wesleyan Quadrilateral, 86
Whitehead, Alfred North, 75, 76, 92, 93
wholeness, 64–65, 78, 99, 143, 169
Whyte, L. L., 175
Wickes, Frances, 178
Wilber, Ken, 200, 201
Wordsworth, William, 168, 200

www.ingramcontent.com/pod-product-compliance
Lightning Source LLC
Chambersburg PA
CBHW062020220426

43662CB00010B/1409